Apple Of My Eye

The story of Apple Records and the end of The Beatles

Andrew Wild

sonicbondpublishing.com

Sonicbond Publishing Limited
www.sonicbondpublishing.co.uk
Email: info@sonicbondpublishing.co.uk

First Published in the United Kingdom 2025
First Published in the United States 2025

British Library Cataloguing in Publication Data:
A Catalogue record for this book is available from the British Library

ISBN 978-1-78952-379-9

Typeset in ITC Garamond Std & ITC Avant Garde Gothic
Printed and bound in England

Graphic design and typesetting: Full Moon Media

Apple Of My Eye

The story of Apple Records and the end of The Beatles

Andrew Wild

sonicbondpublishing.com

By the same author

Books About Music
Pink Floyd Song by Song (Fonthill, 2017)
Queen On Track (Sonicbond, 2018)
The Beatles: An A-Z Guide to Every Song (Sonicbond, 2019)
Solo Beatles 1969-1980 On Track (Sonicbond, 2020)
Crosby, Stills and Nash On Track (Sonicbond, 2020)
Dire Straits On Track (Sonicbond, 2021)
Fleetwood Mac in the 1970s (Sonicbond, 2021)
Eric Clapton Solo On Track (Sonicbond, 2021)
Eric Clapton Sessions (Sonicbond, 2022)
Phil Collins in The 1980s (Sonicbond, 2022)
The Allman Brothers Band On Track (Sonicbond, 2022)
A Mirror of Dreams: The Progressive Rock Revival 1981 To 1983 (Kingmaker, 2024)
Live Aid: The Greatest Show On Earth (Sonicbond, 2024)
Four Sides Of The Circle (Rumble Strips, 2024)
The Beatles On Track 1962-1966 (Sonicbond, 2025) – with Alberto Bravin
A Playground Of Broken Hearts: The Progressive Rock Revival 1984 To 1989 (Kingmaker, 2025)
The Beautiful South + The Housemartins On Track (Sonicbond, 2026)

Biographies
Play On: The Official Biography of Twelfth Night (Twelfth Night, 2009)
One for the Record: The Official Biography of Galahad (Avalon, 2013/2nd edition, 20181
His Love: the Art, Music and Faith of Geoff Mann (Sonicbond, 2023)

Books About Films
James Bond On Screen (Sonicbond, 2022)

Books About Comics
The Perfect Marvel Comics Collection – 1939-1985 (Rumble Strips, 2022)

Local History
108 Steps Around Macclesfield (Sigma Press, 1994/2nd edition, Rumble Strips, 2018)
Exploring Chester (Sigma Press, 1996/re-publication, Rumble Strips, 2018)
Ever Forward (MADS, 1997)

As Editor
Stored In Clocks And Mortal Shadows: Geoff Mann's Poems 1973-1993 (Twelfth Night, 2024)

Plays
The Difficult Crossing (Stagescripts, 2016)
A Difficult Man (Rumble Strips, 2021)

Thank you (once more) to Nick Jackson.

It's a business concerning records, films, electronics and – as a sideline – manufacturing, or whatever it's called. We just want to set up a system whereby people who just want to make a film about anything don't have to go on their knees in somebody's office – probably yours!
John Lennon, New York City Press Conference, 13 May 1968

The Beatles were probably the last people in Britain who should have attempted to run a company: they didn't have the slightest idea of how to go about it, and terrible mistakes were made.
Barry Miles, *The Zapple Diaries*, 2015

Unless explicitly credited otherwise, all quotes from John Lennon, Paul McCartney, George Harrison, Ringo Starr and Neil Aspinall are taken from *The Beatles Anthology* (2000).

Apple Of My Eye

The story of Apple Records and the end of The Beatles

Contents

Introduction

Brian Epstein's death in August 1967 changed everything. When The Beatles' manager died, he had plans in place to set up a small group of companies to keep his clients busy and to create a tax-effective business structure for their earnings. The top rate of income tax was 95%, or 19 shillings in the pound:

> Let me tell you how it will be, there's one for you, nineteen for me,
> Cause I'm the Taxman, yeah, I'm the Taxman.
> Should five per cent appear too small be thankful I don't take it all,
> Cause I'm the Taxman, yeah, I'm the Taxman.
> The Beatles, 'Taxman' (1966)

Beatles & Co. had been established in April 1967. This was an 'umbrella' company set up to channel all of the band's income, with the exception of songwriting royalties. Each of the four Beatles took 5% of Beatles & Co. A new corporation, collectively owned and called Apple, would control the remainder. The name was suggested by Paul McCartney, who was inspired by *Le Jeu De Mourre*, a painting by René Magritte that shows a green apple with the words 'au revoir'.

In parallel, Epstein encouraged diversification of The Beatles' business activities. The first of these, Apple Publishing, was headed by Terry Doran, a Liverpool friend and business associate of Epstein, 'the man from the motor trade'. Apple Publishing, with offices in Curzon Street, London, wanted to find and contract songwriters who would not only have their own successes as recording artists but also be able to place songs with others. The first of these, songwriters Paul Tennant and Dave Rhodes, met Paul McCartney by chance in May 1967. They had been given Terry Doran's number, and Apple funded a number of demos. Brian Epstein was keen for them to form a band as a vehicle for their material and told them he wanted them to be called Focal Point. Their sole single, 'Love You Forever', was released on Deram in May.

Initially, Apple business was conducted from Nems Enterprises' office or at Apple Publishing's office on Curzon Street. Towards the end of June 1967, they paid £76,500 (£1.5m today) for a four-storey building at 94 Baker Street, London. Apple Publishing took up residence.

Re-grouping after Brian Epstein's death, the original plan was for Apple and Nems Enterprises to work closely together, but Clive Epstein was not as close to The Beatles as his late brother. As Ringo Starr explained in a 1970 interview with *Melody Maker*, 'We tried to form Apple with Clive Epstein, but he wouldn't have it ... he didn't believe in us, I suppose ... he didn't think we could do it. He thought we were four wild men and we were going to spend all his money and make him broke. But that was the original idea of Apple – to form it with Nems ... we thought, now Brian's gone, let's really amalgamate and get this thing going; let's make records and get people on our label and things like that.'

The matter was clouded by the involvement of Robert Stigwood, who had merged his management agency with Nems Enterprises earlier in 1967. The plan was for Epstein to continue to manage The Beatles and Cilla Black, and Stigwood would look after the rest of the Nems Enterprises roster, as well as bringing in his own clients, including Cream and The Bee Gees. As part of the deal, Brian Epstein had made a provisional agreement to sell a controlling interest in Nems Enterprises to Stigwood. This was valid until September 1967. The Beatles had no interest in working with Stigwood, and Stigwood did not want to buy Nems Enterprises without The Beatles. Backing out, he formed his own Robert Stigwood Organisation, taking Cream and The Bee Gees with him.

Apple Publishing signed more songwriters as 1967 moved into 1968. George Alexander was the older brother of Angus and Malcolm Young, later of AC/DC, and had an unnamed group along with John Perry, a former member of Tony Rivers And The Castaways, and brothers Geoff and Pete Swettenham. They were signed to Apple Publishing and were given the name Grapefruit by John Lennon, who, with Paul McCartney, attended the band's first recording session at IBC Studios in London on 24 November 1967. As Apple didn't yet have a record company, the single 'Dear Delilah' was licensed to other labels and, to promote the release, Apple introduced the group to the press at a reception on 18 January 1968. 'Dear Delilah', the first release by an Apple artist, reached number 21 in the UK in March 1968 during a nine-week spell in the charts. A second single, 'Elevator', was less successful, despite a promo film directed by Paul McCartney, but a cover of The Four Seasons' 'C'mon Marianne' reached number 35 later that summer. RCA subsequently dropped the band, and they were released from their Apple contracts in November 1968. Other songwriters who were contracted to Apple Publishing included Jackie Lomax, an old friend from Liverpool who was managed by Nems Enterprises, three sets of partners – Paul Tennant and Dave Rhodes, Alan Morgan and Steve Webber, and Benny Gallagher and Graham Lyle – and Dave Lambert, who later joined The Strawbs. Gallagher and Lyle would provided several songs for Mary Hopkin. Ultimately, they formed a band with their friends Tom McGuinness and Hughie Flint, but there was seemingly no discussion of McGuinness Flint signing to Apple Records in a period when new acts were not sought for The Beatles' record company. McGuinness Flint's debut single, 'When I'm Dead And Gone', and accompanying album, *McGuinness Flint*, would both be top ten hits in 1970. But not for Apple.

In the meantime, Apple Films produced the *Magical Mystery Tour* TV feature. The resultant 52-minute programme originally aired on BBC1, in black-and-white, on 26 December 1967. A colour transmission followed two weeks later.

And, in a tale that's hard to believe, The Beatles opened their own clothing shop, the Apple Boutique, on 7 December 1967 on the ground floor of their Baker Street office. Clive Epstein's original suggestion was to set up a chain of shops that sold greetings cards. This was changed to focus on records, but the idea was rejected as it would involve selling the products of their rivals.

Clothing was the next best option. The Apple boutique was modelled on the hugely successful Biba in Kensington, opened in 1964 and run by the Polish-born designer Barbara Hulanicki and her husband Stephen Fitz-Simon. The Beatles' shop opened in December 1967 and was managed by John Lennon's old school friend Pete Shotton, who had been running a small supermarket. Perhaps an early warning was that the exterior mural was far more interesting than the clothing lines.

George Harrison in *Anthology*: 'The painting on the side of the Baker Street shop looked amazing, but everything went wrong. A couple of nearby shopkeepers decided they didn't like the tone of the building, although others liked it because it brought a lot of attention, and Baker Street suddenly became somewhere worth talking about. Before that, other than Sherlock Holmes, Baker Street was nothing; nobody went there except to catch a bus. Now, suddenly, it was really happening. But because of the complaints, the landlord or whoever owned the lease made us paint it out and get rid of it. Once we were told we had to get rid of the painting, the whole thing started to lose appeal.'

The next step was to establish a record company. In December 1967, The Beatles Ltd, formed in June 1963, was re-established as Apple Music Ltd. Apple Music Ltd owned 80% of The Beatles & Co. This arrangement allowed accumulated royalties to be paid to The Beatles as a business, attracting a lower corporate tax rate, rather than as individuals. The original directors were: Clive Epstein, Brian's brother and director of Nems Enterprises; Alistair Taylor, Brian's former PA; and Geoffrey Ellis, a solicitor and accountant.

The Beatles had big ideas. They wanted Apple to be more than simply a tax shelter. It was founded to cover several diverse disciplines: retail, publishing and film production were already operating. A record company would be next. To give a more inclusive name to these different divisions, Apple Music Ltd changed its name again on 12 January 1968, this time to Apple Corps Ltd. Apple Corps controlled Apple Records Ltd, Apple Films Ltd, Apple Music Publishing Ltd and Apple Electronics Ltd, soon to be joined by others. The Apple name was trademarked in most countries, and this foresight paid off many years later when Apple Computers launched the iPod and moved into music distribution. A series of lawsuits netted The Beatles many millions for copyright infringement.

Neil Aspinall, their long-time *aide-de-camp*, was appointed managing director. 'A lot of people were nominated or put themselves forward,' he told Paul du Noyer of *Mojo*, 'But there didn't seem to be any unanimous choice here. So, I said to them, foolishly, I guess, Look, I'll do it until you find somebody that you want to do it. We didn't have a single piece of paper. No contracts. The lawyer, the accountants and Brian, whoever, had that. Maybe The Beatles had been given copies of various contracts, I don't know. I know that when Apple started, I didn't have a single piece of paper. I didn't know what the contract was with EMI, or with the film people or the publishers or anything at all. So, it was a case of building up the filing system, finding out what was going on while we were trying to continue doing something.'

Peter Brown, Alistair Taylor, Tony Bramwell and Mal Evans, all of whom had worked for Epstein or directly for The Beatles, were added to the payroll. American-born record company executive Ron Kass would be Director of Apple Records, and former pop star Peter Asher, still only 23, would report to Kass as Head of A&R. Denis O'Dell, producer on *A Hard Day's Night* and *Magical Mystery Tour,* headed up Apple Films. And Derek Taylor was persuaded to return to the UK.

'At the end of 1967, I got a call from all of The Beatles,' Taylor said in *Anthology*, 'a conference call from Hille House. That was where they had the big Apple launch meeting, and they said, 'Come and join us, and you can run Apple Records.' It sounded like a wonderful treat. We had all changed.'

Taylor had attended a housewarming/album launch event at Brian Epstein's house, Kingsley Hill in Sussex, the previous May. Here, he had reconnected with The Beatles after spending three years working in Los Angeles. Two of the Beatles plied him with LSD. 'We became hippies, really,' Taylor said, 'And The Beatles had changed a lot from being rather charming but world-weary pop stars into being extremely nice, gentle, huggable souls … we believed we were going to make everything very beautiful and that it was going to be, now, a wonderful world. So, the idea of going back to England from California after having had three good years there was, I thought, like going to the Holy Land. When all the stuff on the phone was over and done with – about what I was actually going to do – it was said, 'Well, you don't have to do anything, man. We don't believe in labels or structures or anything. Just come and be – that sort of thing – and we'll pay your fare.' So, I came over in April 1968.' Derek Taylor started at Apple on 8 April 1968.

'As much as a business,' noted author Philip Norman, 'Apple set out to become a kind of alternative welfare state. Plans were announced for an arts foundation that would award regular stipends to deserving applicants, even an Apple school, where The Beatles' own children and those of their followers would be educated side-by-side. John took a particular interest in the school project, insisting it must bear no resemblance to the disciplined academies he and Paul had both attended, and bringing in their mutual childhood friend Ivan Vaughan, now a noted educationalist, to develop it. John's other main protégé or charitable interest – depending on one's point of view – was Magic Alex, by now established in a well-equipped workshop under the banner of Apple Electronics and supposedly at work on life-transforming inventions of every kind.' The school never got off the ground, and Apple Electronics proved to be an expensive white elephant. It operated out of 34 Boston Place, tucked behind Marylebone Station and not far from Baker Street.

In this period, The Beatles were preparing for a long trip to India. A new single, 'Lady Madonna', was recorded in early February before the band flew to Delhi. Their trusted associate, Neil Aspinall, was asked to stay in the UK to set up the Apple office. 'I didn't stay in Rishikesh,' he said, 'because I was supposed to be running the Apple companies. We'd just taken some temporary offices in Wigmore Street … just trying to get all the information we needed – copies of the contracts and files – to find out what had happened in the past, so we could work out where we were going in the future.' The Beatles returned from India in mid-April with beards, life experiences and lots of new songs.

On 19 April 1968, a widely published press advertisement in the UK music press featured new general manager Alistair Taylor posing as a one-man band, announcing 'This man has talent'. The poster further added:

> One day, he sang his songs to a tape recorder (borrowed from the man next door). In his neatest handwriting, he wrote an explanatory note (giving his name and address) and, remembering to enclose a picture of himself, sent the tape, letter and photograph to Apple Music, 94 Baker Street, London, W.1. If you were thinking of doing the same thing yourself – do it now! This man now owns a Bentley!

Apple had arrived, with a large, open-plan office at 95 Wigmore Street, not far from the Asher household and close to busy Oxford Street.

Their free-wheeling, anything-goes philosophy mirrored a similar set-up a mile-and-a-half away along Oxford Street and down Wardour Street.

> In the summer of 1967, [Kit] Lambert moved Track's headquarters from Chesterfield Gardens to 58 Old Compton Street. 'In the early days, there was an air of power and sustainable expansion about Track Records', says Arthur Brown, before offering a vivid, fanciful description of their new HQ: 'You'd never seen an office with so many criminals in your life – an eclectic mixture of intellectuals, artists, businessmen, models, actors, English crime lords and American Jewish mafia. The Who might be ambling in or out, or, in the case of Keith Moon, running up and down the stairs chortling merrily at the top of his pirate voice. Hendrix might be there. Kit might be haranguing Polydor Records on the phone, and Terence Stamp might be holding forth about being on the frontlines when the revolution came. Tea was made, joints were smoked, and cannabis tincture was administered medicinally!'
> Mark Blake, *Pretend You're In A War: The Who And The Sixties* (2015)

John, Paul and Neil travelled to New York City for a series of press conferences, their first since the 'bigger than Jesus' row two years before. On 12 May, at the St. Regis Hotel, they were interviewed by the business press. They also met Ron Kass for the first time aboard a boat, a Chinese Junk, sailing around the Statue of Liberty. The next day, at the Americana Hotel for a more general press conference, Lennon said, 'The aim of this company isn't really a stack of gold teeth in the bank. We've done that bit. It's more of a trick to see if we can actually get artistic freedom within a business structure, and to see if we can create nice things and sell them without charging three times our cost.'

'We're in the happy position of not really needing any more money,' Paul said, 'so for the first time, the bosses aren't in it for the profit. We've already bought all our dreams, so now we want to share that possibility with others.'

A day later, John and Paul appeared on *The Tonight Show With Johnny Carson*, taped in Studio 6B at the Rockefeller Center and hosted by baseball player Joe Garagiola. 'Before Lennon or McCartney had a chance to open their mouths,' writes Richard DiLello, 'they found themselves in the middle of a verbal blizzard of antagonism generated by a sad, gravel-voiced, burned-out movie star who, for decency's sake, shall remain unnamed [It was Tallulah Bankhead]. She tried very hard to throw a wet blanket of ridicule on their about-to-be-announced project. In spite of her, John and Paul told an audience of 11 million viewers that The Beatles were now prepared to use their considerable influence and personal wealth to help the young people of the world. Apple was going to make it possible for an infinite number of artistic ventures to reach fruition. No longer would it be a world in which the young and the creative had to put up with unspeakable humiliations to achieve artistic freedom. The Beatles had formed an organisation which would seek to finance and encourage projects of a cinematic, literary, scientific and musical nature. Apple was the company where you didn't have to come in on your hands and knees to get what you wanted. It was going to attempt to end forever the philistine conspiracy of artistic suppression and tyranny that had run rampant through the world for too long.'

On 22 May, John and George attended a lunchtime launch party and press conference for Apple's second retail venture, Apple Tailoring. This was a bespoke tailoring business located at 161 King's Road in Chelsea, with a men's hairdressing salon in the basement run by Leslie Cavendish, The Beatles' preferred hair stylist. By John Lennon's side, for the first time in public, was Japanese artist Yoko Ono. The tailoring business opened the next day but was divested later that year.

Five weeks later, on 28 June, Paul attended the Capitol Records Sales Conference at The Beverly Hills Hilton Hotel in Los Angeles. All future Beatles recordings, he said, would be on the Apple label. The entire operation was moved to new headquarters at 3 Savile Row in July 1968, the building that is now synonymous with Apple. It had been bought from bandleader Jack Hylton for around £500,000 (over £9m in 2025 value). The building had previously been The Albany Club.

'Inside, in the large entrance hall,' Barry Miles wrote, 'the walls were all white, the telephones were all white and the deep pile carpet was apple green. At the end was the main staircase, with a subsidiary one to the left; there was plaster panelling in all the main rooms, including the entrance hall, dados, entablatures, cornices, and in the back room on the ground floor was a row of columns. To the right of the stairs was the reception and Debbie, the receptionist; a few gold records on the wall, a row of chairs, the music magazines and trade press, with doors leading to Ron Kass's office and the big back room. As head of the record division, Ron had more visitors than anyone except the press office. Displayed on the main staircase was an oil painting of two lion cubs; otherwise, the walls were lined with gold records. On the first floor, in the building's two principal rooms, were the offices of Neil Aspinall and Peter Brown. The front room ran the full width of the building and featured elaborate plaster moulding on the ceiling. Derek Taylor's press office was on the third floor. It was a large room, dominated by Derek's high scallop-backed white wicker chair that he had shipped from Los Angeles when he moved to London to join The Beatles. It was known as the 'throne of Apple', and it was from here that he managed to keep in check the waves of madness caused by John and Paul inviting every nutter, crazy, hustler and conman in the Western world to apply to them for funds. It was also the public face of The Beatles.'

'Maybe forty people were in the whole office working there,' Derek Taylor recalled. 'Maybe fewer, but middle double-figures.'

But there was seemingly no accountability in the business. In a famous story, the post boy stripped all of the lead from the roof. 'Between The Beatles and their employees,' suggested Peter McCabe and Robert D. Schonfeld in their book *Apple To The Core* (1972), 'it was a kind of dual rape. Many members of the staff robbed them left and right, but The Beatles flattered, magnetised, seduced and finally abandoned many who worked for them. The old buddies from Liverpool spent most of their time patting Beatle backs and taking every opportunity to hack off a piece of the empire for themselves. For a while, The Beatles remained aloof from petty office politics. Smiling and unquestioning, they appeared like sheikhs sitting fatly on newly acquired wealth.'

Apple Records was officially founded as pre-production for the band's next album commenced. Sessions would stretch from late May to mid-October. The Beatles had signed a new nine-year contract with EMI in early 1967. Therefore, EMI and its US subsidiary, Capitol Records, agreed to distribute albums and singles until 1976; their group and solo albums and singles would be released under the Apple banner until then. They were also free to sign other acts, and brought on several artists, including James Taylor, Mary Hopkin, Billy Preston, The Modern Jazz Quartet, Badfinger, Doris Troy and Jackie Lomax. In many cases, The Beatles would provide production, songs or performances, especially during the first couple of years.

British songwriter Trevor Bannister was signed to Apple Publishing during this period and made some recordings at Trident Studios for a proposed single. The full-on psychedelic 'Lovers From The Sky' was recorded on 13 May 1968, produced by Traffic's Jim Capaldi, under the group name Contact. Bannister met John and Paul, who asked him to pull together a band for promoting the single, but Bannister was unable to find the right musicians, and the opportunity passed. Likewise, Keith Drewett and Pete Dymond, known as Drew and Dy, recorded a number of demos for Apple after accosting Paul McCartney outside the Apple offices. They were signed as writers to Apple Publishing's subsidiary Python Publishing and, in due course, as recording artists to Apple Records, recording a number of tracks with Paul McCartney at Trident in August. McCartney also worked with a young singer/songwriter from Liverpool called Timon (real name: Stephen Murray), who recorded three tracks that summer, playing piano on 'Something New Every Day'. Although professionally recorded and mixed, the Grapefruit, Contact, Drew And Dy and Timon tracks recorded for Apple were not released until 2021.

Apple missed some aspiring artists who would become major players in the years ahead. A group of British blues musicians called Fleetwood Mac had formed in the summer of 1967 and were keen to sign with Apple. There was a connection: the band's drummer, Mick Fleetwood, was married to Patti Harrison's sister, Jenny. But, without a record company at that stage, Apple were unable to follow up. Fleetwood Mac's debut album, recorded for Blue Horizon, dates from February 1968. Joe Walsh, later of The Eagles, submitted a tape on behalf of his band, James Gang, who had opened for Cream in Detroit and, therefore, may have been encouraged to contact Apple by Eric Clapton. Walsh received a rejection letter from Derek Taylor, and his band duly signed with ABC early in 1969. According to Tony Bramwell, both Gilbert O'Sullivan (who had 13 top 40 hits in the 1970s) and Queen were within Apple's orbit prior to signing record deals. The big-selling progressive rock band Yes recorded some demos for Apple before going with Atlantic and achieving nine top ten albums in the years to come.

The debut album of David Jones of Brixton had flopped after release in June 1967. He was released from his recording contract in May 1968, just as Apple was launched. David Bowie wanted a new recording deal. Bowie's then-manager, Kenneth Pitt, recalled in his memoirs that he had reservations about the label, and if it weren't for his artist's desires, he wouldn't have even considered Apple. Pitt complained about the 'sheer amateurism and downright rudeness that confronted us during the next three months, the time it took Apple to give us a decision.' He also waspishly suggested that Peter Asher's sole qualification as Head of A&R 'was that his sister was the … girlfriend of Paul McCartney.'

Pitt continued: 'It took me some considerable time to make contact with [Asher], but when I did, he told me that the label was not interested in David. I asked him if he would let me have a letter to that effect, and on 15 July, he wrote: 'As we told you on the phone, Apple Records is not interested in signing David Bowie. The reason is that we don't feel he's what we're looking for at the moment. Thank you for your time."

Asher's letter to Pitts was signed on his behalf by his PA, Chris O'Dell. O'Dell had walked into Apple's offices in Wigmore Street, hoping to speak to Derek Taylor, whom she had first met in Los Angeles. By the end of the day, she had reunited with Taylor and chatted with Paul McCartney. She was smitten. 'I stayed at the Apple offices until eight o'clock that night, when Derek left to catch the train to his country home', she recalled in her vivid memoirs. 'I jumped in a taxi for my last night in the bed and breakfast. I didn't have a job yet, but I had already made up my mind that I would show up for work every day until someone gave me something to do.'

Despite replacing Pete Shotton with John Lyndon as manager of the Apple Boutique, poor business practices resulted in estimated losses of £200,000 (over £3.5m in current value). The shop closed down at the end of July 1968, seven months after opening. The Beatles, their staff and friends helped themselves to whatever stock was left the day before a public giveaway. 'It was a big event,' John recalled four years later, 'and all the kids came and just took everything that was in the shop. That was the best thing about the whole shop, when we gave it all away. But the night before, we all went in and took what we wanted. It wasn't much, T-shirts ... It was great, it was like robbing. We took everything we wanted home. And the next day, we were watching, and there were thousands of kids all going in and getting their freebies. We came up with the idea to give it all away and stop fucking about with a psychedelic clothes shop.'

'We decided to close down our Baker Street shop yesterday,' Paul said in a press release, 'and instead of putting up a sign saying, 'Business will be resumed as soon as possible', and then auction off the goods, we decided to give them away. The shops were doing fine and making a nice profit on turnover. So far, the biggest loss is in giving the things away, but we did that deliberately. We're giving them away – rather than selling them to barrow boys – because we wanted to give rather than sell. We came into the shops by the tradesman's entrance, but we're leaving by the front door. Originally, the shops were intended to be something else, but they just became like all the boutiques in London. They just weren't our thingy. The King's Road shop, which is known as Apple Tailoring, isn't going to be part of Apple anymore, but it isn't closing down, and we are leaving our investment there because we have a moral and personal obligation... We want to devote all our energies to records, films and our electronics adventures. We had to re-focus. We had to zoom in on what we really enjoy, and we enjoy being alive, and we enjoy being Beatles.'

Early in the morning on 7 August, after an all-night session for George's 'Not Guilty', Paul McCartney and Francine 'Francie' Schwartz, who worked in the Apple press office, visited the vacant Apple Boutique on Baker Street. 'One evening,' Schwartz wrote in her memoirs, 'Paul had suddenly decided to go down to Apple and paint the storefront windows white. Nobody saw us leave, but by the time we had fingered 'Revolution' and 'Hey Jude' in wet paint on each of the windows, a few reporters had gathered outside, wanting to know who I was and if there were any truths to the rumours [about her relationship with Paul]. Next morning, the *Daily Sketch* ran two half-columns headed 'Paul and Francie paint the town white.' Witty.' This ad-hoc PR backfired, as local residents assumed an anti-Semitic slur.

This off-the-cuff, unplanned act seemed to personify the way that Apple would work. However, with The Beatles attached, and notwithstanding some missteps such as this, Apple Records was bound to be a success. It released 59 albums in the UK between 1968 and 1976. Of these, 26 were hits, including 21 that reached the top ten and seven number ones. It was a similar story in the US, where, of the 62 albums released, 33 entered the *Billboard* Top 100 and 24 made the top ten, with 11 number ones. These are notable statistics, although it's worth stating that despite many hit singles for diverse artists, the only hit album on Apple which was not directly released by The Beatles (group or solo) was Badfinger's *Straight Up*, which peaked at number 31 in the US in 1972.

Behind the business, the story is one of chaos: Hells Angels, the rooftop concert, The Beatles' split, a bitter court case, Badfinger, 10cc, Yoko Ono, Allen Klein. Richard DiLello's memoir, *The Longest Cocktail Party* (1973), is an eye-opening account of how lots of money can be easily squandered. As he writes in the introduction to his book, 'Apple was a noble experiment created in the spirit of the '60s by four musicians who came to represent everything that was best about the '60s. It was birthed with selfless intentions. It was an idealistic blueprint for a new way of doing business, a place where aspiring artists and creators could come to fulfil their dreams without toadying to the corporate masters. And if business was what made the world go 'round, then dreams made it worth living. Apple would attest to that. The Beatles were going to use their own money to fund a new world order, saturated with beauty and art, a long-playing record without end, a soundtrack of non-stop joy. For a brief period, The Beatles and much of the world believed they would succeed. But then reality got in the way and the runners stumbled.'

This was a boutique record label at heart, of that there is no doubt, but what a story there is to tell.

1968

August – September 1968: The First Four

The first four official releases by Apple Records were made available on 26 August 1968 in the US: 'Hey Jude', 'Those Were The Days', 'Sour Milk Sea' and 'Thingumybob'. Two of these, 'Hey Jude' by The Beatles and 'Those Were The Days' by Mary Hopkin, came out on 30 August in the UK, with 'Sour Milk Sea' by Jackie Lomax and 'Thingumybob' by The Black Dyke Mills Band a week later.

But there was another, very much rarer release on Apple, a couple of weeks before these. Tony Bramwell, in his book *Magical Mystery Tours: My Life With The Beatles* (2000), tells the story of APPLE 1:

> It was Ringo's wife Maureen's 22nd birthday on 4 August 1968, and Ron Kass got the idea of doing something really special for her. He phoned his friend Sammy Cahn in Hollywood and got him to rewrite the lyrics to 'The Lady Is A Tramp' so that it related to Ringo and Maureen. Nobody thought Sammy would do it, but he did. Then he amazed us by calling Sinatra and asking him to record it. Frank (presumably with pianist Bill Miller, his long-time musical director) went to Capitol Studios in Hollywood's Capitol Tower, and the finished tape was couriered to Ron in London to be mastered. The printer ran off a single label that read: 'The Lady Is A Tramp', Frank Sinatra, APPLE 1. He took the master to EMI's factory for a test, and APPLE 1 was pressed, both sides the same. Ringo gave the one and only vinyl copy in the world to Maureen on her birthday. Then, Ron ordered the master stampers crushed. The tape was cut up and destroyed.

Proof, perhaps, that no-one could say 'no' to The Beatles. The recording circulates amongst collectors. Sinatra sings, with little enthusiasm, to a simple piano backing. The arrangement is a medley of 'The Lady Is A Tramp' from the 1937 musical *Babes In Arms* and 'But Beautiful' from the 1947 film *Road To Rio*.

> There's no-one like her, but no-one at all
> And as for charm, hers is like wall-to-wall
> She married Ringo and she could have had Paul!
> That's why the Lady is a Champ
> Though we've not met I'm convinced she's a gem
> I'm just FS but to me she's Big M
> Mainly because she prefers me to them
> That's why the Lady is a Champ

Back to business. Outside his own projects and those of The Beatles, John Lennon had little interest in Apple Records. He was not directly involved in any music beyond those of The Beatles, his various solo albums and those he made with Yoko. Likewise, although Ringo was employed as a session drummer and released several solo albums on Apple, he chose not to produce any music by Apple's various signings. 'I wasn't as involved as the others,' Ringo said in *Anthology*, 'but it was fun. A lot of what Apple did related to the four of us, but I wasn't hanging out there every day. At that time, I didn't really want to be in an office. I liked to be in the country.'

It was left to Paul and George to nurture new talent, bankrolled by the first single released on Apple: 'Hey Jude'. With its Parlophone catalogue number R5722 and the now-famous Apple image in the centre label, it would be an immediate and huge hit. It was 1968's top-selling single in the UK and the US (and in other countries around the world). In their home country, it knocked The Bee Gees' 'I Gotta Get A Message To You' from number one on 17 September. In the US, it stayed at number one for nine weeks, from September to November, the longest-ever continuous run at the top of the US charts until 1977 when Debby Boone's 'You Light Up My Life' would extend it to ten.

In the UK, 'Hey Jude' topped the UK singles chart for two weeks and was replaced at number one by another Apple single, Mary Hopkin's 'Those Were The Days'. This remained at number one for six weeks from 25 September, as well as settling at number two in the US behind 'Hey Jude', and was part of a conspicuous success – 13 million sales – for a new record company's first two releases.

Mary Hopkin is a Welsh folk singer who was brought to Paul McCartney's attention by his friend, the model Twiggy, who had seen Hopkin sing Pete Seeger's 'Turn, Turn, Turn' on *Opportunity Knocks*, a long-running ITV talent show hosted by Hughie Green between 1964 and 1978. The show was recorded in Manchester on 3 May – Hopkin's 18th birthday – and broadcast two days later. Hopkin's clear voice and simple production were appealing, and these qualities were evident in McCartney's arrangement of 'Those Were The Days', a Russian folk song with a nostalgic English lyric, which chimed oddly with a singer who had just turned 18. McCartney heard folkies, and the song's co-composer, Gene & Francesca, perform 'Those Were The Days' in a London nightclub some years before and had tucked the song away for future use. Hopkin's version was a massive hit around the world, reaching number one in the UK, Belgium, Canada, Denmark, Finland, France (as 'Les Temps Des Fleurs'), Germany ('An Jenem Tag'), Ireland, Japan, The Netherlands, New Zealand, Norway, Poland, Singapore, Spain ('Que Tiempo Tan Feliz'), Sweden and Switzerland.

The two other singles released by Apple in August 1968 were less successful. Jackie Lomax was a gruff-voiced Liverpudlian, former lead singer of the Merseybeat group The Undertakers, who followed The Beatles' route through local Liverpool venues and a residency in Hamburg before securing a recording contract with Pye. One of their four singles, 'Just A Little Bit', achieved a solitary week in the UK charts in 1964. By 1967, Lomax was informally managed by Brian Epstein and, after Epstein's death, Apple took over responsibility for Lomax's recording career.

His debut single for Apple, 'Sour Milk Sea', was written by George Harrison in India. It was demoed for The Beatles in May 1968 (released in 2018) before being officially recorded the following month, produced by Harrison at EMI and Trident. It rocks hard, with a stinging lead guitar, courtesy of Eric Clapton. The rest of the backing band were no slouches either: George, Paul, Ringo and the keyboard session maestro Nicky Hopkins. The B-side, Lomax's own 'The Eagle Laughs At You', reworks the Bo Diddley beat. The song was re-released in the US in June 1971 (B-side: 'I Fall Inside Your Eyes') to no effect.

Finally, 'Thingumybob' is by the long-established John Foster & Son Ltd Black Dyke Mills Band, a brass band from Bradford. 'Thingumybob' was a Paul McCartney instrumental (credited to Lennon/McCartney) that was the theme to an ITV sitcom of the same name starring Stanley Holloway, which had first aired on 2 August. The song, and its B-side, an arrangement of 'Yellow Submarine', was recorded at 9 am on a Sunday morning in Saltaire on 30 June 1968.

These first four singles were packaged together as a promo-only box set called, appropriately enough, *Our First Four*. Copies were hand-delivered to The Queen, the Queen Mother, Lord Snowdon and the Prime Minister, Harold Wilson. Only 400 were made, and this is now highly sought after by collectors. Plans for a series of Beatles concerts were put in place, with The Royal Albert Hall booked for several days in December 1968.

The Beatles' official biography was published on 30 September. It was written by Hunter Davies. Since its commission, Brian Epstein had died, The Beatles had been to India, Apple had been founded and John Lennon had left his wife for Yoko Ono. 'In the whole realm of non-fiction,' noted Philip Norman, 'there was no hotter topic, and Davies had it all to himself.'

October 1968: Business Problems

By the late autumn of 1968, it had become clear to Apple's management team (and, as a result, to The Beatles themselves) that Apple was overspending and their business plan was becoming unsustainable. Stephen Maltz, The Beatles' accountant and financial adviser, resigned on 30 September and left the company a few days later. His resignation letter is reproduced in his 2015 book *The Beatles, Apple And Me.*

Dear John, Paul, George and Ringo,
As you are aware, I am leaving Apple today, and since I have been connected with you for approximately three years, I feel that this is a good occasion to express some of my views and make certain observations.

After six years' work, for the most part of which you have been at the very top of the musical world, in which you have given pleasure to countless millions throughout every country where records are played, what have you got left to show for it? I am sure you have derived great satisfaction from your work and that materially you have had every comfort you desired. You have had the opportunity of doing whatever you wished to do and to search for whatever you are searching for, but my concern only for you is purely so that you can have enough money to go on doing all these things. Two of you have money in the bank and a vast holding in a public company, but are these shares, in fact, worth to you what they are quoted at? You have shown no inclination so far of diversifying your assets. They are all locked away in a Company solely dependent on you. You, therefore, have no freedom of action as far as that is concerned. All four of you have houses, cars, etc., but you also have tax bills to be paid and tax cases to be won. Meanwhile, the spending goes on. You have already spent the second £400,000 due under the goodwill scheme that has not been approved as yet by the tax authorities. You all have assets in the form of your shares in the Apple companies, but this is only paper until Apple can be built into a position where that paper can be sold, but at the rate Apple is progressing, it seems likely to me that this paper will eventually be valueless. Your personal finances are in a mess. Apple is in a mess, and I believe honestly that the only way you can get out of it is by trusting Neil [Aspinall] and talking to him not as a road manager but as a managing director.

Please believe me when I say that my only wish for you is that you have the millions you so richly deserve, and I hope that I will still have the opportunity of being able to speak to you as frankly and honestly as I have always tried to do.

With all best wishes to you,
Stephen Maltz

John: 'I got a note from an accountant saying, 'You're broke, and if you go on, it's going to all go, whatever you've got left.' He laid it out to all of us, but I think I was the only one who read it.' Alistair Taylor, formerly Brian Epstein's personal assistant and now a director at Apple, called a meeting with The Beatles and Neil Aspinall. Taylor explained that Apple was losing £50,000 *per week*. 'If you allow things to carry on the way they are, you will lose all of your money within 12 months,' he told The Beatles. Lennon's response: 'Don't be a drag, Al.' Taylor suggested that Apple needed a proven businessman to head the company.

I was getting very worried by now, and I called the boys in, sat them down, and said, 'Look, this can't go on!' Neil was with us, and he was more on their side than mine. I said, 'Something has got to be done. We cannot go on like this. Look at us. We're a multi-million-pound company, and you've just got us five guys running this company. I can't speak for everyone, but, for me, it's beyond me to do it like it should be done. I think we need a top

businessman in here to run it. Somebody to control the company.' John then began to realise that money was flying out.
Alistair Taylor quoted in *The Beatles: Off The Record* (2008)

John: 'I'm sure the others wanted it tightened up, but I don't think they were really aware of it. I mean, they could all tell. Sometimes, George would go in and go crazy because of how many people were just lying around drunk there and living on the company. But you couldn't stop it. Somehow, it needed a firm hand to stop it.'

Paul sought the counsel of Lee Eastman, his girlfriend Linda's father and an experienced music lawyer. Paul was convinced that Eastman was the right person to manage The Beatles' financial affairs. The other Beatles were not comfortable with the idea of Paul's future father-in-law running Apple. Thus, the seeds of future discord were planted.

John Lennon's life continued to be chaotic. On 19 October, he was charged with drug possession at Marylebone Magistrates' Court. The following month, he met Richard Beeching, the former chairman of British Railways. Beeching had recommended extensive changes in the loss-making railway network, known as the 'Beeching Axe'. The meeting was unsuccessful. Beeching advised John to 'stick to making records'. A meeting with Cecil Harmsworth King, until recently the chair of IPC, the world's biggest publishing corporation, was similarly unproductive. John Lennon offered the job to Neil Aspinall, The Beatles' oldest and most loyal friend. Neil, at that time, had no wish to accept the role.

November 1968: The White Album, 'Maybe Tomorrow'

With The Beatles busy recording *The White Album,* it would be several months between Apple Records' formation and their first album release. *Wonderwall Music*, released on 1 November 1968, is George Harrison's first solo album and extends his experiments with mixing Indian and Western music styles. As with many instrumental soundtrack albums, the music has little interest outside the film. It's very much 'of its time' and despite the loud presence of Eric Clapton on one track, 'Ski-Ing', this one is for devout collectors only. *Wonderwall Music* has arrangements by John Barham, a graduate of the Royal Academy of Music. He had been introduced to George by Ravi Shankar, and Barham would be the arranger-of-choice on many projects, including the strings on *Let It Be*, *Imagine*, *All Things Must Pass* and others.

In early November, Apple's press office announced that The Beatles had block-booked The Roundhouse in Chalk Farm for the last two weeks of December, with a view to one or more live concerts. This idea was shelved, partly due to Yoko Ono's miscarriage in mid-November.

The Beatles would be released on 22 November 1968 to universal acclaim. A week later, an album celebrated for different reasons would follow: John Lennon and Yoko Ono's *Unfinished Music No.1: Two Virgins*. It's difficult, even almost 60 years later, to be objective about this self-indulgent mess. It was the result of an all-night session of experimentation and is utterly unlistenable. When the most notable aspect of an album is the cover, which shows the couple naked, then the music, such as it is, becomes irrelevant. Astoundingly, *Two Virgins* reached number 124 on the US *Billboard* album charts.

In this period, serendipity brought an American trio to Apple. Guy Masson, Tom Smith and Tony Van Benschoten had the group name Mortimer and were keen to pitch songs for Mary Hopkin. They blagged their way into Apple, sang some of their songs and were noticed by George Harrison, who said, 'Sign them up.' They signed on 30 November and were assigned to Peter Asher, who booked them into Trident Studios for an afternoon to run through their songs. Thirty-nine tracks were recorded. Plans for an album were put into progress, with sessions booked for the following year.

Amidst all this, we meet the heroes and victims of the Apple story. The Iveys were a Welsh band, founded in 1961 by Pete Ham (guitar), Dai Jenkins (guitar), Ron Griffiths (bass) and Roy Anderson (drums). By late 1967, Anderson had been replaced by Mike Gibbins and Jenkins by Tom Evans. Evans and Ham were both accomplished songwriters. Evans wrote the band's debut single, 'Maybe Tomorrow', which was released by Apple in November 1968.

The Iveys were a hard-working, fully professional band from Swansea. Their manager, Bill Collins (father of *The Professionals* actor Lewis), knew Mal Evans when he worked at The Cavern in Liverpool and was also friendly with Paul McCartney's brother, Mike. This association was enough to persuade Evans and Peter Asher to see The Iveys perform at London's famous Marquee Club on 25 January 1968. Mal asked for a tape of the group to play for Paul McCartney. Paul was impressed, but not enough to sign them to Apple. Collins and Evans persevered, and the band were signed to Apple on 31 July 1968. Their debut single, 'Maybe Tomorrow', was recorded at Trident on 9 August. It was produced by Tony Visconti, who was at the beginning of a very illustrious producing career. Despite the over-lush production, 'Maybe Tomorrow' is still a terrific song with a strong chemistry between Ham and Evans. It was a big hit in the Netherlands and Germany. The prospects were good.

Terry Doran left Apple Publishing at this time to manage Grapefruit, who also moved away from Apple. Their Apple demos and masters were eventually released in 2016.

December 1968: James Taylor, Modern Jazz Quartet, Hell's Angels

The developing crisis at Apple was covered at length in a critical article by Alan Walsh, published in *Melody Maker* on 7 December, titled 'Has Apple Gone Rotten?' Walsh noted that Apple had launched with an ambition that was both grand and unusually public and that The Beatles set out to challenge what they saw as a corrupt music business, one preoccupied with quick returns and indifferent to talent or originality unless it promised immediate profit.

Apple, of course, promised an alternative: a company run on benevolence, giving artists the resources and freedom to create without interference. The reality, within six months, was mixed. The Apple Boutique collapsed amid poor management and opportunism, Apple Films failed to establish itself and Apple Electronics produced nothing of consequence. Only Apple Records provided any success.

Derek Taylor summed up the position with frankness. Apple had, in his words, become 'more or less a record company'. Taylor admitted to inefficiency and a lack of structure, yet defended the organisation's atmosphere of generosity and openness, suggesting that people still sought out Apple as a place of warmth and support.

In this spirit, in a busy few weeks, two further, very different albums would come out in early December.

James Taylor is known now for his smooth, Laurel Canyon hits such as 'Fire And Rain' (1970) and 'You've Got A Friend' (1971). His time at Apple was an extended false start. Taylor, born in Boston but raised in North Carolina, had moved to London in 1967, determined to be a successful musician. Through a mutual friend (future session ace Danny Kortchmar), Taylor sent some demos to Peter Asher.

'It was quite late on a rainy winter in early 1968,' Asher wrote later. 'I was at home in my flat and I got a phone call out of the blue from a rather nervous-seeming American with a very pleasant speaking voice. I didn't know him, but he told me his name was James Taylor. James explained that he was in London in search of some kind of musical success. He had made a demo the day before and wondered whether I would like to hear it. We made a plan for him to come over the next day. When he played the demo, I still remember my utter astonishment and delight. These were not traditional rock 'n' roll songs. They had elements of folk to them, but with an R&B groove. The vocals were intense and soulful, but introspective and thoughtful at the same time.'

A three-song demo from the time, released in 2010, shows Taylor's attractive voice, simple guitar accompaniment and depth of songwriting. 'I said that I had a new job as head of A&R for a new label,' Asher recalled, 'and that I would like to sign him.' Asher played the demo for Paul McCartney and George Harrison and, in short order, James Taylor became the first non-British act at Apple. His first album was recorded between July and October 1968 at Trident Studios, produced by Asher. Paul and George guest on 'Carolina In My Mind', and the title phrase of 'Something In The Way She Moves' was borrowed by George for one of his most famous songs.

James Taylor was released in his home country in February 1969. It was reviewed by Jon Landau in *Rolling Stone* issue 31 (19 April 1969).

> James Taylor is the kind of person I always thought the word folksinger referred to. He writes and sings songs that are reflections of his own life and performs them in his own style. All of his performances are marked by

an eloquent simplicity. Mr Taylor is not kicking out any jams. He seems to be more interested in soothing his troubled mind. In the process, he will doubtless soothe a good many heads besides his own. Taylor's music is a mix of country, blues and some antique folk styles. Whichever idiom he is leaning on in any particular song, both his lyrics and his voice flow with a lyricism that connotes a deeply personal style. Taylor is aware of his mastery of his material and, therefore, tends to understate things. His reserve is a sign of his maturity. He sings with resonance and plays with grace; he refuses to let himself get lost in anything that obscures his identity as an artist. There is only one problem with this album: some of the production is superfluous. There are a few string arrangements that serve no real function. The horn arrangements sound a bit too British. And on some cuts, James' voice is not as 'up front' as it should have been. These reservations notwithstanding, this album is the coolest breath of fresh air I've inhaled in a good long while. It knocks me out.

James Taylor is a strong album, sophisticated and elegant even if, at times, the busy production is at odds with Taylor's songs and voice. It was perhaps a year too soon: *Crosby, Stills & Nash* and *Clouds* (both May 1969) would be the foundation for the Laurel Canyon sound, and Taylor would quickly become an important part of that scene.

Under The Jasmin Tree by Modern Jazz Quartet had no patronage from The Beatles. The album was recorded in New York City and made available at the insistence of the first Head of Apple Records, Ron Kass. The Modern Jazz Quartet comprised pianist and composer John Lewis, vibraphone player Milt Jackson and a rhythm section of Percy Heath (bass) and Connie Kay (drums – he played on *Astral Weeks*). Lewis and Jackson had performed with Dizzy Gillespie and Miles Davis. By 1968, the group had been established for almost 20 years. Their first album for Apple oozes professionalism, comprising four instrumental pieces varying from five to 14 minutes in length.

George Harrison had visited San Francisco in August 1967. Here, he met two Hell's Angels and, in an unguarded moment, invited them to visit. They raised the money (funded by the concert promoter Bill Graham) and made plans. Their arrival was heralded by a call from the customs office at Heathrow asking for £250 (almost £3,000 in 2025) to cover shipping charges for two Harley Davidson motorcycles.

From George Harrison to all Apple staff, 4 December 1968:

Hell's Angels will be in London within the next week on the way to straighten out Czechoslovakia. There will be 12 in number, complete with black leather jackets and motorcycles. They will undoubtedly arrive at Apple, and I have heard they may try to make full use of Apple's facilities. They may look as though they are going to do you in, but are very straight and do good things, so don't fear them or uptight them. Try to assist them

> without neglecting your Apple business and without letting them take control of Savile Row.

Neil Aspinall: 'George had said: 'Oh, if you ever come to England, look us up, or something. A couple of months later, the motorbikes were outside Savile Row with these guys saying, 'Well, George said it was okay.' They ended up living at Apple and terrifying everybody.'

Apple's Christmas party was held on 23 December with John and Ringo in attendance. George skipped the event, fearing violence (he was right to worry), and Paul was in Liverpool with his family. 'We had the Hell's Angels' Christmas Party', Neil Aspinall recalled. 'I can remember that everybody was getting hungry, and then a huge turkey came in on a big tray with four people carrying it. It was about ten yards from the door to the table where they were going to put the turkey down, but it never made it. The Hell's Angels just went 'woof', and everything disappeared: arms, legs, breast, everything. By the time it got to the table, there was nothing there. They just ripped the turkey to pieces, trampling young children underfoot to get to it. I've never seen anything like it.'

'They proceeded to ruin the kids' party,' Ringo recalled, 'and then we couldn't get rid of them. They wouldn't leave, and we had bailiffs and everything to try to get them out. It was miserable, and everyone was terrified, including the grown-ups. It was like the edgy Christmas party.'

A few days later, they were asked to leave by George. This encounter was described by Richard DiLello in his book *The Longest Cocktail Party*.

> 'Well, are you moving all of your stuff out of here tonight?' George asked rhetorically.
>
> There was a hush so deep it seemed as if the molecules in the air had stopped moving. All eyes turned on George. An intense seesaw struggle to maintain a psychological cool bounced from one end of the room to the other in a duel of eyeballs. The silence seemed to stretch out forever.
>
> 'Hey, man,' [one of the Hell's Angels] said, 'I just wanna ask you one question. Do you dig us or don't you?'
>
> 'Yin and yang, heads and tails, yes and no', replied George Harrison.
>
> This answer to that question completely fucked everyone's mind. No one knew quite what to say or how to say it.
>
> George turned and left the room. 'Good-bye, everyone!' he hurled over his shoulder.
>
> One of the micro boppers, still shattered by the aura of this charismatic young man who had just dazzled them all, finally found her vocal cords.
>
> 'Gosh, he sure is beautiful', she moaned.

In this same period, Apple were courted by a trio of musicians who would become one of the most popular and influential bands of 1969-70. David

Crosby had been in The Byrds, Stephen Stills was formerly of Buffalo Springfield and Graham Nash had co-founded The Hollies. By the end of 1968, they were united as an acoustic trio: Crosby, Stills & Nash.

Crosby had met The Beatles in August 1965 when they socialised together. The same happened the following summer when he attended the press conference for the release of *Revolver*. Crosby later attended sessions for *Sgt. Pepper's Lonely Hearts Club Band* in February 1967 (there are rumours that he sings on 'Lovely Rita'). So, he had an 'in' when he wanted to find a record deal for his new band with Stills and Nash. They travelled to London together in December 1968 to rehearse and finalise some legal matters. Barry Miles, Paul McCartney's friend, was one of the people who understood the trio's potential.

'One Sunday before Christmas, we went to a flat in Moscow Road to hear what Graham Nash had described on the phone as 'one of the happiest sounds you have ever heard", Miles wrote in *International Times*. 'The new supergroup of Graham, Dave Crosby and Steve Stills had been the subject of much rumour and discussion – the living proof is even better than predicted.'

Crosby, Stills and Nash were able to sing the whole of their new album with just voices and guitars.

'We invited George Harrison over to listen,' Stills told Dave Zimmer in the band's official biography, 'to see if Apple might be interested in us.' As Crosby clarified on Twitter in January 2022. '[It was a] live audition. [We] sang the whole first record in London to George and Peter Asher.' The trio received a letter the next day explaining that Crosby, Stills & Nash 'would not be a good fit'.

'After we finished, [George] went, 'Wow!", Stills recalled. 'Then, he turned us down! The English attitude toward American musicians was a lot more competitive than I expected. 'Flippin' Yanks, tryin' to steal our thunder, eh?' And little ol' naïve Stephen from down there in Florida was just tryin' to be friendly. A little encouragement from our limey mates wouldn't have hurt.'

Nash talked to Harrison about this in 1983. Graham said, 'George told me he'd heard us on tape, but I don't remember making any tapes in England then. We could have. But, anyway, George tells me, 'It's damn lucky CSN didn't end up on Apple, because things were so totally chaotic, you would have been swallowed up in the bullshit'.'

'They turned us down,' Nash recalled years later. 'How could you listen to that first album sung by the three of us and go 'No thanks'. I never understood that.'

'Apple passed on a number one record there,' Crosby tweeted. 'Everybody makes mistakes. Bet they regretted it later.'

There may also have been a hangover from a well-publicised spat between Graham Nash and George Harrison. The Hollies, who formed in 1962, had played the same club scene as The Beatles. They were performing at The Cavern in Liverpool when they were seen by Parlophone's Ron Richards and were offered an audition with EMI. The Beatles and The Hollies shared the bill as part of an eight-hour promotion at The Cavern on 3 February 1963, and the Manchester group were signed to EMI that spring. As EMI artists, they had access to Beatles demos and recorded their version of 'If I Needed Someone' on 17 November 1965 (about a month after The Beatles' own). George expressed displeasure when interviewed by *New Musical Express* in December 1965. 'Tell people that I didn't write it for The Hollies', George is quoted as saying, 'I think it's rubbish the way they've done it! They've spoilt it. The Hollies are all right musically, but the way they do their records, they sound like session men who've just got together in a studio without ever seeing each other before. Technically good, yes. But that's all.' Nash responded the following week in the same paper, 'Not only do these comments disappoint and hurt us, but we're sick and tired of everything The Beatles say or do being taken as law. The thing that hurt us the most was George Harrison's knock at us as musicians. And I would like to ask this: if we have made such a disgusting mess of his brainchild song, will he give all the royalties from our record to charity? I'll tell you this much: we did this song against a lot of people's advice. We just felt that after nine records, we could afford to do something like this without being accused of jumping on The Beatles' bandwagon. We thought it was a good song. And still do. About the crack about us sounding like session men, I suppose he means we don't have any soul in our discs. Rubbish. We don't profess to be a soul R&B-type group, and we never have. My opinion of The Beatles hasn't changed. I still think they're great, and I'm not going to say anything stupid like, 'I'm going to burn all their records in my collection.' No. I like their music. But knocking comments like the one about us are a load of bollocks.'

This exchange from three years before might have been a factor in Apple's dismissal of Crosby, Stills & Nash, who flew back to Los Angeles a few days before Christmas 1968. They signed with Atlantic Records the following month, recorded and released their debut album that spring, teamed up with Neil Young, performed at Woodstock and had a number one album with *Déjà Vu* in 1970.

Amidst this chaos, Apple confirmed that The Beatles' proposed live concert, previously scheduled for the Royal Albert Hall and the Roundhouse, had been postponed until 18 January 1969.

1969

January 1969: Get Back, Allen Klein, Yellow Submarine

During the whole of January, John, Paul, George and Ringo rehearsed and recorded hours of material for their proposed live concert and next album, *Get Back*. The concert idea was dropped after George quit the band for a few days, with their 40-minute rooftop performance as an eventual compromise.

An interview with John Lennon by Ray Coleman was published in *Disc & Music Echo* on 13 January 1969. This made Apple's business problems public for the first time.

> Apple is losing money. If it carries on like this, we'll be broke in six months.
> Q: Are you happy with the way that Apple is shaping?
> No, not really. I think it's a bit messy and it wants tightening up. We haven't got half the money people think we have. We have to live on, but we can't let Apple go on like it is. We started off with loads of ideas of what we wanted to do, you know, an umbrella of different activities. But, like one or two Beatles things, it didn't work out because we weren't quick enough to realise that we needed a business brain to run the whole thing. You can't offer facilities to poets and charities and film plans unless you have money coming in. It's been pie-in-the-sky from the start. Apple's losing money every week because it needs closely running by a big businessman. We did it all wrong, you know, Paul and me running to New York City, saying we'll do this and encourage this and that. It's got to be a business first. We realise that now. It needs a broom, and a lot of people there will have to go. It needs streamlining … It doesn't need to make vast profits, but if it carries on like this, all of us will be broke in the next six months.

If the other Beatles were uncomfortable with the idea of Paul's future father-in-law running Apple, they nevertheless agreed to have Lee Eastman and his son John act as business advisors. They signed a document granting the Eastmans the authority to negotiate contracts on their behalf. John Eastman used those rights to parley the acquisition of Brian Epstein's former company, Nems Enterprises, which Clive Epstein was now looking to sell to cover taxes due following Epstein's death. These were due on 31 March 1969. Here was a part of The Beatles' legacy that they deserved to own.

EMI chair Sir Joseph Lockwood agreed to lend The Beatles £1m against future royalties to buy Nems Enterprises and to keep 25% of their own royalties, which funnelled into Nems Enterprises' account as management commission. This last clause, added by Brian Epstein in 1967, would legally stay in place until 1976, even if the Nems Enterprises management contract was terminated: it's worth spelling out here, that had The Beatles left Nems Enterprises at any time between 1967 and 1976, then Nems Enterprises remained recipients of 25% commission on all income through the term of the contract.

'[John] Eastman spent a week negotiating for Nems Enterprises on the basis of the loan that Lockwood was prepared to make The Beatles,' Clive Epstein said in 1972. 'But he loaded the offer with so many conditions and warranties that he ended up talking himself out of the deal. In my opinion, he was a little too young to be negotiating at that level.'

The plans for John and Lee Eastman to act as The Beatles' business managers and the sale of Nems Enterprises were both disrupted by the arrival of Allen Klein. Klein was an accountant by trade and had entered the music industry by skilfully renegotiating Sam Cooke's agreement with RCA. This not only enriched the soul singer considerably but also Klein himself, who ended up owning the rights to all of Cooke's recordings. Klein subsequently became the American business manager of the successful producer Mickie Most. His work for Most gave Klein access to several musicians and, in time, he would negotiate vastly improved deals for The Animals, Herman's Hermits, The Kinks, Lulu, Donovan and Pete Townshend. Klein's business plan was to shelter money from Britain's high tax rates and reinvest it to earn far more than he was obliged to pay out. Klein famously renegotiated The Rolling Stones' contract with Decca, so that Jagger, Richards and co. earned considerably more than The Beatles despite selling fewer records. Money talks.

Klein had seen John Lennon's comments in *Disc & Music Echo* and, through a mutual friend of Derek Taylor, pressed for a meeting with the musician. They met at The Dorchester Hotel in London on 27 January after Lennon had been working on The Beatles' next single, 'Get Back'. 'Both John and Yoko were extremely nervous when they arrived at the hotel', wrote McCabe and Schonfeld. 'They'd heard plenty about this awesome figure, who managed The Rolling Stones and had said years ago that one day he would have The Beatles. They were surprised to find an equally nervous, bright-eyed, stocky individual in a sweater and sneakers, alone in his hotel room, with no assistants and no lawyers. During the course of the evening, Klein impressed Lennon with his knowledge of the pop industry and The Beatles' work. He knew all about their current position. Had John Eastman taken the trouble to learn a little more about the group, Klein might never have obtained even an audience.'

John Lennon was impressed enough to immediately appoint Allen Klein as his personal manager. He scribbled a note to EMI's chairman Sir Joseph Lockwood: 'Dear Sir Joe – from now on, Allen Klein handles all my stuff.' The following day, John met Klein again, accompanied by George Harrison, Ringo Starr, Paul McCartney and Lee Eastman. Klein would describe this meeting in a subsequent court case.

> On 28 January 1969, at 3 Savile Row, London, W1, at about 9 pm, I met Mr Lennon, the Plaintiff [Paul McCartney], Richard Starkey [Ringo Starr] and George Harrison and had a general discussion about the proposed purchase

> of Nems. I informed them that, for my part, I could not recommend Mr Lennon to proceed with the purchase while (as was the fact) the relevant information about the position of The Beatles (and their companies) themselves remained to be ascertained. The Plaintiff said that the proposal was strongly recommended by John Eastman, and he (the Plaintiff) was pressing it. I therefore suggested that there was no point in debating the matter in the absence of John Eastman, and it was agreed that we have another meeting on Saturday 1 February, with John Eastman present.
>
> During the meeting on 28 January, I said that I was going to make enquiries into Mr Lennon's financial position. Mr Starkey and Mr Harrison asked me to do the same for them. (At this stage, the Plaintiff had left the meeting) I spent the remainder of that week largely in the offices of Bryce Hammer & Co, chartered accountants (who were The Beatles' personal accountants) with Mr Harry Pinsker, a partner in that firm, obtaining the information that I required. By the end of the week, I had a reasonable amount of information about the personal position of The Beatles, but, as I had not had time to make a full investigation into the affairs of their companies, I was not really in a position to assess their true financial position overall.

As Klein noted, Paul McCartney and John Eastman left the meeting early. Starr and George Harrison sided with John Lennon and Allen Klein, and here we have the schism that split The Beatles apart.

'I liked Allen', Ringo said later. 'He was a lot of fun, and he knew the record business. He knew records, he knew acts, he knew music. A lot of people we spoke to were trying to get in with the music crowd but didn't know anything about the music business.'

George, for his part, thought, 'Well, if that's the choice, I think I'll go with Klein because John's with him and he seemed to talk pretty straight. However, years later, we formed a different opinion. Because we were all from Liverpool, we favoured people who were street people. Lee Eastman was more like a class-conscious type of person. As John was going with Klein, it would be much easier if we went with him, too.'

Away from these business problems, Apple released 17 singles and 11 albums in 1969. The first of these was the soundtrack to the film *Yellow Submarine*. This included four new songs by The Beatles (recorded in mid-1967 and early 1968), as well as two previously released tracks and a whole side of George Martin's orchestral score. 'Only A Northern Song', 'All Together Now', 'Hey Bulldog' and 'It's All Too Much' are all good if non-essential songs, effectively off-cuts from other projects, but with The Beatles' name on the front cover, *Yellow Submarine* was a big hit and added greatly to Apple's coffers. The original idea of a five-song EP (adding 'Across The Universe') might have been more artistically valid.

A cover of Jerry Goffin and Carole King's 'Road To Nowhere' would be released as the first of two singles by the Scottish band White Trash, formerly known as The Pathfinders. They comprised Timi Donald (drums), Frazer Watson (guitar), Ronnie Leahy (organ), Ian Clews (vocals) and Colin Morrison (bass). The band had been brought to Apple by Tony Meehan, former drummer for The Shadows, turned record producer, who had recorded The Beatles' audition for Decca in 1962. 'Road To Nowhere' reminds the listener of an organ-heavy variant of 'If I Were A Carpenter'. It adds little to King's magnificent original.

Meanwhile, the Apple board were told about John's desire to bring on Allen Klein at a meeting on 31 January. Paul was still hopeful that the band's rooftop show would rekindle the others' appetites for playing together. John closed that down immediately. He then went on to officially appoint Klein with the words, 'I don't give a bugger what anyone else wants. I'm having Allen Klein for me.'

February 1969: Business Troubles

From *Cash Box*, 2 February 1969:

> Apple Corps, the Beatle enterprise, is to take over Nems Enterprises, the company built up by the foursome's late manager, Brian Epstein. The largest holding in Nems is the 70% owned by Epstein's mother, who inherited shares after his death, and The Beatles themselves have 20%. There is further interlinking represented by a 7.2% Nems stake in the publicly quoted Northern Songs, in which John Lennon and Paul McCartney have 15% each, and Northern Songs directors have a financial interest in some Nems contracts. Rumours that Apple has been experiencing fiscal strain were substantiated recently by comments attributed to Lennon to the effect that if the company's expenditure continued at its present level, it would be bankrupt within six months. Apple publicity director Derek Taylor remarked in a BBC radio interview that it seemed the company had too many people on its payroll and was trying to help too many causes and projects financially. Lennon approached Lord Beeching, a noted figure in British industry and former chief of British Rail, for business guidance and assistance for Apple last fall, but received a polite refusal. Another top businessman, at present anonymous, is said to be taking over the administrative reins of the company to organise it on a sounder footing. It is estimated that Apple receives about £750,000 annually in Beatle record royalties, while a further £250,000 goes to Nems. These amounts will obviously swell when proceeds from the massive sales of the foursome's current double album start to flow. By acquiring Nems, Apple will strengthen its own financial health and also obtain a slice of Northern Songs.

Klein's appointment as a business advisor to Apple was announced on 3 February, and The Beatles, Klein and John Eastman met again that day. Later, Klein met Clive Epstein and his accountant at the Dorchester Hotel. 'I asked

Clive Epstein if he would be willing to wait and defer a decision with regard to his disposal of Nems Enterprises for about three weeks,' Klein stated in a later affidavit, 'until I had had an opportunity to assess the financial position of The Beatles and their companies. Clive Epstein agreed to defer a decision [on the sale of Nems Enterprises] for at least three weeks.' Klein returned to New York City the following day after a very productive stay in London.

Clive and Queenie Epstein were ill-suited to the demands of the music business. As McCabe and Schonfeld observed, 'As head of the Nems entertainment complex, [Clive Epstein] appeared as a roller skater among a herd of rhinos. Within a few months, the struggle of managing the company had exhausted him, and he confided to friends that all he wanted was time to relax and a chance to concentrate on his furniture business.'

On 14 February, John Eastman wrote to Clive Epstein, as reproduced in *The Beatles: A Diary Volume 1: The Beatles Years* (2009) by Barry Miles.

> As you know, Mr Allen Klein is doing an audit of The Beatles' affairs vis-à-vis Nems and Nemperor Holdings Ltd. When this has been completed, I suggest we meet to discuss the results of Mr Klein's audit as well as the propriety of the negotiations surrounding the nine-year agreement between EMI, The Beatles and Nems.

This shocked Clive Epstein, who read it as an insult towards his late brother. He immediately replied.

> Before any meeting takes place, please be good enough to let me know precisely what you mean by the phrase 'the propriety of the negotiations surrounding the nine-year agreement between EMI, The Beatles and Nems'.

Unwilling to be part of potentially difficult negotiations with The Beatles, Eastman and Klein, Clive Epstein reopened negotiations with Triumph Investment Trust, a firm of London merchant bankers. On 17 February, Triumph acquired 70% of the shares of Nems Enterprises for £750,000. Later that year, they acquired a further 20%.

February 1969: Post Card And Is This What You Want?

Mary Hopkin's debut album *Post Card* was very much a pet project for Paul McCartney, who chose the songs and produced the recording sessions at EMI, Trident and Morgan studios between October and December 1968. *Post Card* comprises an intriguing mix of show tunes ('Someone To Watch Over Me', 'Lullaby Of The Leaves', 'There's No Business Like Show Business'), 50s throwbacks ('Inch Worm', Young Love', 'The Honeymoon Song'), songs in languages other than English ('Prince En Avignon', 'Y Blodyn Gwyn') and compositions by Donovan ('Lord Of The Reedy River', 'Happiness Runs (Pebble And The Man)', 'Voyage Of The Moon'), Harry Nilsson ('The Puppy

Song', later a big hit for David Cassidy) and George Martin ('The Game'). Paul plays acoustic guitar on two songs and bass on two others.

The album is beautifully produced, but some of the material is very sophisticated for a young singer. The three songs by Donovan work the best. As Hopkin said in the sleeve notes to the reissue, 'I thought Donovan was like a little elf, this magical person. They sat on either side of me, him and Paul, playing their acoustic guitars. I was on a stool between them, sitting there like a tiny mouse, singing this beautiful music.'

The release had been celebrated at a launch party on 13 February in the revolving restaurant in London's Post Office Tower. An impressive guest list included Donovan, George Martin, Brian Jones, Jimi Hendrix, Tony Visconti and Eric Clapton. 'Mary was holding up well', wrote Richard DiLello. 'Beseeched for autographs, chased by questions, asked again and again for just one more smile for the camera, fending off advances, she carried the whole thing with a surprising expertise for a girl who had had to make the transition from knee socks to world stardom in less than a year.' With little tact, Paul appeared at the reception in public for the first time with Linda Eastman, hence generating press coverage that ignored Mary Hopkin.

'Those Were The Days' was added to the US release, and *Post Card* was the first non-Beatles album from Apple to crack the *Billboard* top 30 in spring 1969.

If *Post Card* was Paul's baby, then Jackie Lomax's album, *Is This What You Want?,* recorded in the same period, is very much George Harrison's. This takes nothing away from Lomax's terrific songs (all but one are his), his powerful singing or his photogenic good looks. With 'Sour Milk Sea' and its B-side, 'The Eagle Laughs At You', already in the can, much of the album was recorded in Los Angeles between 16 October and 11 November. George flew to the US for his first sessions there, immediately after the conclusion of *The Beatles*. In addition to Jackie and George, the famous session players Larry Knechtel (piano), Joe Osborn (bass) and Hal Blaine (drums) from The Wrecking Crew comprised the core band. The opening song, the robust, soulful 'Speak To Me', sets the standard for an enjoyable album, very much in the Joe Cocker/Leon Russell style. The failure of *Is This What You Want?* to have any commercial success was unexpected and unfortunate.

Sessions for Mortimer's album began in February 1969. Peter Asher had been working from Apple's Los Angeles office for several months, giving Mortimer time to write new songs. They had enough material for an album, which would be recorded over several sessions that spring.

Peter Asher's other client, James Taylor's only single for Apple, 'Carolina In My Mind', was released in February/March 1969. The B-side, 'Taking It In', is taken from *James Taylor*. It crept into the lower reaches of the *Billboard* charts (reaching a high of number 118) and was re-released in October/ November 1970 with a different B-side following Taylor's success with 'Fire And Rain' and *Sweet Baby James*.

Outside music, Allen Klein returned to London to meet with Leonard Richenberg of Triumph Investment Trust at Savile Row on 25 February. After several sessions, Richenberg agreed to accept £750,000 in cash and 25% (over £300,000) of accrued royalties for their share of Nems Enterprises, as well as taking £50,000 for Nems Enterprises' 23% stake in the film company Subafilms. They also agreed to take 5% of The Beatles' gross record royalty from 1972 to 1976, rather than 25% for the next nine years. 'Richenberg says he was satisfied with it,' noted McCabe and Schonfeld, 'as he knew that Klein would soon roast EMI's chairman, Lockwood, to get The Beatles' royalty rate increased.' Nems Enterprises surrendered all of its rights in all contracts affecting The Beatles.

The Triumph deal had the immediate effect of holding back The Beatles' royalty payments, as it was not clear to EMI whether earnings should be channelled through Triumph or paid directly into Apple. EMI decided to freeze £1.3m in royalties (over £22m in 2025 value) until the situation was clarified. This went to court, which found in Apple's favour on 1 April. This was the first of many expensive court cases in the following years. 'It's fair to say that had we got Nems Enterprises, a lot of our later financial problems would never have occurred', Neil Aspinall said in *Apple To The Core*. 'It cost The Beatles a lot more to free themselves from Triumph later. You could say the deal was crucial.'

March 1969: 'Goodbye', 'New Day'

The astounding success of 'Those Were The Days' demanded a follow-up. This time, Paul McCartney provided his own song, 'Goodbye'. This was recorded over two days, 1-2 March 1969, with the arrangement closely following a home demo recorded by Paul the previous week. Mary Hopkin sang and played acoustic guitar, while Paul played bass guitar, acoustic guitar, ukulele and drums. Backing vocals, horns and strings were later added. The B-side, 'Sparrow', was written by Apple-signed songwriters Benny Gallagher and Graham Lyle. Hopkin sang and played guitar once again, and Paul added maracas.

'Although I'm flattered that Paul wrote 'Goodbye' especially for me,' Hopkin told *Goldmine* in 2007, 'it was, I believe, a step in the wrong direction for me. I'm so grateful that he chose 'Those Were The Days' as my first single. I think 'Those Were The Days', being originally a Ukrainian folk song, has a timeless quality, but 'Goodbye' is set firmly in the 1960s pop era.'

Nevertheless, 'Goodbye' reached a height of number two in April, sandwiched between 'The Israelites' by Desmond Dekker And The Aces and 'I Heard It Through The Grapevine' by Marvin Gaye. After being available for years on bootlegs, Paul's original demo was officially released in 2019. Outside the UK, Apple would release two songs recorded for local markets: 'Lontano Dagli Occhi' in Italy and 'Prince En Avignon' in France.

The day after 'Goodbye' was recorded, and in utter contrast, John Lennon performed with Yoko Ono at Cambridge University.

'Talking about John and Yoko, did you hear about their concert last night?'
'What concert?'
'It was Yoko's concert at Lady Mitchell Hall in Cambridge, and she just wailed and screamed and moaned, and John accompanied her on feedback guitar.'
'Wailing, screaming, and moaning? Well, it makes sense, doesn't it? I mean, after all, she isn't your average, everyday girl-next-door, now is she? If you ask me, this is just the beginning of John and Yoko. They're getting quite far out – '
Richard DiLello, *The Longest Cocktail Party* (1973)

Engineer and co-producer Glyn Johns was asked to compile an album from the January recording sessions to be called *Get Back*. His first attempt was mixed between 10 and 13 March and presented to The Beatles in April. This comprised:

Side One
'One After 909' (30 January 1969)
'Rocker (Instrumental)' (22 January 1969)
'Save The Last Dance For Me' (22 January 1969)
'Don't Let Me Down' (22 January 1969)
'Dig A Pony' (22 January 1969)
'I've Got A Feeling' (22 January 1969)
'Get Back' (23 January 1969)

Side Two
'For You Blue' (25 January 1969)
'Teddy Boy' (22 January 1969)
'Two Of Us' (24 January 1969)
'Maggie Mae' (24 January 1969)
'Dig It' (24 January 1969)
'Let It Be' (31 January 1969)
'The Long And Winding Road' (26 January 1969)
'Get Back (Reprise)' (23 January 1969)

At The Beatles' request, the 23 January version of 'Get Back' (side one, track seven) was replaced by the single version. A longer edit of 'Dig It' was preferred, and some dialogue was added before 'The Long And Winding Road'. This version of the *Get Back* album was released as part of the deluxe reissue of *Let It Be* in 2021, although the version of 'For You Blue' used there is a later mix with a new vocal from George Harrison. The album was scheduled for release in July 1969, and then pushed back first to September and then to December to coincide with the planned theatrical film.

With The Beatles' own success seemingly guaranteed with each new single and album, their protégées were less profitable. Jackie Lomax's 'Sour Milk Sea' had been an unexpected chart failure. Ahead of the release of his album, *Is This What You Want?,* a hastily arranged session took place at Apple Studios on 11 March for a quick follow-up single. Paul produced a cover of The Coasters' 'Thumbin' A Ride'. The band was extraordinary: Paul played drums, George Harrison was on guitar and backing vocals, Klaus Voormann and Billy Preston provided bass and organ with backing vocals credited to 'Patti And The Rascals'. A Lomax original, 'Going Back To Liverpool', was recorded for the B-side.

George Harrison was recording overdubs the following day when he learned that the police had carried out a drug raid at his home, Kinfauns in Surrey. Paul McCartney, meanwhile, married Linda Eastman at Marylebone Register Office that same day.

'Thumbin' A Ride' and 'Going Back To Liverpool 'were reported as making up Lomax's next single, according to *New Musical Express* on 22 March. However, a new Lomax song, 'New Day', produced by Lomax with Mal Evans and using Lomax's live band, was subsequently released as the A-side. 'Thumbin' A Ride' was used as the B-side in the US, and a track from *Is This What You Want?*, 'Fall Inside Your Eyes', would be used in the UK. 'Going Back To Liverpool' was eventually made available as a bonus track on the 1991 and 2004 reissues of *Is This What You Want?*, but oddly not on the 2010 remaster. Once again, Jackie Lomax failed to chart. He'd be given one more chance with Apple.

The American songwriter and comedy actor Stephen Friedland performed under the alias Brute Force. The childish and tiresome 'King Of Fuh' caught the ear of John Lennon and George Harrison and despite zero chance of airplay (sample lyric: 'the mighty Fuh king, all hail the Fuh king'), it was given a strings overdub (recorded on 10 January 1969, the day that George quit The Beatles) and limited release as a 7" single. If you really want to hear it, it's easily available on the 2010 compilation *Come And Get It: The Best Of Apple Records*.

By late March, with Allen Klein officially appointed as The Beatles' manager and with both John and Paul on their respective honeymoons, news came through that their partner in their Northern Songs publishing company, Dick James, had sold his shares to Associated Television Corporation (ATV). 'They had no idea that James was planning to sell', noted McCabe and Schonfeld in *Apple To The Core*. 'That he had done so without first consulting them made them furious. And as for Associated Television Corporation, a household name in communications and entertainment, they saw it as an unforgivable sell-out to the establishment. John [then in Amsterdam for his Bed-In] forgot all about acorns and his peace message. ATV's bid brought out the fighter in him. 'I won't sell', he declared. 'They are my shares and my songs, and I want to keep a bit of the end product. I don't have to ring Paul. I know damn well he feels the same as I do.'

> Despite their disagreement on other issues, [John and Paul] were united in fury against James for having sold them down the river without even the courtesy of a warning. The managerial duel between John Eastman and Allen Klein at this point was still far from resolved, but once again, Klein took the initiative, putting forward a strategy for Apple to snatch Northern Songs from Lew Grade's open jaws. At present, John and Paul each owned 15% of the company, and another token 1.6% was held jointly by George and Ringo. Klein's plan was to offer £2 million for the 20% that would secure them a hair's-breadth majority stake. The money was to come from a firm of merchant bankers on collateral, including John's entire holding in Northern, 650,000 shares. While these arrangements were going forward, it emerged that, on Eastman's advice, Paul had quietly increased his own holding to 750,000 shares, which would form no part of the collateral. John was vociferously upset by what he saw as Paul's underhanded behaviour and selfishness.
> Philip Norman, *John Lennon: The Life* (Harper, 2009)

Individually and collectively, The Beatles opposed the ATV bid. With ATV now owning around 35% of Northern Songs against The Beatles' 29%, it was still possible for the musicians to broker a deal to gain a majority. A consortium of stockbrokers, however, sniffed blood and a quick profit, and quickly amassed around 14% of Northern Songs stock, which would now be offered to the highest bidder. This would tip the balance either to ATV or The Beatles.

April 1969: 'Get Back'

Karma took Billy Preston to The Beatles. The Beatles had first met Preston when he was a member of Little Richard's band and they shared a bill in Hamburg in November 1962. Preston subsequently joined Ray Charles' band, and George Harrison became re-acquainted with the keyboardist when Harrison went with Eric Clapton to see Charles at the Royal Festival Hall in London in early 1969.

'Before Ray came on,' George recalled, 'there was a guy on stage playing the organ, dancing about and singing 'Double-O Soul'. I thought, 'That guy looks familiar', but he seemed bigger than I remembered. After a while, Ray came on and the band played for a few songs, and then he reintroduced ... Billy Preston! Ray said, 'Since I heard Billy play, I don't play the organ any more – I leave it to him.' I thought, 'It's Billy!' Since we had last seen him in Hamburg in 1962, when he was just a little lad, he had grown to be six feet tall. So, I put a message out to find out if Billy was in town, and told him to come into Savile Row, which he did. He came in while we were down in the basement, running through 'Get Back', and I went up to reception and said, 'Come in and play on this because they're all acting strange.' He was all excited. I knew the others loved Billy anyway, and it was like a breath of fresh air. It's interesting to see how nicely people behave when you bring a guest in because they don't really want everybody to know that they're so bitchy.'

Paul said, 'Billy was brilliant – a little young whizz-kid. We'd always got on very well with him. He showed up in London and we all said, 'Oh, Bill! Great – let's have him play on a few things.' So, he started sitting in on the sessions because he was an old mate, really.'

His presence not only fleshed out the sound but also improved the mood. 'I don't think Billy Preston made us behave a bit better', Ringo said, 'I think we were working on a good track and that always excited us. His work was also a part of it, so suddenly, as always when you're working on something good, the bullshit went out of the window and we got back down to doing what we did really well.'

Preston stayed for the rest of the sessions, including the famous rooftop show on 30 January. The first music to be made available was the single 'Get Back', explicitly credited to 'The Beatles with Billy Preston', which was released on 11 April 1969 in the UK and three weeks later in the US. It was number one for six weeks in the UK from 23 April, and for five weeks in the US from 24 May.

With Klein looking after the biggest band in the world, it would be inevitable that the British media would sniff around looking for stories. On 13 April, an article, headlined 'The Toughest Wheeler-Dealer In The Pop Jungle', would be published in *The Sunday Times*.

> [Allen Klein's business practices are] a startling blend of bluff, sheer determination and financial agility, together with an instinct for publicity and the ability to lie like a trooper. He is a veteran of some 40 lawsuits, and dealings in one of his shares were halted by the American Stock Exchange. In one of his better-known achievements, he himself took over one of his own companies and saw the value of the stock go up by $15 million.

For two weeks, between 10 and 24 April, Apple and The Beatles pushed hard to buy Northern Songs outright by improving their current stake. Details of The Beatles' offer were revealed on 18 April as a joint bid by Apple Corps, equally owned by the four Beatles, Subafilms (76.1% owned by Apple) and Maclen (Music), a licensing/royalty administration operation (20% owned by Apple), with Paul and John controlling the balance in equal proportions. The existing stake would be used as collateral for a loan needed to finance the bid.

Paul, advised by John Eastman, it seems, refused to commit his shares in Northern Songs as loan collateral. It was crucial that The Beatles showed solidarity at this point, but Paul was over-cautious. The broad outline of the band's offer was announced on 24 April. They would make a public offering of £2.1 million to acquire a further 21.3% of Northern's shares, taking their holdings to 51%. The guarantee was made up of Apple shares, John Lennon's entire holding in Northern Songs and ABKCO's shares in the MGM film corporation.

The Beatles issued a statement on 30 April, which reads thus:

We, The Beatles, would like to draw the attention of Northern Songs' shareholders to the following reasons why the ATV offer should be rejected and our offer accepted.

1. If our offer succeeds, the Board of Northern Songs will be reorganised. Mr David Platz, an experienced music publisher, will be appointed to the Board and, in addition, invitations to become Directors will be issued to one of the Directors of our Merchant Bankers, Henry Ansbacher and Co. Limited, to an experienced Solicitor and to a Chartered Accountant with experience of the entertainment industry. As ATV is likely to be the largest shareholder other than ourselves, it would also be invited to appoint a representative to the Board. None of us intends to join the Board, nor would we interfere with the management of the Company. We recognise that our talents lie chiefly in composing and entertaining, rather than in financial management. Mr Allen Klein, who is working with us on other projects, would not become a Director of Northern Songs.

2. We have already undertaken, but only if our offer succeeds, to enter into new contracts as composers with Northern Songs, each for an additional period of two years on competitive commercial terms. We are also willing, subject to the provisions of the 1969 Finance Bill, to offer other of our entertainment interests to Northern Songs at an independent valuation. Any such interests offered would be proven high revenue earners and would not include any ventures which have proved unprofitable under our own personal management.

3. The position of minority shareholders in Northern Songs would be no different from that of minority shareholders in numerous other quoted companies in which members of the Boards and their families possess control.

4. Having made its offer without consulting us, the owners of some 30% of the issued capital and the principal revenue earners of Northern Songs, ATV originally stated that it intended to keep any shares which it acquired, but has since suggested that it might be a 'weak holder' of those shares. ATV has apparently questioned the value of Northern Songs shares following a successful bid by us, despite having been willing to make an offer … for control. In fact, were we working happily and independently, ATV would be in a stronger position as a minority shareholder with a representative on the Board than it would be as a controlling shareholder with us unhappily serving out our existing contracts.

5. By accepting our offer, Northern Songs shareholders would obtain a substantially higher price for part or all of their holdings … than they could by accepting the ATV offer. It must be emphasised that … the value of this package cannot be assessed with complete accuracy and, in any event, Northern Songs shareholders would be surrendering voting Ordinary shares in exchange for only a relatively small proportion of equity shares with no voting rights.

Having profited by having a stake in The Beatles' past compositions, if you want to ensure that they happily continue to earn further profits for Northern Songs, you should reject the ATV offer and accept The Beatles' offer in respect of your entire shareholdings.

May 1969: 'The Ballad Of John And Yoko'

'Get Back' was still at number one in the UK when an impatient John Lennon insisted that a new song should be recorded and released *immediately*. 'The Ballad Of John And Yoko' describes the bizarre circumstances of John and Yoko's wedding in Gibraltar.

The facts are these:

12 March 1969. On the day before Paul wed Linda, John and Yoko were in Southampton, enquiring whether they could get married at sea, on the romantic setting of the cross-channel ferry, the Dragon.

> Standing in the dock at Southampton/Trying to get to Holland or France

They flew, instead, on a private charter to Paris and spent several days at the Plaza Athénée hotel, plotting their next move.

> Finally made the plane into Paris

Apple employee Peter Brown learned that they could marry in Gibraltar.

> Peter Brown called to say: 'You can make it OK/You can get married in Gibraltar near Spain.'

20 March 1969. John and Yoko charter another aeroplane and fly from Paris to Gibraltar, landing at 8:30 am. The three-minute ceremony, with Peter Brown as a witness, took place at the British Consulate at 9:00 am, officiated by the registrar, Mr Cecil Joseph Wheeler. After paying four pounds and 14 shillings for the marriage licences and posing for photographs (the photographer, David Nutter, was the second witness), the happy couple returned to Paris after just 70 minutes in Gibraltar. A few days later, after lunch with Salvador Dali, they travelled to Amsterdam.

> Drove from Paris to the Amsterdam Hilton

25 to 29 March 1969. The Amsterdam Bed-In. Room 902.

> Talkin' in our beds for a week

31 March 1969. John and Yoko fly to Vienna to premiere their film *Rape* and take part in a press conference inside a white bag. *The Daily Mirror*

reported that 'a not inconsiderable talent ... seems to have gone completely off his rocker.'

> Made a lightnin' trip to Vienna/Eatin' chocolate cake in a bag
> Newspaper said 'She's gone to his head/They look just like two gurus in drag.'

1 April 1969. They return to London for a TV interview on Thames Television's Today. They were, according to Lennon, 'willing to be the world's clowns' for peace. As part of this, they planned to send acorns to 50 world leaders. Beleaguered staff from the Apple press office were tasked with finding dozens of acorns out of season. Allegedly, they resorted to digging holes in London parks, trying to find where squirrels might have hidden them.

> Caught the early plane back to London/Fifty acorns tied in a sack

John visited Paul's house on 14 April, insisting that a new song depicting these events should be recorded that same evening, even though George was out of the country and Ringo was away filming. 'The Ballad Of John & Yoko' was recorded, in its entirety, in a single session and the B-side, George's rocking 'Old Brown Shoe', would be laid down later the same week (the first full band session at EMI for six months and, in effect, the start of *Abbey Road*). The single would be released in late May and was the last UK number one for The Beatles for 54 years.

Unfinished Music No. 2: Life With The Lions, also released in May, marked John and Yoko's second experimental (read: unlistenable) album. Side one is a live recording from a Sunday afternoon concert at Cambridge University on 2 March 1969. John's loud guitar feedback accompanies vocalisations from Yoko, which can best be described as 'screeching'. The first lasts for 45 seconds. This continues for another 26 minutes. Percussion and saxophone add minor interest in the final few moments.

John discussed the event with Andy Peebles in 1980. 'We arrived in Cambridge', John said. 'It was supposed to be an avant-garde – that word again – jazz thing, right? And there was a guy called John Tchicai, who was apparently a famous avant-garde sax guy or jazz sax guy – I didn't know any of them. A few people whose names I don't remember, they were there, too. And I turned up as her band, you know. And the people were looking and saying, 'Is it? Is it?' You know. I just had a guitar and an amp, and that was the first time I'd played that style, just pure feedback and whatever it is on that track. And the audience were very weird because they were all these sort of intellectual artsy-fartsies from Cambridge, you know, and they were uptight because the rock 'n' roll guy was there, even though I wasn't doing any rhythm. If you hear it, it's just pure sound. Because what else can you do when a woman's howling, you know, you just go along with it, right? Well, the reaction I got from the – quotes, unquotes – avant-garde group ... was the same reaction that she got from the rock 'n' roll people, like, 'What's she doing here?' ... this little tight-knit avant-garde scene would be saying, 'What the hell ... who the hell is he? He's one of those pop...' So we're both getting shtick for not being in the right bag.'

John is protesting too much. This is unlistenable. Incredibly, the released mix is an edit of an even longer original. Side two was recorded at Queen Charlotte's Hospital in London in November 1968. It's a field recording which captures the sounds and experiences of Yoko's pregnancy and subsequent miscarriage from 4 to 25 November 1968. The most listenable track is called 'Two Minutes' Silence'. John described it as, 'It is saying whatever you want it to say. It is just us expressing ourselves like a child does, you know, however he feels like then. What we're saying is make your own music. This is Unfinished Music.' The best summary of *Unfinished Music No. 2* is George Martin's pithy quote on the cover, which simply says, 'No Comment'.

George Harrison's *Electronic Sound* was released the same day. This comprises two lengthy pieces performed on a Moog 3-series synthesiser, recorded at Sound Recorders, Los Angeles ('No Time Or Space', 3 November 1968, during sessions for *Is This What You Want?*) and at George's home ('Under The Mersey Wall', February 1969). The session for 'No Time Or Space' remains contentious. George asked for a demonstration of the synthesiser from musician and engineer Bernie Krause. Krause obliged, but George recorded the output without Krause's knowledge. As Krause wrote in his autobiography, *Into A Wild Sanctuary*, 'Had I been aware that he was recording my demonstration, I would never have shown examples of what [his partner] Paul [Beaver] and I were considering for our next album. As I showed him the settings and gave some performance examples, Harrison seemed impressed with the possibilities.'

A few weeks later, George bought his own synthesiser and it was set up at his home. Krause was invited to fly to the UK to collaborate on new music, and George cued up 'my first electronic piece done with a little help from my cats'. According to Krause, he realised that he was hearing the tape made in Los Angeles the previous year. George, it seems, planned to include the recording on *Electronic Sound* without Krause's permission or compensation.

George recorded the second piece, 'Under The Mersey Wall', himself, and a planned co-credit for Krause was abandoned, with his name painted out of the cover artwork. The most interesting part of the album is the title of one of the two pieces, a play on 'Over The Mersey Wall', the name of a newspaper column in the *Liverpool Echo* by another George Harrison.

Unfinished Music No. 2 and *Electronic Sound* came out on the short-lived Zapple label. This had been set up to cater for experimental and spoken word albums.

> We want to publish all sorts of sounds. Some of these sounds will be spoken, some electronic, some classical. We'll be producing recorded

> interviews, too. Some of the people we put on record will be well known, some not so well known. This means that you'll get plenty of variety. We don't want Zapple to become a one-track record label. We'll publish almost anything provided it's valid and good. We're not going to put out rubbish, at any price.
>
> Derek Taylor's original press release, launching Zapple

Paul's friend Barry Miles, co-owner of the Indica Gallery and editor of independent newspaper *International Times*, was asked to source content. He was given an office on the top floor of Savile Row.

'At Zapple, we planned to record a series of live poetry readings,' Miles wrote in *The Zapple Diaries*, 'each featuring five or six poets: the 'Liverpool Scene' poets – Adrian Henri, Brian Patten, Roger McGough; the New York City Poetry Project poets; and the poets and writers surrounding City Lights Books in San Francisco. Paul was keen on the idea of a record of William Burroughs talking about different drugs, as well as reading from his work, and he also wanted to release BBC radio plays, such as its production of *Ubu Cocu* by Alfred Jarry, that he had listened to on his car radio while driving to Liverpool one time and which he had enjoyed very much. He thought it would be good to have such a performance readily available. We talked about setting up a deal with the BBC for a separate series of such recordings. None of it would have cost very much money compared to many of the other Apple projects.'

Miles flew to the US in January 1969 with the intention of recording works by the poets Lawrence Ferlingetti (1919-2021), Michael McClure (1932-2020), Charles Olsen (1910-1970), Allen Ginsberg (1926-1997), Gregory Corso (1930-2001), Richard Brautigan (1935-1984), Charles Bukowski (1920-1994), Kenneth Patchen (1911-1972), Diane di Prima (1934-2020) and others. Apple paid for flights, accommodation, studio rentals and so on. Despite Miles successfully making several recordings in New York City and Los Angeles, none of these would be released by Apple. A spoken-word album by Brautigan was expected as the third Zapple release, with a planned release date of 23 May, two weeks after *Unfinished Music No. 2* and *Electronic Sound*. Acetates were made and artwork approved, but Zapple ceased operating before the album could be pressed. A series of performances by Lawrence Ferlinghetti had been recorded and edited and would have been Zapple 4, but Zapple was closed down in June 1969 with just two releases on their roster. Miles held on to his recordings and made some others later in 1969 and successfully produced a number of them for other labels. *Ferlinghetti* would be released on Fantasy later in 1969. Brautigan's recordings were released as *Listening To Richard Brautigan* on Harvest Records in 1970, and Ginsberg's *Songs Of Innocence And Experience* came out on MGM that same year. Ginsberg would, on a verbal contract from John Lennon in 1971, record an album for Apple to have been called *Holy Soul And Jelly Roll*. Apple declined to release the album, which remained unheard until 1994. The Olsen recordings were made available on Folkways in 1975 as *Charles Olson Reads From Maximus Poems IV, V, VI*. A planned album by Ken Kesey, to be called *Paperback Record*, did not materialise. Allen Ginsberg would work with Paul McCartney in 1996 on the track 'Ballad Of The Skeletons', and Charles Bukowski's *At Terror Street And Agony Way* finally emerged in 1998, by which time the poet was dead.

The Iveys' 12-track debut album *Maybe Tomorrow* was made available only in Japan, West Germany and Italy in May 1969. It was also scheduled for release in the UK and the US, but it seems that all non-Beatles releases were halted by Allen Klein so that Apple's finances could be refocused and the profligate spending brought under control. The single 'Dear Angie' was also put on ice. This was the first of many blows for this band.

Mortimer's album was completed in mid-April, and Peter Asher played it to anyone prepared to listen. One of these, Paul McCartney, suggested that one of his songs would make a good addition and potential single. This was called 'On Our Way Home'. Paul had an acetate of a Beatles recording from 24 January 1969, which had been mixed during sessions in mid-March (this version can be heard on *Anthology 3*). Asher took Mortimer back to Trident to record 'On Our Way Home'. It was added as the first song on Mortimer's album and was slated as a single, Apple 16, for a September release.

With Allen Klein behind his desk at Apple, heads started to roll.

> Klein brought a new uncertainty to Apple and the possibility of eagle-sudden dismissals. Apple employees gaped in disbelief as they saw their idyllic employment situations crumble. Chris O'Dell was an Apple secretary when Klein brought his Seventh Avenue urgency to the damasked drawing rooms of the Mayfair townhouse. She observed that he wasn't prone to bouts of nostalgia. 'He just moved in and started firing people', she said. 'It took him more than a year to do it, but in that time, he got rid of everybody he could possibly clear out, either by taking their work away, so that there was nothing for them to do, or by making their jobs so uncomfortable they felt obliged to quit.'
>
> Peter McCabe and Robert D. Schonfeld, *Apple To The Core* (1972)

Ron Kass was falsely accused of 'financial impropriety' and was forced to resign on 8 May. He was succeeded by his former deputy, Jack Oliver. 'Magic' Alex Mardas was let go after costing Apple an estimated £180,000 (over £3m in 2025 value), as was contracts manager Brian Lewis. Perhaps most surprisingly, Alistair Taylor was sacked after seven years with The Beatles.

'He was one of the Liverpool group of totally loyal staff who adored the boys and were there out of love, not for the money', Barry Miles recalled. 'Alistair … was, like Neil Aspinall, Mal Evans and Peter Brown, more of a royal courtier than a record business employee. It turned out that their loyalty was misplaced. Rather than let Klein fire him, Peter Brown told him the news.

Alistair choked back tears and spent the rest of the day trying to reach Paul and John on the phone, but they wouldn't take his calls.'

The rout had begun.

'Klein went through Apple like a Rottweiler through a basket of newborn puppies,' wrote Philip Norman, 'slashing costs, axing idealistic or unproductive projects … firing all staff members he deemed nonessential, creating an atmosphere of terror and insecurity that was normal to American business but still almost unknown in Britain. That many marked for termination considered themselves personal friends of John or George, as much as large-salaried and expense-accounted employees, made no difference. Concerned that, here and elsewhere, Klein seemed to be throwing out the baby with the bathwater, Neil Aspinall protested to John, but even he received short shrift. Back came a telegram that seemed to take little account of Neil's long-time loyalty and selflessness. 'Don't bite the hand that feeds you', it said.'

By early May, it seemed that The Beatles would retain control of Northern Songs, and therefore millions of pounds of potential publishing income. They needed to secure an extra 20% and their proposed deal, in which Allen Klein would have no part in the new company's management structure and in which John and Paul would extend their creative involvement beyond the present expiration date of 1973, was attractive to the balance-holding consortium of investors. Sadly, at a meeting with their potential partners, John announced he was 'sick of being fucked around by men in suits, sitting on their fat arses in the City.' Allegiances were switched to ATV, and the Lennon-McCartney catalogue became lost to the songwriters forever.

Notably, Paul's song 'You Never Give Me Your Money' was written in this period.

Another key date in the disintegration of The Beatles would be 9 May 1969. Allen Klein had been working for The Beatles for three months without a formal management contract. His demands were not unreasonable: a three-year contract which could be terminated with three months' notice at the end of each year. Klein would receive 20% of gross income from any source, plus 20% on all new deals until the end of their term. Apple would also pay for a house in London for Klein and cover 'reasonable expenses' incurred by Klein in the course of his duties. John, George and Ringo signed Klein's management contract on 8 May, with the intention of meeting Paul the next day to secure his signature.

Paul: 'I remember being at Olympic Studios one evening when I think we were supposed to be doing something on *Abbey Road* [they were there to listen to mixes of the *Get Back* album]. We all showed up … and Allen Klein showed up, too. The other three said, 'You've got to sign a contract, he's got to take it to his board.' I said, 'It's Friday night [9 May was a Friday]. He doesn't work on a Saturday, and anyway, Allen Klein is a law unto himself. He hasn't got a board he has to report to. Don't worry, we could easily do this on Monday. Let's do our session instead.'

Paul did not want to be pushed into a management contract without a review by his legal team. 'There was a big argument,' Paul recalled, 'and they all went, leaving me at the studio.' He stayed at Olympic and recorded a song with Steve Miller. Its title: 'My Dark Hour'. 'I had to do something,' Paul said, 'thrash something, to get it out of my system.'

Earlier that evening, the smiling, happy Beatles were shown on *Top Of The Pops* singing 'Get Back' on the roof of Savile Row. A few days later, they re-created the cover of *Please Please Me* at EMI's offices on 13 May for the proposed *Get Back* album. In truth, they could hardly have been further apart.

Paul went on holiday for a month with Linda and her daughter Heather on 15 May, travelling to Provence in France and the Greek Island of Corfu, where he finished writing 'Every Night'.

Back in London, plans to release an album by Delaney & Bonnie & Friends (scheduled release date: 30 May) reached the acetate stage, and it was allocated a catalogue number before being scrapped.

June 1969: 'Give Peace A Chance'

John and Yoko's Amsterdam bed-in 'honeymoon' was followed by a second in Montreal in June, after initial plans (and a visit) to The Bahamas proved impractical. Here, they wrote and recorded an anti-war song, 'Give Peace A Chance', although, laughingly, it was published as a Lennon/McCartney composition. The performance, deliberately simple and built around one chord with a sing-a-long chorus, was recorded on 1 June 1969, in Room 1742 at The Queen Elizabeth Hotel in Montreal in the company of journalists and various celebrities, including psychologist and author Timothy Leary, Abraham 'The Singing Rabbi' Feinberg, political activist Joseph Schwartz, singer Petula Clark, comedian and actor Dick Gregory, poet Allen Ginsberg, US-domiciled British DJ Roger Scott, self-proclaimed 'Fifth Beatle' Murray The K and Apple's press officer Derek Taylor.

Lennon played acoustic guitar along with Tommy Smothers of The Smothers Brothers. Additional backing vocals were overdubbed the following day. 'Give Peace A Chance' was released as a single in the first week of July, with Ono's delicate 'Remember Love', recorded immediately after 'Give Peace A Chance', as the B-side. Lennon plays the chord changes from 'Sun King' and Yoko sings gently. If this had Vashti Bunyan's name on it, and not Yoko Ono's, it might be regarded as a minor classic. 'Give Peace A Chance' was a sizeable hit, reaching number two in the UK and number 14 in the US.

Denis O'Dell and Peter Asher both resigned from Apple this same month. 'Allen Klein brought in his own people and fired a lot of people who were working at Apple', Neil Aspinall recalled. 'It didn't all take place in one day, but over a period of nine months. For example, he would rather have Les Perrin (a PR man with his own outside company who worked for The Rolling Stones, amongst others) than let Apple have its own press department. Ron

Kass went, Denis O'Dell went after *Let It Be*, Peter Asher went. It wasn't just slimming down, it was end of story.'

> The latest name on the growing list of executive and creative talent to part company with Apple is A&R chief Peter Asher, who leaves the company at the end of next week. Asher's resignation from Apple follows the recent departure of Ron Kass, head of the record division. Asher joined Apple a year ago. He told *Record Retailer* last week, 'Apple has been changing a great deal recently, which has made it more and more difficult for me to do my work with the same enthusiasm and effectiveness as before.' Asher goes to America next month and plans to spend at least a year there. He will continue to manage Apple artist James Taylor.
> *Record Retailer*, 4 June 1969

Neil Aspinall, indispensable and unsackable but now without a clear role at Apple, set to work on a pet project. 'In '69,' he told *Mojo* in 1996, 'in all that chaos, the traumas – things were falling apart, but they were still making *Abbey Road* – Paul called me saying, 'You should collect as much of the material that's out there, get it together before it disappears.' So, I started to do that, got in touch with all the TV stations around the world, checked what we had in our own library, like *Let It Be*, *Magical Mystery Tour*, the promo clips, what have you. Got newsreel footage in, lots and lots of stuff. We edited something together that was about an hour and three-quarters long.' This idea would eventually materialise as *The Beatles Anthology* 25 years later.

July 1969: That's The Way God Planned It

One artist who was guaranteed the support of The Beatles was Billy Preston. He had been quickly signed to Apple, and from February to July 1969, George Harrison worked on what would become Preston's fourth album, *That's The Way God Planned It*. Not only did Harrison produce nine of the songs, but he played guitar and, again, got some friends to help him out: Keith Richards, Eric Clapton, future Apple artist Doris Troy, Ginger Baker and Madeline Bell all took part. Three of the songs were older recordings left over from Preston's sessions for Capitol the previous year.

Although the album failed to do well in the charts, Preston did have a hit single in the UK and Europe with the irrepressible title track, which combines Preston's effortlessly funky soul with the best of the UK's rock musicians: Eric Clapton, Keith Richards and Ginger Baker play on the song alongside Preston and Harrison.

'Do What You Want To' is a strong opener, a tough rock-soul track with a winding guitar lick and Baker's hammering drums. The opening verses of the lead single and title track are practically a duet between Preston's gospel-tinged vocal and Eric Clapton's bluesy lead guitar. The central section includes a beautiful trade-off between Preston's swirling Hammond and Clapton's gently picked electric guitar, and the closing guitar solo has real power. Such was the strength and energy in this take that a couple of glaring mistakes were left in.

George was so impressed with Doris Troy, one of the backing singers and co-composer of three of the songs on *That's The Way God Planned It*, that he offered her a deal with Apple, too.

The single mix of the joyous title track reached number 11 in the UK. A longer edit would be included on the album of the same name, released in August 1969 (UK) and September 1969 (US). A tentative alternative take recorded at Olympic Sound Studios in March 1969 has George Harrison, not Eric Clapton, on lead guitar. This was released in 2010 on the remastered re-release of the album. Another of the tracks from the album, the upbeat 'Everything's Alright', would be lifted as a single in October/November 1969. It failed to chart.

The sessions for *Abbey Road* started on 1 July. John and Yoko were on a holiday in Scotland with their children, where, after a crash, they were hospitalised. The badly damaged Austin Maxi, which Lennon was driving, would be transported to the couple's Tittenhurst Park estate, where it was displayed in the garden. You couldn't make it up.

Amongst many interesting ideas that emanated from the Apple offices, one of the most unlikely was a link with a British frozen food manufacturer. A four-track EP was available only through mail order in the UK as part of a Walls' Ice Cream promotional campaign in July 1969. It included four songs: The Iveys' 'Storm In A Teacup' (the first release of this fabulous song), James Taylor's 'Something's Wrong' (from *James Taylor*), Jackie Lomax's 'Little Yellow Pill' (from *Is This What You Want?*) and Mary Hopkin's 'Pebble And The Man' (from *Post Card*). The sleeve notes gave a potted history of the four acts:

> The Iveys – Pete Ham, Ron Jones, Tom Evans and drummer Mike Gibbons are the new Apple Corps group. An exciting quartet who are thought to be the most enjoyable group since The Beatles.
> James Taylor – James is a Boston, Massachusetts man. Taciturn, 20 and talented. At 18, he was in New York City in a group called The Flying Machine, and now two years later, he's in London with an Apple contract and a new album produced by Peter Asher. This track is just one from his first LP.
> Jackie Lomax – John Richard Lomax was a Merseyside boy, born in Wallasey in 1944. He joined the Undertakers group and went with them to Germany in 1962. In 1966, he went to America and went solo. His first record for Apple was 'Sour Milk Sea' by George Harrison – he wrote the flip himself, and has written 'Little Yellow Pill'. Jackie's singing and writing are emotive and exciting – he'll be on the scene for always.
> Mary Hopkin – Mary has been singing since she was four years old, in chapel, in South Wales Working Men's Clubs (where they know good voices

when they hear them) and on Welsh TV. She was chosen for *Opportunity Knocks,* where she appeared successfully for eight weeks. Twiggy heard her, told Paul McCartney – the result was a number one chart-topper with 'Those Were The Days'. These are certainly the days for Mary – at 18, she's a star, and sounds like staying up there.

This EP is now a sought-after collector's item.

George Harrison's well-publicised love of Eastern philosophies led to a surprise hit single for Apple in the autumn of 1969. 'Hare Krishna Mantra', which features the *Hare Krishna, Hare Rama* refrain later used in 'My Sweet Lord', had been recorded in mid-July at EMI. George played harmonium and added guitar and bass, as well as directing the voices. 'First I played the entire song on a pedal harmonium,' he says in the sleeve notes of the 1993 reissue, 'and then I played my guitar through a Leslie speaker and had someone beat time with a pair of kartals and Indian drums. All the devotees came in later to overdub the 'answering' singing. There were so many of them banging drums and singing that it was very difficult to keep any kind of separation, so the feeling of the recording is very much live.'

For the B-side, George recorded the trance-like 'Prayer To The Spiritual Masters'. Credited to Radha Krishna Temple (London) and bolstered by two appearances on *Top Of The Pops*, the single was a commercial success, peaking at number 12 in the UK charts during a nine-week run between September and November.

August 1969: 'Que Sera, Sera'

Paul McCartney had overseen Mary Hopkin's first two singles, 'Those Were The Days' (a number one in the UK) and 'Goodbye' (number two). Paul also produced her proposed third single, a folkie reworking of the Doris Day oldie 'Que Sera, Sera'. This was recorded in a single session, on 17 August, a day off between recording and mixing duties for *Abbey Road*. The basic track features Paul on acoustic guitar and Ringo on drums. Paul added bass guitar and lead guitar, and Hopkin sang and played acoustic guitar.

'At the time, it was just one of Paul's fun ideas', Hopkin told *Goldmine* in 1992. 'It was one sunny afternoon, we were sitting in Paul's garden, and he said, 'Do you like this song?' I said, 'Well, I used to sing it when I was three!' And he said, 'My dad likes it, let's go and do it.' And so Ringo came along; it was all done in an afternoon. I was sort of swept along with Paul's enthusiasm, really. By the time I was halfway through the backing vocals, I said, 'This is awful.' I really thought it was dreadful and I didn't want it released.'

Hopkin's wishes prevailed. Despite being scheduled as Apple 16 on 12 September, it was released only in France. A plan to issue the B-side 'The Fields Of St Etienne' as the A-side – recorded in the same session as 'Que Sera, Sera' with the same musicians and a lush orchestral overdub – came to nothing. The song was re-recorded with Gallagher and Lyle and issued as the B-side to the US release of 'Que Sera, Sera' in June 1970.

The Beatles' final photographic session took place at John's Tittenhurst estate on 22 August.

James Taylor started to record a new album for Apple in August 1969, recording an early version of 'Fire And Rain' amongst others, but he broke both hands in an accident and was unable to work. Unhappy with the developments at Apple, Peter Asher took the opportunity to move back to Los Angeles as James Taylor's manager. He told *Disc & Music Echo*, 'When I joined Apple, the idea was that it would be different from the other companies in the record business. Its policy was to help people and be generous. It didn't mean I actually had a tremendous amount of freedom; I was always in danger of one Beatle saying, 'Yes, that's a great idea, go ahead', and then another coming in and saying he didn't know anything about it. But it did mean that it was a nice company to work for. Now that's all changed. There's a new concentrative policy from what I can see, and it's lost a great deal of its original feeling.'

Asher and Taylor met Paul McCartney to ask for release from their contract.

> 'So, James Taylor came,' McCartney recalled of their meeting, 'and he and Peter said, 'We don't want to stay on the label. We like you, we like the guys, but we don't like this Klein guy, and we don't like what's going to happen."
>
> Klein was against a no-strings release of Taylor, insisting there at least be a sizeable payment made. McCartney refused, as did the other Beatles, who felt, as Paul put it, 'We should just give him his contract back.'
>
> 'Klein said, 'We should keep him!" as McCartney recalled ruefully for this writer in March 2001. 'But I said, 'Look, man, we're artists here, this is the idea of Apple. We should let him go. He's given us a great album, he's made money for us, why do we need to keep him in a slave thing?"
>
> 'So, I think he [James] was grateful for that', added McCartney. 'I hate to see artists keeping each other to contracts, it's not cool.'
>
> Timothy White, *James Taylor: Long Ago And Far Away* (2011)

A formal letter from Taylor's lawyer, dated 17 September, pointed out that Taylor had been under 21 when his Apple contract had been signed, and due royalties had not been paid.

Taylor was released from his five-year contract with Apple, due to run until 1973. After a period of recovery, his breakthrough album, *Sweet Baby James*, would be recorded in December 1969 for Warner Bros. It was a top ten hit in both the UK and US, the first of many successful releases for a major talent who, like David Bowie, Fleetwood Mac, Crosby, Stills & Nash, Joe Walsh, McGuinness Flint, Yes, Hot Chocolate and 10cc, slipped through Apple's fingers. Taylor's debut album deserves to be more than a footnote in his illustrious career. 'Carolina On My Mind' and 'Rainy Day Man' are undeniably beautiful songs.

Asher's other protégés, Mortimer, were given a deal with Apple that included payback of money that the band owed to their previous record company. Allen Klein was not prepared to fund this, and Mortimer's unreleased album was abandoned. *On Our Way Home* was finally released in 2016. It's very good indeed, and sounds a lot like America, who were founded in London the following year.

September 1969: Abbey Road

Since May, Allen Klein had been arguing for a better royalty rate from Capitol. For all the bluster that Klein embodied, he did follow through with his promise to improve The Beatles' income. Subject to fulfilling a minimum of two new albums a year until 1976, either collectively or individually, their improved rate would earn them 58 cents each until 1972 and 72 cents from 1972 to 1976. This compares with six cents per album before 1966 and 39 cents from 1966 to 1969. Reissues of early recordings would attract a 50-cent royalty per record until 1972, and 72 cents after that.

This was timed well, as the massive-selling *Abbey Road* would be released on 1 October 1969. 'Something'/'Come Together' followed a month later, thus marking the end of The Beatles' active time as a working band. As usual, acts would flurry to record cover versions – Ike and Tina Turner's soulful re-tread of 'Come Together' would be released before the end of the year, George Benson's *The Other Side Of Abbey Road* came out only a matter of weeks after The Beatles' album and Joe Cocker's impassioned 'She Came In Through The Bathroom Window' followed soon after. Apple wanted a slice of this pie and arranged for a cover of 'Golden Slumbers-Carry That Weight' by White Trash (now renamed, unfortunately, to Trash) as their second and last single. The version is almost identical to the original, but with cheesy organ replacing George Harrison's guitar solo. The buying public were not fooled, and the single stalled at number 35 in November 1969.

Just prior to *Abbey Road*'s release, on 20 September, Allen Klein called a meeting for the signing of the revised Capitol contract. John, Paul and Ringo were in attendance. The tone was hostile, especially from John, who accused Paul of dominating the band over the last few years – which is true, as without Paul's drive, they might have split up after *Sgt. Pepper* – and for writing what he unfairly called 'granny music'.

Paul was all for carrying on with further band activity. As he said in *Many Years From Now* (1997), 'I propounded the theory, 'I think we should get back to our basics. I think we've got out of hand, we've overwhelmed ourselves, and I think what we need is to re-establish our musical identity and find out who we are again, and so we should go back to little gigs.' At that point, John looked at me and said, 'Well, I think yer daft!' Which was a little bit of a show-stopper. He said, 'Well, I wasn't gonna tell you till after we'd signed the Capitol contract. Klein asked me not to tell you. But, seeing as you asked me, I'm leaving the group.' So, everyone went, 'Gulp!' The weight was dropped, our jaws dropped along with it, everyone blanched except John, who coloured a little and said, 'It's rather exciting. It's like I remember telling Cynthia I wanted a divorce.' And I think from what he was saying, there was an adrenaline rush that came with telling us. So, that was it. We signed the new Capitol deal in a bit of a daze, not quite knowing why we'd done it. That's my recollection.'

'I don't remember about John saying he wanted to break up The Beatles', George said later. 'I don't remember where I heard it. Everybody had tried to leave, so it was nothing new. Everybody was leaving for years. The Beatles had started out being something that gave us a vehicle to be able to do so much when we were younger, but it had now got to a point where it was stifling us. There was too much restriction. It had to self-destruct, and I wasn't feeling bad about anybody wanting to leave because I wanted out myself. I could see a much better time ahead being by myself, away from the band. It had ceased to be fun, and it was time to get out of it. It was like a straitjacket.'

'I started the band,' John said. 'I disbanded it. It's as simple as that. My life with The Beatles had become a trap. When I finally had the guts to tell the other three that I, quote, wanted a divorce, unquote, they knew it was for real – unlike Ringo and George's previous threats to leave. I must say I felt guilty for springing it on them at such short notice. After all, I had Yoko; they only had each other.'

Ringo: 'We didn't go public about the break-up immediately.'

'I never wanted The Beatles to be has-beens', John told *New Musical Express* two years later. 'I wanted to kill it while it was on top. Remember, I said ten years ago, 'I'm not going to be singing 'She Loves You' at 30'.'

The news would not leak for several months, as those present agreed to say nothing so that *Abbey Road* could reach its market potential. But, with the exception of a handful of housekeeping sessions in 1970, which Lennon did not attend, The Beatles ended on this day in London. Paul would now only attend the Apple offices when called for business meetings, and even then, he usually sent John Eastman in his place.

The ownership of The Beatles' publishing rights rumbled on. The minor investors divested in September 1969, and Allen Klein pulled together an attractive deal to tidy up the legal loose ends. The broad scope of this was that ATV would buy all of the band's remaining Northern Songs shares in exchange for loan stock and cash; The Beatles would withdraw outstanding writs lodged against Northern Songs by Maclen (Music); John and Paul would re-sign as songwriters until 1976 and George and Ringo would switch from Apple Publishing to Northern Songs, also until 1976; Lenmac, the PRS payments collection company formed in 1964, would be sold back to John Lennon and Paul McCartney; and Apple would get sub-publishing rights in the United States.

It was a good deal for both sides, and contracts were drawn up. Paul and the Eastmans, however, were still wary of Allen Klein and would not be party to an agreement negotiated by Klein on Paul's behalf. The two Beatle factions could not agree. Lennon and McCartney, defeated, sold their Northern Songs shares in October 1969.

Twelve years later, McCartney and Yoko Ono offered £21 million to buy The Beatles' publishing copyrights from ATV. The offer was declined. Then, in 1984, ATV Music was put up for sale. Neither McCartney nor Ono chose to bid, and it was sold to Michael Jackson for what now seems the bargain price of £24.4 million. The catalogue was subsequently acquired by Sony Music. MPL Communications, Paul's principal conduit for his creative and business assets, owns a handful of copyrights that predate the formation of Northern Songs, such as 'Love Me Do' and 'PS I Love You'.

October 1969: Hot Chocolate, 'Cold Turkey'

The British soul-disco band Hot Chocolate would enjoy 12 top ten singles in the 1970s and 1980s. Their one single for Apple was a reggae version of 'Give Peace A Chance', released on 17 October 1969. The band went to the Apple office with a mixed master tape, looking to release the song as a single. Named by Mavis Smith of the Apple press office, the single was not a hit. They would need to wait just a few months before their long association with RAK and producer Mickie Most would bear fruit with big-selling songs such as 'You Sexy Thing', 'So You Win Again' and 'No Doubt About It'.

The Plastic Ono Band's second single, 'Cold Turkey', came out a week later. It's difficult to like this loud, dissonant song driven by Eric Clapton's wailing lead guitar. Lennon claimed that it refers to food poisoning from Christmas leftovers, but the lyric, intent and delivery are surely driven by heroin withdrawal. It's unpleasant, and perhaps that was the point.

> The song is self-explanatory. [It] got banned, even though it's anti-drug. They're so stupid about drugs, you know. They're not looking at the cause of the drug problem: Why do people take drugs? To escape from what? Is life so terrible? Are we living in such a terrible situation that we can't do anything without the reinforcement of alcohol or tobacco? Aspirins, sleeping pills, uppers, downers, never mind the heroin and cocaine.
> John speaking to *Playboy* in 1980

On the positive side, the single release of 'Cold Turkey' marks the first appearance of bassist Klaus Voormann on a solo Beatles song. Voormann had met Lennon, McCartney, Harrison, Stu Sutcliffe and Pete Best in Hamburg in August 1960. He moved to London in 1963, designed the album sleeve for *Revolver* in 1966, joined Manfred Mann for three years – he plays on the big hits 'Semi-Detached Suburban Mr James', 'Ha! Ha! Said The Clown', 'Mighty Quinn' and 'Fox On The Run' – and then became a session musician. Voormann was usually the bassist of choice for Lennon, Harrison and Starr between 1970 and 1976

A second album by the Modern Jazz Quartet, *Space*, would also be released in late October. It had been supervised by Peter Asher prior to his departure from Apple. 'I was thrilled,' he wrote in the sleeve notes of the 2010 re-release, 'because I, too, was a big jazz fan. But I'm sure they were deeply suspicious. This idea of this white English kid supervising [band leader and pianist] John Lewis is clearly absurd. I was at least able to convince them that I knew their music. I wasn't some rock 'n' roller who'd been detailed to work with them. I was a huge MJQ fan. I knew their albums. I knew exactly how they played. And I tried to play a role.' *Space* is an intriguing album that includes a very groovy ten-minute jazz arrangement of the Adagio from *Concerto De Aranjuez*.

November 1969: The Wedding Album, 'Come And Get It'

John and Yoko's *Wedding Album* was the third and final in a succession of collaborative experimental albums by the couple. 'By this time,' write McCabe and Schonfeld, 'they were well on their way to rivalling Richard Burton and Liz Taylor for the title of world's biggest bores, but still the avid publicity seeking didn't stop.' The 7 November release coincided with Yoko's miscarriage and Lennon's £150 fine for possession of cannabis resin. Side A comprises 23 minutes of Lennon and Ono's heartbeats overdubbed with the sound of them calling each other's names. It's ideal to get rid of unwanted guests. Side B is a sound collage (25 minutes long) called 'Amsterdam', comprising sounds recorded during the couple's honeymoon. One is never quite sure if they are taking the piss.

From the ridiculous to the sublime: 'Come And Get It' provided a breakthrough for The Iveys, the first of their four top ten hits in the US under their new name, Badfinger. The band had received a letter from Paul McCartney, no less, at the end of July, inviting them to meet him the next day at EMI studios. Paul had seen a feature in the 5 July issue of *Disc & Music Echo* which quoted two of Badfinger's musicians.

> 'We do feel a bit neglected,' said Ron Griffiths. 'We keep writing songs for a new single and submitting them to Apple, but The Beatles keep sending them back saying they're not good enough.'
>
> 'Mind you,' adds Tom Evans, 'we've had a lot of things most groups could not expect. The Beatles bought all our gear for us, all the equipment and a group van, and we've had all kinds of concessions ... all we need now is a hit single, or even just a new single, hit or not, and we'll be happy! We're going to keep on writing, and we're determined to come up with something The Beatles like. At first, we were adamant about not recording anything but one of our own songs, but now we'd record anything, so long as it was good...'

Paul had an idea. Midway through sessions for *Abbey Road*, on the same day that The Beatles recorded 'Sun King' and 'Mean Mr. Mustard', he went in early to lay down a demo of a new song of his called 'Come And Get It', ostensibly for the soundtrack of a film called *The Magic Christian* starring Peter Sellers and Ringo Starr.

As Paul told Mark Lewisohn in the essential *The Beatles Recording Sessions* (1988), 'I did a demo of 'Come And Get It' which took about 20 minutes – it was before a Beatles session. [Engineer] Phil McDonald was there, and I got in – I always used to get in early because I lived just around the corner – and all the equipment was set up from the day before, so I ran in and said, 'Just do this, Phil, go on, it'll only take 20 minutes' and I threw it away. I mean, it's really nice. I said, 'Look, lads, don't vary, this is good, just copy this down to the letter. It's perhaps a little bit undignified for you, a little bit lacking in integrity, to have to copy someone's work that rigidly, but this is the hit sound. Do it like this and we're all right, we've got a hit. No one will know anyway. And if they do say anything, say, 'Yes, Paul did the arrangement, big deal, it's not unheard of."

The Iveys were given a week to work up an arrangement and went into EMI on 2 August to record 'Come And Get It' in a single session. It has a spirited lead vocal by Tom Evans. In the coming weeks, they would record two further songs with Paul: 'Rock Of All Ages' (with Paul on piano) and 'Carry On Till Tomorrow'. These were Paul's last set of production sessions for Apple, other than his own releases. 'Rock Of All Ages', the B-side to 'Come And Get It', is a simple rocker. 'Carry On Till Tomorrow', however, is an intense ballad not too far from the soon-to-conquer-all soft-rock of America and CSNY. The driving lead guitar and gorgeous orchestration in the central section are beautifully produced.

Bassist Ron Griffiths left the band during this period. This led to a rethink about the band's name. They rejected Fresh, The Glass Onion, Tendergreen, Hyena's Nose and The New, The Old, Paul's suggested Home and John's pithy Prix. The Badfinger name was suggested by Neil Aspinall. 'Come And Get It' by Badfinger, with 'Rock Of All Ages' as the B-side, was released on 5 December 1969 in the UK, and on 12 January 1970 in the US. The band had a big hit with the song, peaking at number seven in the US and number four in the UK. Paul's demo was released on *Anthology 3*, and again, with much-improved sound quality (and in stereo) on the 2019 deluxe re-release of *Abbey Road*.

December 1969: Delaney & Bonnie, Live Peace In Toronto

On 1 December 1969, George Harrison attended a Delaney and Bonnie Bramlett concert at The Royal Albert Hall in London. The following night, he travelled to Bristol for what would have been his first stage appearance since The Beatles' final concert on 29 August 1966. He was spooked by local press reports that he would join the band on stage, but Harrison remained with the tour for the next week, playing two shows each night. He appeared in Birmingham, Sheffield, Liverpool and Croydon. George didn't perform at the

Newcastle shows on 5 December as he was visiting his sick mother. The core of the Bramlett band would record much of *All Things Must Pass* in 1970 and quickly morph into Derek And The Dominos.

The final Apple release of a busy, difficult year was The Plastic Ono Band's impromptu concert at the Toronto Rock And Roll Revival Festival on 13 September. *Live Peace In Toronto 1969* (released on 12 December 1969) comprises all 40 minutes of a ramshackle eight-song set to 20,000 people by John and Yoko with a scratch band made up of Eric Clapton, Klaus Voormann and future Yes drummer Alan White. The lineup was pulled together at such short notice that they rehearsed, unamplified, as they crossed the Atlantic by plane.

The set-list was also ad hoc. Three oldies (a ragged 'Blue Suede Shoes', a raucous 'Money (That's What I Want)' and a hit-and-miss 'Dizzy Miss Lizzy', which introduces the vocal stylings of John's wife) preceded three Lennon originals, namely 'Yer Blues' with a two-note Lennon guitar solo and some Clapton blues wailing, the yet-to-be-recorded 'Cold Turkey' and the already-inevitable 'Give Peace A Chance'. So far, so acceptable.

Yoko Ono, thankfully mostly silent up until then, performed the B-side of 'Cold Turkey', the atonal 'Don't Worry Kyoko (Mummy's Only Looking For Her Hand In The Snow)'. The set closed with 'John John (Let's Hope For Peace)', which adds electric guitar feedback to Yoko's screaming for what seems like a lot longer than 12 minutes. If you've never heard this album, then keep it that way.

As Apple established an office in New York City, at 1700 Broadway, rough cuts of the *Get Back* film were assembled. The producers noticed that two songs included in the film were not present on the proposed soundtrack album. 'Across The Universe' had been recorded in February 1968, and Glyn Johns remixed it for the proposed new album. 'I Me Mine' would require a new recording, and this took place in January 1970.

The year ended with George, Patti, Paul and Linda seeing in the new year with Ringo and Maureen at a party in London. John and Yoko were in Denmark, where they declared 1970 as Year 1 AP (After Peace). They issued a statement: 'We believe that the last decade was the end of the old machine crumbling to pieces. And we think we can get it together, with your help. We have great hopes for the new year.'

1970

January 1970: Magic Christian Music

With John still in Denmark – and never wholly committed to George's songs in any case – it was a three-piece Beatles who convened at EMI Studios with George Martin to record 'I Me Mine' on 3 January. The song had made the cut of the *Get Back* film (as it was still called), but had not been recorded during the sessions at Apple the previous year. George (acoustic guitar), Paul (bass) and Ringo (drums) recorded 16 takes of the basic track in a relaxed session. Overdubs onto the final take included two electric guitars (George), acoustic guitars (George and Paul), Hammond organ (Paul) and electric piano (Paul).

'I Me Mine' was added to the proposed album track list, and Glyn Johns remixed much of the existing material once more. Paul's 'Teddy Boy' was dropped at this stage. This revamped version of *Get Back* from January 1970, therefore, comprised:

Side One
'One After 909' (30 January 1969)
'Rocker (Instrumental)' (22 January 1969)
'Save The Last Dance For Me' (22 January 1969)
'Don't Let Me Down' (22 January 1969)
'Dig A Pony' (22 January 1969)
'I've Got A Feeling' (22 January 1969)
'Get Back' (23 January 1969)
'Let It Be' (31 January 1969)

Side Two
'For You Blue' (25 January 1969)
'Two Of Us' (24 January 1969)
'Maggie Mae' (24 January 1969)
'Dig It' (24 January 1969)
'The Long And Winding Road' (26 January 1969)
'I Me Mine' (3 January 1970)
'Across The Universe' (4 and 8 February 1968)
'Get Back (Reprise)' (23 January 1969)

Once again, this album was rejected by The Beatles.

Badfinger's *Magic Christian Music* was released on 9 January, as 'Come And Get It' headed into the top ten in the UK. After release in the US the following month (with 12 tracks in a different order), it started a long run in the US charts, reaching a high of number seven. *Magic Christian Music* comprises the three songs from the soundtrack to *The Magic Christian* ('Come And Get It', 'Rock Of All Ages' and 'Carry On Till Tomorrow', all produced by Paul McCartney), four new tracks ('Crimson Ship', 'Midnight Sun', 'Walk Out In

The Rain' and 'Give It A Try') and seven older songs from The Iveys' *Maybe Tomorrow* album.

Magic Christian Music showcases Badfinger's stylistic breadth, but its patchwork nature results in a confused and confusing collection of songs. 'Crimson Ship', co-written by Tom Evans and Pete Ham about Paul McCartney, has a harmonised dual lead vocal by the two songwriters. It has some tasty lead guitar to recommend it, though it, too, is piano-based. 'Midnight Sun' is a basic riffing rocker, brilliantly sung by Pete Ham. Ham's 'Walk Out in the Rain' is a gorgeous ballad with melancholy lyrics. Inexplicably left off the American edition of the LP, 'Give It A Try' is bubbly power pop which sounds a little forced. It was written as a proposed single. The idea was nixed by Apple.

Badfinger soon expanded back to a four-piece with the addition of guitarist Joey Molland. Molland, from Liverpool, had played with several bands, notably with Gary Walker and as part of The Merseys. He does not play on any of the songs on *Magic Christian Music,* but would be a strong influence on the band's direction going forward. Badfinger's classic lineup was in place, but would last fewer than four years. *Magic Christian Music* sold moderately well in the US, reaching number 55, but in the UK, neither this nor any other Badfinger albums would trouble the chart compilers.

Follow-up singles from Billy Preston, Jackie Lomax and Mary Hopkin were released in the early weeks of 1970, as well as a first Apple single by Doris Troy. The effortlessly funky 'All That I've Got (I'm Gonna Give It To You)' was Billy Preston's third single for Apple. Produced by George Harrison, and with George and Ringo on bass and drums, respectively, even a spirited performance on *Top Of The Pops* wasn't enough to guarantee a hit.

Jackie Lomax's last single for Apple was another George Harrison production called 'How the Web Was Woven', which features a thrilling piano part by Leon Russell, who was in town recording his first solo album. One gets the feeling that Lomax wasn't really engaged. The B-side, a cover of Leiber and Stoller's 'Thumbin' A Ride', was produced by Paul McCartney, but the single failed to chart, and Lomax left Apple.

As he told *Rolling Stone* later that year, 'He [Klein] came in and put a stop to everything going out of the company, to get a chance to re-evaluate things … Klein never spoke to me to find out what I was into. They stopped answering my phone calls. I owed them a certain number of sides a year, but all I cut was a single that George produced. Finally, I had a solicitor's letter sent to them asking what was going on. They said the man in charge of the matter would get back to me in three weeks. Well, I got some pride, so I had another letter sent saying, 'I consider our association terminated'. They haven't yet answered that one.'

He joined the bands Heavy Jelly and Badger with a conspicuous lack of success.

Mary Hopkin's 'Temma Harbour' gave the Welsh singer her third big hit in the UK. The song was produced by Mickie Most, whose arrangement mixed chirpy folk with steel drums. In the US, 'Temma Harbour' stalled at number 39, but at home, it peaked at number six in mid-February in a lightweight top ten which also included 'Love Grows', 'Leaving On A Jet Plane' and, ahem, 'Two Little Boys'.

February 1970: 'Instant Karma!'

Mary Hopkin's highest position with 'Temma Harbour' on 15 February was one place above 'Instant Karma!', credited to Lennon/Ono/Plastic Ono Band.

John and Yoko had spent four weeks in Denmark with Ono's ex-husband, Tony Cox. Two days after returning to the UK, on 27 January, Lennon woke up with the idea for a song. An hour later, he'd composed 'Instant Karma!'. Keen to record it immediately, he phoned George Harrison and together they gathered a band comprising two of the musicians from the Toronto concert – Klaus Voormann and Alan White – and the ever-present Billy Preston.

The American producer Phil Spector had called in to ABKCO's New York City office a few weeks beforehand to pitch his services to The Beatles. Klein persuaded The Beatles to meet him, and Spector landed in London on 27 January. Later that evening, he was with Lennon and Harrison recording 'Instant Karma!'. The song was recorded in ten takes, with backing vocals by Yoko, Mal Evans and several revellers from the Hackett Club on Piccadilly, a five-minute walk from the Apple offices on Savile Row. It was released on Apple on 6 February and went to number five in the UK. John played the song on *Top Of The Pops*, with Yoko sitting beside him, wearing a white blindfold and knitting. In the US, it was the first solo single by a member of The Beatles to sell a million copies, reaching number three. The B-side is Yoko's delicate 'Who Has Seen The Wind?'.

The Beatles had signed a new nine-year contract with EMI/Capitol in early 1967. This guaranteed that Capitol would end their practice of chopping up Beatles albums for the US market. It didn't stop them from creating new compilations, and the second of these, *Hey Jude*, was released on 26 February 1970. This must have angered The Beatles considerably, as they had a new single ready to roll. Nevertheless, the year-old 'Let It Be' duly became the band's 19th number one in the US, but peaked at number four in the UK.

George Harrison worked hard on the follow-up to Radha Krishna Temple's hit single. 'Govinda' was recorded at Trident in January. A gentle rock backing of acoustic guitar, organ, bass and drums accompanies the devotees' voices (bolstered by the likes of Donovan and Mary Hopkin) and tinkling bells. An overdubbed orchestra, harp and tubular bells enable the sound to swell gloriously and hypnotically. George's efforts paid off, and the Temple achieved another hit in the UK, peaking at number 23.

Chris O'Dell, one of the first Apple employees, left in November 1969 to spend time in Los Angeles. She returned in February 1970. 'I took the stairs to Derek's office', she wrote later. 'That's when I began to feel a strange kind of tension in the air and an eerie silence. The place seemed empty and silent. It was the silence that affected me most. That deep stillness, an unspoken hush where you wait for something to happen – you're not sure what – and you hold your breath, waiting, wondering and knowing somehow that whatever it is, it's not going to be good. The next morning, I went to work as usual … acting as if my four months in Los Angeles were just a weekend fling. I was home, even if the place felt like a graveyard. Somehow, we'd bring it back to life.' O'Dell set to work with Neil Aspinall, cataloguing film footage of The Beatles.

Billy Preston's 'All That I've Got (I'm Gonna Give It To You)' was co-written by Doris Troy, whose own 'Ain't That Cute' would be her first single for Apple in February. Troy was a gifted American singer-songwriter, a member of The Sweet Inspirations. Her only solo success was the original 'Just One Look' in 1963, later a hit for The Hollies. She moved to London in 1969, sang on 'You Can't Always Get What You Want' and Billy Preston's sessions for Apple. Her debut album was recorded between the autumn of 1969 and the spring of 1970, co-produced by Troy and George with contributions from Eric Clapton, Ringo Starr, Klaus Voormann, Bobby Keys, Jim Price, Gary Wright, Billy Preston, Stephen Stills and Peter Frampton. The lead single, 'Ain't That Cute', is a powerful, commercial soul-rocker with some stinging lead guitar from Clapton and tasty Harrison fills. Troy was a phenomenal singer, and George's production of 'Ain't That Cute' (which he also co-wrote) highlighted her powerful vocals in a tight rock arrangement and blasting horns. The middle-eight, which pivots into a minor-to-major, features slightly unexpected harmonic shifts and tilts toward Beatles-esque, is pure George and could be straight off *All Things Must Pass*. Sadly, it failed to chart despite encouraging reviews.

As Paul continued to record songs for his debut solo album, he went into EMI on 15 February and laid down 'Every Night' in a single session. A week later, he repeated this feat with the incomparable 'Maybe I'm Amazed', then again on 25 February with 'Man We Was Lonely'.

March 1970: Phil Spector

With a release date for the *Get Back* film finally scheduled, the session tapes were given to Phil Spector in March 1970. Spector chose several different takes for his version of the album, now called *Let It Be* after the newly-released single of the same name (after a brief consideration of *The Long And Winding Road*). Spector re-ordered the tracks and added orchestra and choir to 'The Long And Winding Road', 'Across The Universe' and 'I Me Mine'. Ultimately, just six tracks on *Let It Be* were wholly live performances in accordance with the original concept: 'I've Got A Feeling', 'One After 909' and 'Dig A Pony' from the rooftop performance, and 'Two Of Us', 'Dig It' and 'Maggie Mae' from studio sessions.

Paul McCartney was deeply upset with Spector's treatment of some songs, particularly 'The Long And Winding Road'. He unsuccessfully attempted to

This page: The Beatles in 1968 on their Mad Day Out, and in 1969, just before the band broke up. (*Alamy*)

Left: The Beatles launched Apple to release their own records and their pet projects. They hit immediately with 'Hey Jude'. (*Apple*)

Right: Paul McCartney chose the songs, produced and played on Mary Hopkin's first album, *Post Card*. (*Apple*)

Below: James Taylor showed great promise with his debut album. He needed to leave Apple to fulfil it. (*Apple*)

Right: John Lennon and Yoko Ono's *Unfinished Music No.1: Two Virgins*. When the most notable aspect of an album is the cover, which shows the couple naked, then the music, such as it is, becomes irrelevant. (*Apple*)

THE MODERN JAZZ QUARTET UNDER THE JASMIN TREE

Left: Apple supported a number of non-pop/rock artists at Apple, including the sophisticated jazz of The Modern Jazz Quartet ... (*Apple*)

John Tavener

Right: ... and the experimental classical composer John Tavener. (*Apple*)

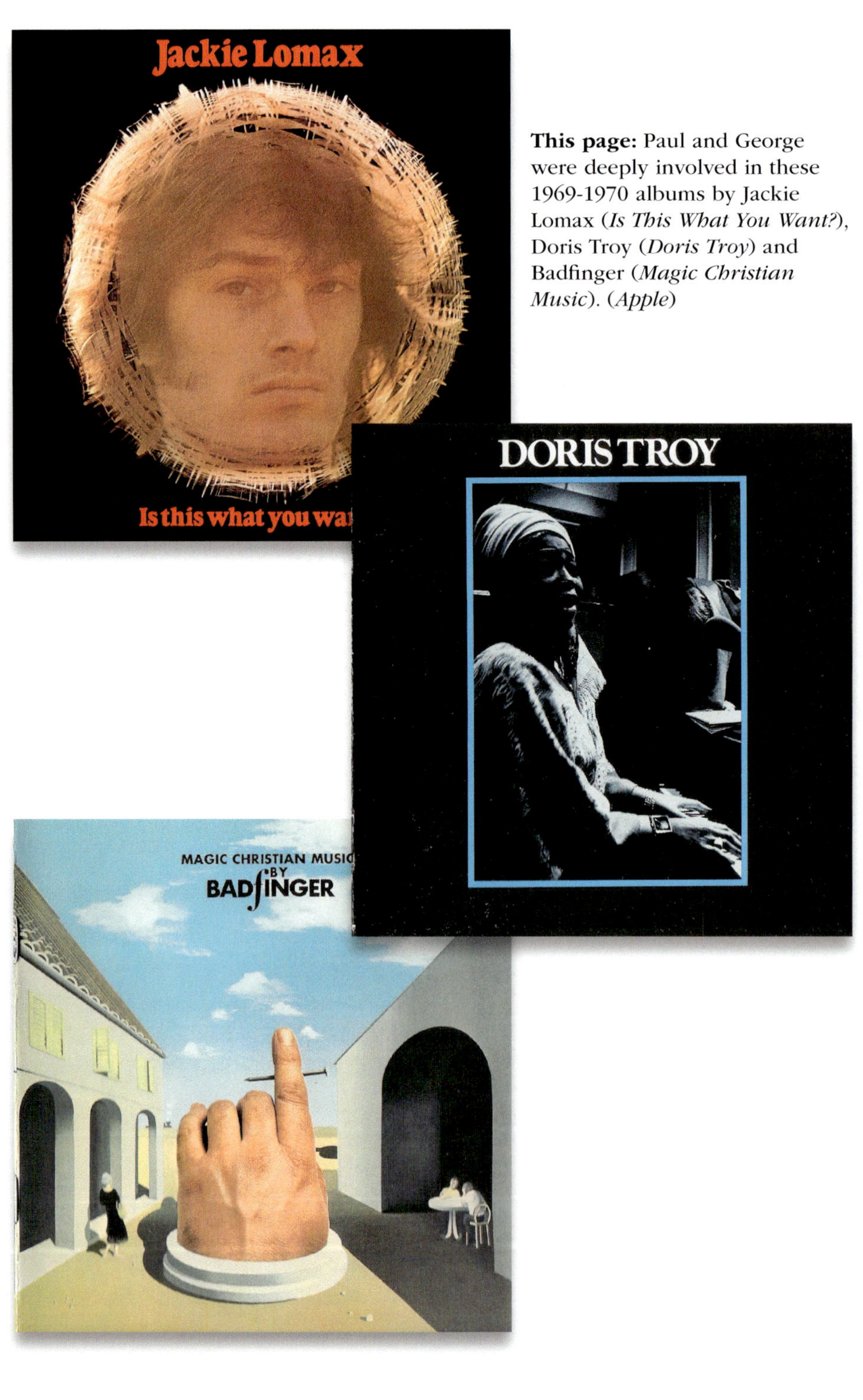

This page: Paul and George were deeply involved in these 1969-1970 albums by Jackie Lomax (*Is This What You Want?*), Doris Troy (*Doris Troy*) and Badfinger (*Magic Christian Music*). (*Apple*)

Right and below: Billy Preston's *That's The Way God Planned It* and *Encouraging Words* also received heavy input from Paul and George. (*Apple*)

Above: Above: These twin albums – *John Lennon/Plastic Ono Band* and *Yoko Ono/ Plastic Ono Band* – were recorded during the same set of sessions with a core band of John Lennon, Klaus Voormann and Ringo Starr. They were released on 11 December 1970. (Apple)

Above: John, Paul, George and Ringo in the Apple offices in 1968 with Mary Hopkin and Yoko Ono.

Above: James Taylor: one of many talented artists to slip through Apple's fingers. (*Alamy*)

Left: John Tavener, an English composer of choral religious works, whose cantata, *The Whale*, was released on Apple.

Above: Badfinger, the heroes and victims of the Apple story, with George Harrison.

Left: Jackie Lomax with George Harrison. The Beatles' magic didn't rub off despite a series of great singles.

Right: John and Yoko. 'We're only trying to get us some peace.' (*Getty*)

Left: Solo albums from the ex-Beatles helped to fill Apple's coffers in 1970. These include Harrison's *All Things Must Pass* ... (*Apple*)

Right: ... Starr's *Beaucoups Of Blues* ... (*Apple*)

Left: ... Lennon's *Imagine* ... (*Apple*)

Right: ... and McCartney's *RAM*. (*Apple*)

Left: Joey Molland's presence on Badfinger's *No Dice* adds a much rockier sound to the album, which is full of great music. (*Apple*)

Right: George's *Concert For Bangladesh* took place on 1 August. George and Ringo performed on stage together for the first time since 1966. The shows were a pioneering charity event in aid of the displaced Bengali refugees of the Bangladesh Liberation War. (*Apple*)

Left and below: Yoko Ono's musical talent has confounded listeners for almost 60 years. These double albums, released in September 1971 and February 1973, are fully committed and start to move towards a more conventional rock sound. (*Apple*)

Left: Apple released Starr's marvellous 'It Don't Come Easy' single in 1971. (*Apple*)

Right and below: Further Apple releases in 1971 include the exquisite *Earth Song/ Ocean Song* by Mary Hopkin and Radha Krshna Temple's soothing self-titled album. (*Apple*)

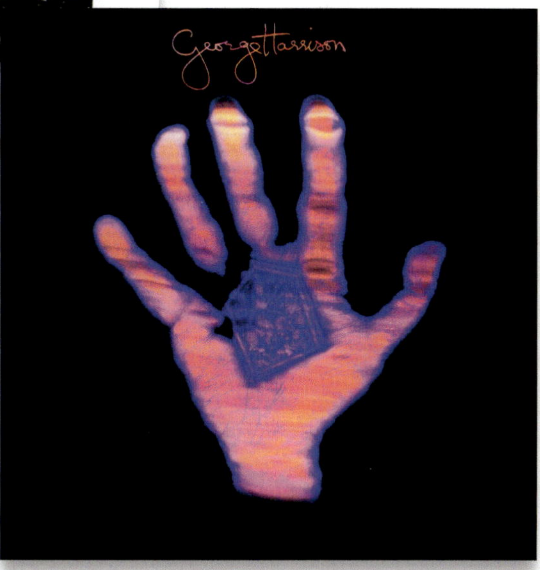

Right: George Harrison's 1973 *Living In The Material World* album. (*Apple*)

Left: Billy Preston and George Harrison giving it large on George's solo tour of 1974. (*Getty*)

Below: Wings: Paul, Linda, Jimmy, Denny and Geoff. (*Getty*)

Above: George donated a manor house to the Hare Krishna movement in 1973.

Below: Allen Klein with John and Yoko – Paul McCartney's refusal to work with him exacerbated The Beatles' personal and business problems. (*Getty*)

Left and below: Badfinger's *Straight Up* and *Ass* are full of great songs, despite their chequered paths to release. (*Apple*)

Left: As well as Harrison's *Material World*, the other ex-Beatles each released marvellous solo albums in 1973, including McCartney's *Band On The Run*... (*Apple*)

Right: ... Lennon's *Mind Games* ... (*Apple*)

Left: ... and Starr's *Ringo*. (*Apple*)

Right: Further Beatles activity in 1973 – the phenomenally successful 'Red' album collects Beatles songs from the first half of their career. (*Apple*)

Left: The Beatles also released the equally successful 'Blue' album in 1973, a compilation of songs from the second half of their career. (*Apple*)

Right and below: A final roll of the dice for Apple – two compilation albums which wrapped up the commercial viability of John (until 1980) and Ringo (forever). (*Apple*) halt the release of Spector's version, and this was a contributing factor to his public announcement that he was leaving The Beatles the following month. Lennon, for his part, defended Phil Spector, saying in his famous *Playboy* interview in 1980, 'He was given the shittiest load of badly recorded shit with a lousy feeling to it ever, and he made something of it.' Spector would produce much of the solo material released by George Harrison and John Lennon between 1970 and 1971.

Chris O'Dell attended Pattie Harrison's birthday party at Friar Park on 17 March and claims that all four Beatles were present. If true, this is likely to be the last time that Lennon, McCartney, Harrison and Starr were together.

Mary Hopkin, meanwhile, had been selected to sing the UK entry in the ever-popular Eurovision Song Contest. Hopkin sang each of the six shortlisted songs for the UK entry in a televised *A Song For Europe* on 7 March, and the winner was selected following a postal vote. Over 120,000 viewers chose the chirpy 'Knock, Knock Who's There?' as their preferred candidate.

The Eurovision Song Contest was held in Amsterdam on 21 March. Mary Hopkin was the pre-contest favourite to win but came second to another 19-year-old, Ireland's Dana, who sang the syrupy 'All Kinds Of Everything'. 'Knock, Knock Who's There?' was released as a single on 23 March, produced by Mickie Most. It was Hopkin's biggest hit since 'Those Were The Days', peaking at number two in the UK behind 'Bridge Over Troubled Water' and was still in the top five when 'All Kinds Of Everything' went to number one. The B-side of 'Knock, Knock Who's There?' was 'I'm Going To Fall In Love Again', the runner-up in the *A Song For Europe* vote.

It's probably safe to say that no-one expected great things from Ringo Starr's solo career. And yet his first solo album, *Sentimental Journey*, was a sizeable hit. In truth, *Sentimental Journey* is a vanity project album of pop and jazz standards recorded to please his mother. Arranged by some of the very best musicians money could buy – Elmer Bernstein, Quincy Jones, Oliver Nelson, Chico O'Farrell and Johnny Dankworth, with Paul contributing the arrangement for 'Stardust' – there is a great deal of craft on *Sentimental Journey*, released on 27 March 1970 in the UK (number seven) and 24 April 1970 in the US (number 22).

'I did the first album,' Ringo told *Innerview* in August 1977, 'because we all know I didn't know what [else] to do. And I decided I gotta get off me ass and get a job. So, I thought 'I'll go in and do all these standards, you know, because I always liked them anyway – and it's me, right? So it's part of me. I'm not one of those people who won't admit to their past and their musical influences. So, I thought, "That's what I'll do."

But Starr is no Frank Sinatra. His lead vocal contributions to The Beatles' albums were written or selected to make the most of his limited range, and on this material, his talents as a singer are sorely exposed. There was, no doubt, a lot of goodwill shown to *Sentimental Journey* and the events of mid-April surely helped it reach a top ten placing that month. *Sentimental Journey* remains a curiosity for die-hards: I doubt anyone has listened to it end-to-end since 1970.

The sessions for the album included an original song, 'You Gotta Play Your Dues'. This was first recorded on 12 February at EMI with Ringo, George, Klaus Voormann and Stephen Stills (on piano). Another version would be laid down a week later, and a third on 8 March at Trident Studios, produced by George Harrison, who also helped considerably with the writing and arrangement. Voormann and Stills again contributed on bass and piano. For now, it was left on the shelf.

Despite recording a handful of songs for Apple for a proposed album in spring 1970, Trash were dropped from Apple at this time.

April 1970: Derek Taylor Leaves Apple, Paul Leaves The Beatles

1 April 1970 marked the last session for the last Beatles album: final overdubs for *Let It Be*. From the band whose name would go on the cover, only Ringo attended. To the wider public, it was still 'business as usual' for The Beatles. But not for long.

On the day that Phil Spector completed work on *Let It Be*, 2 April, Paul McCartney was interviewed by Ray Connolly for London's *Evening Standard*. Paul stated: 'Strictly speaking, we all have to ask each other's permission before any of us does anything without the other three. My own record [*McCartney*] nearly didn't come out because Klein and some of the others thought it would be too near to the date of the next Beatles album. I had to get George, who's a director of Apple, to authorise its release for me. Give us our freedom, which we so richly deserve. We're beginning now to only call each other when we have bad news. The other day, Ringo came around to see me with a letter from the others, and I called him everything under the sun. But it's all business. I don't want to fall out with Ringo. I like Ringo. I think he's great. We're all talking about peace and love, but really, we're not feeling peaceful at all. There's no one who's to blame. We were fools to get ourselves into this situation in the first place. But it's not a comfortable situation for me to work in as an artist.'

This interview would be published on 21 April, by which time Paul had made global headlines with a statement in the form of a self-answering questionnaire. 'I didn't want to do any interviews at the time,' Paul recalled, 'because I knew the first thing they'd ask about was The Beatles and all that stuff, and I didn't really want that. I didn't want to face the press, and I said so. Derek at the office said, 'We should do something.' I said, 'I'll tell you what, you do a questionnaire of anything you think the press would want to know and I'll try and answer honestly.'

'For the release of Paul's solo album,' Derek Taylor said, 'we did a questionnaire in the press office, a general issue thing: 'Will you ever appear with The Beatles? Do you believe in this? What are your plans?' etc. I thought he very generously answered – in an uptight way, but nevertheless answered

– the questions, more or less ruling out a reunion or working with The Beatles: 'And I'm now working with Linda and this is the way I want it to be...'

Q: Is your break with The Beatles, temporary or permanent, due to personal differences or musical ones?
A: Personal differences, business differences, musical differences, but most of all because I have a better time with my family. Temporary or permanent? I don't know.
Q: Do you foresee a time when Lennon-McCartney becomes an active songwriting partnership again?
A: No.

The Daily Mirror received an advance copy of the statement on 9 April. Its front-page story the following day shouted 'Paul Is Quitting The Beatles'. Paul phoned John, who was at a clinic in London for Primal Therapy, to inform him of the statement's release. John recalled, in an interview with *Penthouse* in 1971, 'Paul rang me up. He didn't actually tell me he'd split; he said he was putting out an album. He said, 'I'm now doing what you and Yoko were doing last year. I understand what you were doing.' All that shit. So I said, 'Good luck to yer.''

A press release issued the same day seemed to confirm the worst. 'They do not want to split up,' it read, 'but the present rift seems to be part of their growing up … at the moment, they seem to cramp each other's styles. Paul has called a halt to The Beatles' activities. They could be dormant for years.' The first that John heard of Paul's separation from the group was the following morning. When asked about it, John quipped, 'You can say I said, jokingly, 'he didn't quit, he was fired.''

A statement from Apple on 10 April (in Derek Taylor's unmistakable prose) read: 'Spring is here and Leeds play Chelsea tomorrow and Ringo and John and George and Paul are alive and well and full of hope. The World is still spinning, and so are we, and so are you. When the spinning stops, that'll be the time to worry, not before. Until then, The Beatles are alive and well and the beat goes on, the beat goes on.'

Taylor: 'That was a very unhappy time. That was the pits.'

Ironically, Paul was the fourth Beatle to actually leave the group. Both Ringo and George had quit in August 1968 and January 1969, respectively, but had been persuaded to return. John's decision to 'divorce' the others in September 1969 was kept under wraps. In the end, Paul's public statement that he was leaving The Beatles was terminal, simply because none of the others liked the idea that he had made the first move.

Times columnist William Mann wrote on 11 April, 'If The Beatles were just another pop group, there would be no cause for alarm in Paul McCartney's suggestion announced yesterday, that he may never work with them again.

The others would simply find another bass guitarist and lead singer and go on roughly as before. But The Beatles' image and influence on pop culture in the last ten years have depended on four distinctive personalities working well together. They would not be the same without Paul.'

McCartney contains relaxed recordings of a happy house husband. It's as self-indulgent as *Two Virgins* or *Life With The Lions*. The difference here is that *McCartney* is a charming album made by a man who, at the time of recording, didn't seem weighed down at all by the imminent dissolution of The Beatles – that would come later – nor by the seemingly loose and simple performances on his first statement outside the band.

Paul wrote, played and sang everything on his debut album, other than some harmonies from Linda. The album is modest, relaxed, seemingly effortless and frequently sublime. 'The Lovely Linda' is trite, but still very appealing, setting up the mood for the album to follow. 'That Would Be Something' is a typically melodic McCartney composition, with heavily echoing electric guitar, bubbling bass and a simple, repeating lyric. 'Valentine Day' was improvised on the spot, and sounds like it, but 'Every Night' is the first classic song of Paul's solo career: unashamedly romantic, rough-and-ready and oozing with talent. The lyrics reflect his state of mind in 1969-1970, the final lines hinting at his preferred domesticity rather than the rock 'n' roll lifestyle ('But tonight I just want to stay in/and be with you'). 'Hot As Sun' is one of Paul's earliest songs, dating back to 1958. 'Junk' was written in India and demoed for the *White Album* in May 1968. It's one of those lost classics of the McCartney back catalogue. It's hauntingly beautiful, not much more than an acoustic guitar, lightly tapped drums, a counterpointing bass and a terrific lead vocal. 'Man We Was Lonely', like 'Every Night' and 'Maybe I'm Amazed', was recorded at Abbey Road. This one dates from 25 February 1970. Paul plays guitar with lots of tremolo, bass drum, bass and a steel guitar sound made by working his Telecaster with a drum peg. Linda sings harmony. Its simplicity may annoy some, but it's nothing less than delightful. 'Oo You' is an improvisation recorded by Paul at home. It's a louder, groovier remake of 'Why Don't We Do It In The Road?'. A more formally composed, polished version of the similarly improvised 'Momma Miss America' may have brought out more of McCartney's skills as a songwriter. Nevertheless, this instrumental has some wobbly pulsing bass and terrific jangly piano, all reminiscent of the later 'Nineteen Hundred And Eighty-Five'. The second half started as another improvisation called 'Rock And Roll Springtime' and goes on for a few minutes too long. 'Teddy Boy' was recorded twice by The Beatles but never finished satisfactorily. It feels over-long at 2:25. The album closes with 'Singalong Junk', an instrumental version of 'Junk' and the experimental, heavily percussive 'Kreen-Akrore', separated by not only Paul's classiest song on *McCartney* but one of the best of his entire solo career: 'Maybe I'm Amazed'. His singing revisits his full-bodied voice from 'Oh! Darling' and 'I've Got A Feeling', and is the equal of anything he's recorded. Likewise, the lead guitar break is lyrical, fluid and uplifting, and the songwriting is direct and heartfelt. Paul plays piano, drums, bass, rhythm and solo guitars and, with Linda, two tracks of backing vocals.

Commented George Harrison in May 1970: "That Would Be Something' and 'Maybe I'm Amazed' I think are great, and everything else I think is fair, you know – is quite good – but umm, a little disappointing. But I don't know. Maybe I shouldn't be disappointed, maybe ... it's best not to expect anything and then everything's a bonus, you know. I think those two tracks, in particular, are really very good. And the others, I mean, just don't do much for me.'

At this time, Badfinger were offered, but turned down, another Beatles-written song, 'It Don't Come Easy', as a potential new single. They were convinced that they could succeed with their own original material and went into the studio on 18 April 1970 to record four new songs. Of these, 'I Can't Take It' (Ham), 'No Matter What' (Ham) and 'Without You' (Ham/Evans) would see release later in the year on the album *No Dice*.

George and John both left the UK at the end of April. George met with Bob Dylan and recorded some sessions with him. John and Yoko headed to Los Angeles and would not return to the UK until September.

May – August 1970: Let It Be, The Press Office Closes

Apple-related activity continued in May 1970 before easing off during the summer months. The Beatles' last album, *Let It Be*, was released on 8 May (UK) and 18 May (US). In America, the single 'The Long And Winding Road' would be their final number one. The film premiered on 20 May 1970 at The London Pavilion, Piccadilly Circus. Badfinger sessions for their next album continued at EMI that same month. 'No Matter What' was put forward as a single, but Apple declined. George started work on *All Things Must Pass* at EMI on 26 May.

With no Apple releases scheduled for the next three months, Ringo flew to Nashville for two days of sessions. Here, he recorded 13 songs for his next album.

Derek Taylor had started a six-month sabbatical in March, with a plan to write a book about Apple. He would visit the Apple offices weekly, and the day-to-day workload would be managed by Richard DiLello and Taylor's assistant, Mavis Smith. Smith resigned from Apple on 20 June. Six weeks later, the press office was closed permanently, and the remaining employees, including Richard DiLello, were dismissed.

John Eastman wrote to Allen Klein suggesting that The Beatles' partnership should be dissolved, but a reply was not forthcoming. Trying a more direct response, Paul McCartney wrote to John Lennon suggesting that 'they let each other out of the trap'. John responded with a photograph of himself and Yoko and a hand-drawn speech bubble asking, 'How and Why?'. Paul replied with a letter which read, 'How? By signing a paper which says we hereby dissolve the partnership. Why? Because there is no partnership.' John responded with a card which read: 'Get well soon. Get the other signatures and I will think about it.'

Badfinger continued recording tracks for their next album in July and August, mainly at EMI.

September 1970: Four New Albums

Doris Troy's self-titled album was released on 11 September 1970. It's a fun, upbeat, soulful album and highlights Troy's awesome singing voice. She takes on Stephen Stills' 'Special Care' with real power. The Dorothy Fields/Jimmy McHugh standard 'Exactly Like You' is full-on gospel, as is her cover of Joe South's 'Games People Play'. The glorious 'Gonna Get My Baby Back' features Harrison, Starr and Stills. The spiritual 'Jacob's Ladder' closes the album on a rousing high note. This would be issued as a single, backed with a stunning version of 'Get Back'. Chris O'Dell, who left Apple to work for Peter Asher in Los Angeles during this period, described Troy as 'a large, sturdy woman with a booming voice … she lavished love and laughter on everyone.'

Billy Preston's second album for Apple, *Encouraging Words*, had been mostly recorded between December 1969 and April 1970, initially taking place immediately after George's tour with Delaney And Bonnie And Friends. The album sessions employed most of that band. Three songs – 'Encouraging Words', 'Right Now' and 'Sing One For The Lord' – date from the sessions for *That's The Way God Planned It* in the spring of 1969. Producer George Harrison gifted 'My Sweet Lord' (released as a single) and 'All Things Must Pass' to Preston, and these versions predate George's by two months. *Encouraging Words* includes a super-funky cover of 'I've Got A Feeling' and the unsuccessful single 'All That I've Got (I'm Gonna Give It To You)'.

As with *Doris Troy, Encouraging Words* was released on 11 September 1970. Both albums suffered from a lack of promotion from Apple Records due to the lack of an active press office. Despite receiving good reviews from several music critics, neither made any commercial impact.

Doris Troy continued to sing back-up for multiple artists and bands, including Pink Floyd's *The Dark Side Of The Moon*, Carly Simon's 'You're So Vain' and sessions for Humble Pie, Kevin Ayers, Edgar Broughton, Dusty Springfield, Nick Drake and others.

At the end of the month, Ringo's second album, *Beaucoups Of Blues*, was released. This unapologetic country album shows Ringo at home and in his element among the cream of Nashville session musicians.

> I did the country album because I still like country and western music. And that happened by accident. We were playing on George's album [*All Things Must Pass*], and Pete Drake was there. I had lent him my car, and he noticed I had all these country tapes, besides the rock tapes and any other tapes in the car. And he said, 'Ah, you like country', and I said, 'Yeah, I really dig it.'

And he said, 'You should come and do an album in Nashville.' I said, 'I'm not looking to spend three months in Nashville', and he said, 'What are you talking about? We do an album in a week!' He was leaving, and I said 'I'll be there a week from Saturday. You get it together, and I'll fly in.' And we went in. I was getting up at ten in the morning, learning five songs and going in at seven at night, and we'd cut five songs.
Ringo Starr, *Innerview*, August 1977

The musicianship on *Beaucoups Of Blues* is peerless – every song was custom-written for Ringo – but, as with *Sentimental Journey*, the album is let down by Ringo's uncertain vocals, despite their obvious sincerity. Either way, this style suits Ringo perfectly. The album is a lot of fun and remains one of Ringo's best solo releases.

In complete contrast, Apple's other album released on 25 September 1970 would be one of the most remarkable on the label. *The Whale*, a cantata for chorus and orchestra, was written by John Tavener, a young classical composer who was described by *The Guardian* as 'the musical discovery of the year'. During his career, Tavener became one of the best-known and popular composers of his generation. He was knighted in 2000. *The Whale* tells the Old Testament story of the prophet Jonah, who disobeys God, flees on a ship, is thrown overboard during a storm and is swallowed by a whale. Jonah repents and travels to Nineveh to convert the city to the ways of the Lord.

In 2004, Sir John said: "The Whale' is a piece written by an angry young man. I was angry because the world didn't see the cosmos in metaphysical terms. I was also angry because what I saw of so-called classical music in those days was very po-faced. I wrote *The Whale* as a reaction in a way. The piece is very fantastical.'

Indeed, *The Whale* has both unconventional scoring (the traditional orchestra and chorus are augmented by non-musical instruments such as a whip and a football rattle) and dynamic rise and fall in its recounting of the biblical story. It opens with BBC radio newsreader Alvar Lidell, one of the most distinctive broadcast voices of the 20th century, as the narrator, reading an encyclopaedic description of the sea mammal. *The Whale* was premiered in London on 24 January 1968, and heard again at a Proms concert on 1 August 1969.

But why Apple? As the story goes, Tavener had met John and Yoko at a dinner party. The composer played a recording of one of his operas, and John was intrigued by the mixture of music and sound effects. In a remarkable coincidence, Tavener's brother, Roger, was at that time employed to carry out building work on Ringo Starr's home. Roger discussed the possibility of *The Whale* being released on Apple and provided Starr with a recording made for the BBC. With two ex-Beatles now supportive, *The Whale* was recorded for Apple in July 1970. Almost by accident, The Beatles' record label gave a leg-up to one of the UK's most prolific and well-regarded classical composers.

Meanwhile, John Lennon, with Phil Spector, recorded his first solo album at EMI in late September and through October.

October 1970: 'Think About Your Children', 'No Matter What'

Mary Hopkin's fifth single, 'Think About Your Children', once again produced by Mickie Most, came six months after her immense success with 'Knock, Knock Who's There'. Notwithstanding the song's message of unity and positivity, it would be her lowest chart placement to date. It had been written by Errol Brown and Tony Wilson of former Apple artists Hot Chocolate.

Hopkin started to record her second album at this time. As she said to *NME* that November, 'I'm about halfway through my second album, but it's difficult getting the time to finish. I'm not even sure how it's going to work out. It's supposed to be on one theme – children – and I want it to be good. But it's such a shame having to cram everything in and then not being happy about it or doing it as well as I should.' This album would remain unfinished.

Badfinger's second single, 'No Matter What', was a strong follow-up to 'Come And Get It', even though it sounded nothing like it, in a dissimilar musical style and with a different singer. It was written by Pete Ham and produced by Mal Evans. 'No Matter What' was one of the band's favourites, but Apple Records were not keen, and it was not until Al Steckler, the American director of Apple in New York City, heard a recording that the song was accepted for Badfinger's next album. At Apple's request, the song was remixed by Geoff Emerick. It sounds a lot like The Beatles, especially the backing vocals, spiralling guitars and George-esque slide solo. Backed with an edit of 'Carry On Till Tomorrow', 'No Matter What' reached the top ten in both the US and the UK.

John and Yoko once again flew to the US in late October, staying there until late December.

November 1970: No Dice, All Things Must Pass

'No Matter What' was the key track on Badfinger's next album, *No Dice*, released a few weeks after the single. Joey Molland's presence adds a much rockier sound to the album, which is full of great music. *No Dice* opens with the powerful rocker 'I Can't Take'. This is full-strength Badfinger with driving guitar, great singing and an upbeat arrangement of a genuinely brilliant song. This lays the foundation for an excellent album which, despite the obvious Beatles parallels in songs such as 'Believe Me' and 'It Had To Be Me', still stands up as a classic. Reviews were strong:

> The album is literally a quantum jump over their uneven debut album, *Magic Christian Music*, and Badfinger is certainly on the way to fulfilling their enormous promise. To be sure, the types of songs that Badfinger excelled at before are here once again: great rockers ('I Can't Take It', 'Love Me Do', 'Better Days' and 'Watford John') and gorgeously done pop rock 'n' roll

('No Matter What' and 'Believe Me'). The difference is that, this time around, everything else is good as well: the whole album flows well, Pete Ham sings his best McCartney-esque voice, their guitarist now plays like Eric Clapton and the material is all very good: the whole album adds up as close to the monster Badfinger may well make, in time. Without doubt, Badfinger's most noticeable trademark is Pete Ham's ability to write, sing and even look uncannily like Paul McCartney. And it even goes beyond that, for the group's similarities to The Beatles, in their late Beatles studio-type sound and the good group singing that the late Beatles so direly lacked, are really boggling. It's as if John, Paul, George and Ringo had been reincarnated as Joey, Pete, Tom and Mike of Badfinger. And, in general, this album sounds like nothing so much as what might have happened had the post-*Pepper* Beatles gotten it together after their promising double *The Beatles*. Badfinger is becoming that good, and they may well get better. Don't miss them.
Mike Saunders, *Rolling Stone*, 2 December 1970

Village Voice critic Robert Christgau was cautiously approving. 'I don't think these guys imitate The Beatles just so Paul will give them more hits,' he wrote, 'they've got hits of their own. But from the guitar parts (play 'Better Days' right after 'I Feel Fine') and harmonies (the Paul of 'I've Just Seen A Face' atop the Paul of 'Long Tall Sally') to concept and lineup, an imitation is what this is, modernised slightly via some relaxed countrification. They write almost well enough to get away with it, too. But somehow, the song that stands out is 'Blodwyn', a simulated (I think) English folk ditty about a swain and a spoon that has nothing to do with the Fab Four at all.'

Neither Saunders nor Christgau, both writing at the time of the album's release, made any mention of what would become Badfinger's best-known song, Ham and Evans' 'Without You'. The Badfinger original sounds unfinished, lacking conviction. It would take a remarkable cover version early in 1972 to bring out the song's inner qualities.

The band commenced a three-month US tour to promote *No Dice*, which would reach number 30 on the *Billboard* charts. It was not a hit in the UK, perhaps underlining Badfinger's image at home as a singles band when albums were the new rock currency.

But trouble was brewing. The band's manager, Bill Collins, signed them to a deal with business manager Stan Polley, who offered to help with the band's uncertain finances by establishing a group corporation, providing salaries to the four members. Polley, who managed Al Kooper and Al Christie, provided shady contracts which allowed him to retain the majority of the earnings and leave next to nothing for the band. This would have long-lasting repercussions.

By November 1970, The Beatles' business issues came to a head. The British tax authorities, the Inland Revenue, issued a writ against Apple for failing to pay income tax. Paul's only option, it seemed, was to sue his bandmates. Paul and George met socially in New York City at the end of the month or in the first days of December, but the meeting did not go well. They agreed to meet with the others back in London in the new year.

Against this background, George Harrison emerged as the most successful ex-Beatle. By mid-1970, George had a huge stockpile of songs ready to go. Some of these, such as 'All Things Must Pass', 'Hear Me Lord', 'Isn't It A Pity' and 'Let It Down', were offered to The Beatles during the *Get Back* rehearsals in January 1969. 'Wah Wah' was written immediately after quitting those fraught sessions on 10 January 1969. 'I've had songs for a long time, and lots of new songs,' George told Howard Smith at WABC-FM radio in New York City on 1 May 1970. 'I've got ... enough songs for about three or four albums, actually. But if I do one, that'll be good enough for me.'

George entered EMI Studios either in late April 1970, just before flying to New York City for sessions with Bob Dylan, or, more likely, in mid-May on his return. *The Beatles Monthly* reports that pre-production began on 20 May 1970, with sessions proper, according to Easter and Madinger, starting on 26 May 1970.

Either way, George recorded 15 songs, accompanied by just an acoustic or electric guitar, in the presence of Phil Spector. Formal sessions for the backing tracks lasted for around five weeks, with many notable musicians including Eric Clapton, Gary Wright, Ringo Starr, Billy Preston, Peter Frampton, Dave Mason and Gary Brooker, along with members of Badfinger and the soon-to-be-formed Derek And The Dominos. Overdubs were completed between mid-July and mid-August. During this fraught period, Harrison had to deal with the death of his mother, the deep infatuation of his friend Eric Clapton with his wife Patti, EMI's concern over studio costs, the co-writing and recording of Ringo's single 'It Don't Come Easy', producing and playing on solo albums by Doris Troy and Billy Preston, and working with a profoundly unreliable co-producer. Spector, variable at best, turned his attention to John Lennon's first solo album for a month in October 1970. Final editing for *All Things Must Pass* took place in New York City in late October/early November 1970. George Harrison's talent as a musician and songwriter, hidden in plain sight for years, is evident in this extravagant, highly personal and very successful album. In 1971, the chief ex-Beatle wasn't Lennon or McCartney, but George Harrison.

Does the album stand up? It opens with 'I'd Have You Any Time', a wonderful, warm production of a quite gorgeous chord progression. This gentle ballad is an unexpected downbeat opening to *All Things Must Pass*. George in 1977: 'I liked the first song that was on the album, 'I'd Have You Anytime', and particularly the recording of it because Derek And The Dominos played on most of the tracks, and it was a really nice experience making that album because I was really a bit paranoid, musically. Having this whole thing with The Beatles had left me really paranoid. I remember having those people in the studio and thinking, 'God, these songs are so fruity! I can't think of which song to do.' Slowly, I realised, 'We can do this one', and

I'd play it to them and they'd say, 'Wow, yeah! Great song!' And I'd say, 'Really? Do you really like it?"

'My Sweet Lord' still sounds truly astonishing. George's hymn to Krishna, 1971's best-selling song, let's not forget, opens with layers of chiming acoustic guitar, and we get to hear George's signature slide guitar for the first time as the sound builds with strings and backing vocals. The pure simplicity of the song's composition is remarkable, and the complexity of the production is quite awe-inspiring. George got into a lot of trouble as 'My Sweet Lord' sounds a lot like The Chiffons' 'He's So Fine'. Bright Tunes, owners of the copyright to 'He's So Fine', filed for copyright infringement – this eventually went to court in 1976 and ruled against Harrison, who was fined over $1.5m. By this time, Bright Tunes' catalogue had been bought by Allen Klein, resulting in further litigation that would not be concluded until 1998.

Phil Spector's wall-of-sound is much in evidence on 'Wah-Wah', a glorious, driving, majestic rocker that George wrote after temporarily quitting The Beatles in January 1969. '[In the] *Let It Be* movie, there's a scene where Paul and I are having an argument,' George told *Crawdaddy* in 1977. 'And we're trying to cover it up. Then the next scene, I'm not there, and Yoko's just screaming, doing her screeching number. Well, that's where I'd left, and I went home to write 'Wah-Wah'. It had given me a wah-wah ... I had such a headache with that whole argument.'

'Isn't It A Pity', in contrast, is deeply moving and powerful: anyone who has lived through regret can respond to its universal message of love and forgiveness. Perhaps the chord progression is just too close to 'Hey Jude'. The lyrics, poetic and heartfelt, talk of spiritual salvation and friendship – 'Isn't it a pity, isn't it a shame/How we break each other's hearts, and cause each other pain/How we take each other's love without thinking any more/Forgetting to give back, now isn't it a pity'. Spector's superb production builds and builds, but the tension is never allowed to release. Along with 'Maybe I'm Amazed', 'Imagine' and 'Photograph', this song represents a pinnacle of each ex-Beatle's solo career. 'What Is Life' is a bright, exultantly commercial song written as George was on his way to a Billy Preston recording session in 1969. It has multiple acoustic guitars played by the members of Badfinger, strings, horns and backing from the nascent Derek And The Dominos. 'If Not For You' is a Bob Dylan song recorded by him in August 1970 for his *New Morning* album. Harrison thought enough of it to record it himself for *All Things Must Pass*. In contrast to other songs on the album, the arrangement is restrained. Dylan also inspired 'Behind That Locked Door', a country waltz which is wonderfully rich in its simplicity. The arrangement and chord changes are very reminiscent of The Band. Phil Spector's multi-layered production is given full rein on the exquisite 'Let It Down', which is dynamic, passionate, sexy and splendid. Is 'Run Of The Mill' about Paul? Or Patti? 'Everyone has choice when to or not to raise their voices/It's you that decides which way you will turn/While feeling that our love's not your concern/It's you that decides'. The production is mostly acoustic, with added horns – a welcome contrast to the walls of overdubs heard elsewhere on this album. The lyrics of 'Beware Of Darkness' are amongst George's best. They portray a powerful and poetic message: 'Watch out now, take care/Beware of the thoughts that linger/ Winding up inside your head/The hopelessness around you/In the dead of night/Beware of sadness'. The Dylan-esque 'Apple Scruffs' was recorded late in the sessions for the album: it's a touching tribute to the die-hard fans who kept vigil outside recording studios and offers a refreshing change of pace and feel. The pedestrian 'Ballad Of Sir Frankie Crisp (Let It Roll)' offers a guided tour of Friar Park with George's wry humour in evidence, and the gospel-influenced spiritual rock song, 'Awaiting On You All', is almost buried under Phil Spector's massive production. The utterly majestic 'All Things Must Pass' was presented to The Beatles in January 1969, and they recorded a creditable version, with fully realised harmony vocals, on 8 January 1969 after extensive rehearsals earlier that same week. George's own more thoughtful and contemplative arrangement was recorded in late May/early June 1970 at Abbey Road. As with other songs on the album, the lyrics have a strong spirituality and deal with the transient nature of human existence. All in all, it's a terrific song, certainly the equal of anything else Harrison wrote, in or out of The Beatles. A song very much of its time, 'I Dig Love' is one of the lesser songs on *All Things Must Pass* – the trademark slide guitar and dense production are in place, but the spiritual messages heard elsewhere on the album are replaced with a trite, repetitive and over-simplistic paean to free love. The album ends with 'Art Of Dying', a driving, horn-laden rocker, a second slower, sedate and stately version of 'Isn't It A Pity' and the superb 'Hear Me Lord', a deeply personal plea for spiritual forgiveness. The third disc of studio jams need not trouble us.

All in all, *All Things Must Pass* is an unqualified masterpiece, enhancing the reputation of both George Harrison and Apple Records. The single 'My Sweet Lord' would be number one in America by the end of the year, further adding to the Apple coffers.

With George in the studio, Apple were, according to Apple publicist Tony Bramwell, approached by two young songwriters with big ideas. Tim Rice and Andrew Lloyd-Webber had achieved some success with *Joseph And The Amazing Technicolor Dreamcoat,* which had been performed in 1968 and released as an album in 1969. They now had a bolder plan, a musical based on the Gospels' accounts of the Passion, which they called *Jesus Christ Superstar*. As Bramwell writes in his memoirs:

> Many things slipped through the net in Klein's reign, including a big stage musical that ran and ran for years. The first big musical in London after *Hair* was *Jesus Christ Superstar*, the first of a dynastic series of musicals from Andrew Lloyd Webber and Tim Rice. *Jesus Christ Superstar* was brought to Apple as a new project because Ian Gillan from Deep Purple sang on the

demo [Gillan sang on the final master, not the demo] and another friend, Johnny Gustafson, the bass player from Liverpool's the Big Three, played on it [he actually sang the track 'Simon Zealotes/Poor Jerusalem']. I can remember hearing it around the building at the time, with everyone singing snatches of the very catchy big theme song.

It should be noted that Tim Rice makes no mention of this in his autobiography and that the album was released on MGM before Bramwell left Apple.

Released first as an album in October 1970, *Jesus Christ Superstar* made its stage premiere in October 1971. It ran for over eight years in London between 1972 and 1980, and it held the record for longest-running West End musical before it was overtaken by *Cats* in 1989.

By the end of 1970, James Taylor achieved his breakthrough with the American number-three single 'Fire And Rain'. Suddenly, Taylor's sole album for Apple was a serious asset. It was re-promoted with the re-release of 'Carolina On My Mind' as a single, which reached number 65. Apple enjoyed a long run in the album charts with *James Taylor*.

December 1970: John And Yoko's Solo Albums, Paul Breaks Cover

The release of *All Things Must Pass* was followed two weeks later by the twin albums *John Lennon/Plastic Ono Band* and *Yoko Ono/Plastic Ono Band*. Officially his fifth album outside The Beatles, *John Lennon/Plastic Ono Band* is Lennon's true solo debut. It is stark, uncomfortable, self-revelatory and compelling, and remains an eviscerating listen. Aurally, Phil Spector's sparse production is the direct opposite of his work on *All Things Must Pass*, sessions for which overlapped with *John Lennon/Plastic Ono Band*. 'This time, it was my album', John told *Rolling Stone*. 'It used to get a bit embarrassing in front of George and Paul 'cause we know each other so well: 'Oh, he's trying to be Elvis, oh he's doing this now', you know. We're a bit supercritical of each other. So, we inhibited each other a lot. And now I had Yoko there and Phil there, alternatively and together, who sort of love me, okay, so I can perform better.'

Acclaim for the album was not universal. As Beatles specialist Tim Riley has said: 'For Lennon fans, the album proved revelatory, a vocal flashpoint; to others, it sounded wrenching, forced and draining. It dropped from the charts quickly, and his public exorcism faded from the stage, outmanoeuvred by Santana's *Abraxas* and *Led Zeppelin III*.' (*Los Angeles Review Of Books*, 2019).

Austere tolling bells open 'Mother', and the album, before Lennon's full-throated voice cuts in. His simple piano chordings are supported by Klaus Voormann's spare bassline and Ringo's sharp drum patterns. Lennon's voice is exposed and mournful, building to the quite remarkable, painful and instinctive release of 'momma don't go, daddy come home'. Here is one of the great rock singers taking everything to the limit, emotionally and physically. It's remarkable stuff. 'Mother' was released as a single in the US on 28 December 1970, reaching number 43. Lennon's heavily tremoloed guitar – chords and riffs copped from 'Sun King' – and double-tracked vocals are the signature sounds of 'Hold On', a comforting and self-reassuring song with plenty of wide-open spaces in the arrangement. Ringo's drumming is, as usual, outstanding. 'I Found Out' is an angry blues characterised by a low, rumbling guitar and a very tight rhythm section with Ringo's rolling drums and Klaus' tumbling bass. The only truly political song on *John Lennon/ Plastic Ono Band* is 'Working Class Hero'. It's a successor in a way to 'Revolution' and a forerunner to 'Power To The People' and *Sometime In New York City*. The song features just Lennon singing and accompanying himself on his acoustic guitar: this is the tortured artist laid bare. His middle-class upbringing has absolutely no bearing on his politics or his credibility in terms of writing a song such as this. Lennon's spirit and self-awareness transcend any class structures. The message in this song – that class divisions are ultimately divisive – still rings true. 'Isolation' is an extraordinarily direct and heartfelt song – only Lennon could have written it – which warns that fear and vulnerability are universal, no matter who you are. The song expectedly slams shut, ending side one of the original album with a jolt.

Side two opener 'Remember' is urgent and piano-driven, with direct lyrics. It's a terrifyingly honest and often poignant song. The warmly-produced 'Love' is based around Phil Spector's piano and John's acoustic guitar and earnest vocals. The lyrics don't merit much re-evaluation, but there's no doubt of the sincerity of the performance. In direct contrast to 'Love', 'Well Well Well' is a loud blues-rock song, with a sharp, raw guitar sound and a vocal performance that ends in a scream. Dating from The Beatles' India trip in early 1968, 'Look At Me' is a quiet acoustic song that uses the same finger-picking technique as 'Julia' and 'Dear Prudence'. Lennon lays himself bare in his simply worded, introspective questioning of what one's life is supposed to mean. Finally, we have 'God', one of the most remarkable songs of Lennon's career.

> This therapy forced me to have done with all the God shit. All of us growing up have come to terms with too much pain. Although we repress it, it's still there. The worst pain is that of not being wanted, of realising your parents do not need you in the way you need them.
>
> John Lennon, interviewed by *Red Mole*, 21 January 1971

If the opening line doesn't stop you in your tracks – 'God is a concept by which we measure our pain. I'll say it again' – then the rest of the song will, as Lennon lists the idols in which he no longer believes: '… magic, I-Ching, bible, tarot, Hitler, Jesus, Kennedy, Buddha, mantra, Gita, yoga, kings'. Then, 'Elvis' and 'Zimmerman' (Bob Dylan). Finally, conclusively, 'I don't believe in Beatles'. Eight years earlier, he was singing 'She loves you. Yeah! Yeah! Yeah!' And then he ends the idealistic 1960s in four words: 'I was the dream weaver, but now I'm reborn. I was the Walrus, but now I'm John. And so dear friends, you just have to carry on. The dream is over'. Quite how Beatles fans were supposed to react is uncertain, but the effect today, especially after 8 December 1980, when the song's writer was shot in the back by someone who saw him as a false god, is unsettling indeed. The lovely, fluid piano – full of trills and accents in stark contrast to the direct lyrics – is played by Billy Preston. If you're not moved by this astonishing song, then listen again. The album closes with 'My Mummy's Dead', short, powerful and chillingly disturbing.

Yoko Ono/Plastic Ono Band was recorded with the same musicians in a single afternoon in October 1970. It's jarring, yes, and not always an easy listen, but one cannot doubt the commitment, nor the quality of the band: John, Ringo and Klaus rock hard here. Ornette Coleman's band back 'Aos'.

By the end of 1970, as Apple released *From Then To You*, a collection of The Beatles' Christmas recordings, most of the staff at 3 Savile Row had left. The Georgian townhouse was put up for sale, and the business was transferred to a small office at 54 St. James's Street, about half a mile away. Peter Brown left to work for RSO in New York City, and Derek Taylor, who had spent the last six months on sabbatical writing a book called *As Time Goes By*, moved to the Warner/Elektra/Atlantic record label. Their original roadies, Neil Aspinall and Mal Evans, remained.

A business meeting between the four Beatles was scheduled for January 1971 in London. The others were astounded when, before Christmas, Paul McCartney issued a writ to dissolve The Beatles' partnership, which opened in the Chancery Division of the High Court on 31 December 1970. 'Paul is the greatest bass guitar player in the world,' Ringo told the subsequent hearing, 'but he is also very determined; he goes on and on to see if he can get his own way ... I am as shocked and dismayed as George that, after Paul's promises about all of us meeting in January … the solicitor's letter should have been sent … and the writ issued on 31 December. Nothing happened to my knowledge which would have provided Paul with a good reason for going back on the arrangements for the January meeting. My own personal view is that all four of us together, having the opportunity to consult our separate advisers if necessary, could even yet work something out satisfactorily.'

The Times reported the three main reasons cited for the claim:

> (1) The Beatles had long since ceased to perform together as a group, so the whole purpose of the partnership had gone.
> (2) In 1969, Mr McCartney's partners, in the teeth of his opposition and in breach of the partnership deed, had appointed Mr Klein's company, ABKCO Industries, Ltd., as the partnership's exclusive business managers.
> (3) Mr McCartney had never been given audited accounts in the four years since the partnership was formed.

Allen Klein was not named as a defendant, but was clearly the trigger for the lawsuit. 'Paul didn't want to do it, obviously,' John Eastman said, 'yet the accounts were in such dreadful shape. It took a lot of courage on his part. He kept putting off the decision because it hurt him so much to do it. It was a heart-rending decision for him. Only the greatest provocation made him do it.'

1971

January 1971: Beatles In Court

The year started with headlines that no Beatles fan wished to see.

> Paul McCartney Takes Court Action To Leave Beatles
> Paul McCartney, one of The Beatles who, with John Lennon, wrote the songs that established and maintained their international reputation, yesterday started a High Court action to dissolve all his remaining connections with his three fellow Beatles and their company.
> The most impressive feature in the life of young people in the past decade seems to be finally on the brink of dissolution.
> **Geoffrey Wansell, *The Times*, 1 January 1971**

> Lawsuit Spells Breakup for Beatles
> The Beatles, collective folk heroes of the 1960s, finally broke apart today.
> Paul McCartney brought suit in the High Court here to end the partnership. He named as defendants the other members of the pop group: John Lennon, George Harrison and Ringo Starr.
> The writ claimed that their relationship as 'The Beatles and Company' should 'be dissolved'. It asked for an accounting of assets and income, still thought to be running to $17 million a year.
> For many months, there has been talk of a final Beatle bust-up. The four have long since given up personal appearances together.
> The legal conflict that began today makes it unlikely that The Beatles will again perform as an entity. In a way, the fact that one of the four should go to law against the others symbolised the end of an innocent pop age.
> **Anthony Lewis, *New York Times*, 1 January 1971**

Paul's intention had been to sue only Allen Klein. However, he was advised that Klein's appointment as The Beatles' manager went against his wishes and breached the partnership agreement they made as Beatles & Co. in April 1967. As John, George and Ringo opposed the dissolution of their partnership, Paul would need to sue each of them, collectively, as well as Apple Corps. The case had its preliminary hearing in the Chancery Division of the High Court on 31 December 1970. A full hearing was fixed for 19 January but was adjourned until 19 February.

Renewed success for Badfinger was the backdrop to new solo singles by all four of the now ex-Beatles in the early months of 1971. Paul, at this time, was in New York City working on *Ram*, and John and Yoko were in Japan. The fifth John Lennon/Plastic Ono Band single, 'Power To The People', was written in mid-January after John had met left-wing activists Tariq Ali and Robin Blackburn for an interview for their *Red Mole* magazine. It features a very basic chorus, a honking saxophone from Rolling Stones alumnus Bobby Keys and some gospel-tinged backing vocals. It was another major hit for

Apple. The B-side, Yoko's 'Open Your Box', is effortlessly funky, but one wishes that Yoko was a more considered vocalist. Her singing here, whilst fully committed, is not an easy listen. *All Things Must Pass* spent the first of seven consecutive weeks at the top of the Billboard charts from 2 January. From 6 February, it would spend eight weeks at number one in the UK. 'My Sweet Lord' was released as a single in the UK on 15 January 1971. It was number one for five weeks from 24 January. In the US, with 'My Sweet Lord' concluding four weeks at number one, 'What Is Life' would be issued as a follow-up.

Badfinger's 'No Matter What' landed in the US top ten and helped drive *No Dice* to a high of number 28. The single went even higher in the UK, to number five, week commencing 31 January 1971. The band went into EMI with Geoff Emerick on 9 January to record a follow-up, 'I'll Be The One', and new songs for a fourth album. This was finished by March 1971, but the tapes were rejected by Apple. 'Name Of The Game' was remixed by George Harrison and Phil Spector on 23 April and subsequently overdubbed and mixed again by Al Kooper in New York City, but again was vetoed by Apple. George Harrison was asked to help, as his schedule allowed.

February – April 1971: Solo Singles, Ronnie Spector

The Beatles' court case commenced on 19 February 1971. Paul and Linda had returned to the UK the previous day and attended the opening sessions.

With awkward timing, Paul's breezy 'Another Day' was released the same day. This was his first solo single and would peak at number two in March. The song dates to the *Get Back* sessions in January 1969 despite the spurious Paul and Linda co-composing credit. 'Another Day' is an update of Paul's third-party observational song-writing style, similar in message to 'Eleanor Rigby', if less striking in execution. It features some powerful bass playing and is catchy enough (annoyingly so), but it is too fluffy and lasts a verse and chorus longer than it really should. The B-side, 'Oh Woman, Oh Why', is a sturdy blues rocker with a gritty vocal from McCartney, in every way superior to its A-side.

The trial ran for seven days, and The Beatles' personal and professional business was reported extensively in the press. John, Ringo and George stayed away from court but did submit written declarations.

Amidst this turmoil, Jack Oliver, the head of Apple Records since 1969, would resign in late February. The responsibility of running the record label transferred to Al Steckler, working out of the New York office. In this same period, Apple opened a small office on Sunset Boulevard in Los Angeles, conveniently close to the Capitol Records HQ.

Paul McCartney would return to New York City on 1 March for further *Ram* sessions and was still in the US when judgment in the court case was given on 12 March. The ruling, presented as a form of compromise, in fact handed McCartney an unqualified victory. Control of The Beatles' business was placed in the hands of the court's receiver, with all financial matters suspended until the four could agree on terms for ending the partnership. From this point, Klein's authority extended only to the solo careers of Lennon, Harrison and Starr.

Justice Stamp was careful to state from the bench that he passed no judgment on Klein's character, though his ruling suggested otherwise. The irony was clear: Klein had steadied Apple's finances, renegotiated contracts and strengthened the position of every Beatle, McCartney included. Yet, his reputation was always his greatest liability.

This judgment, in effect, removed Klein as manager of The Beatles' assets. 'I knew the partnership would be dissolved. I know the English law', Klein said the following year. 'The only reason for opposing it was the horrendous tax consequences that could result. But that old judge, [Mr. Justice] Stamp, he didn't understand what it was all about. He got lost. He got Beatlemania.'

Three years after the Chancery ruled in his favour, McCartney was asked about Klein in an interview with *Rolling Stone*. 'Even a murderer has a great line in his own defence,' he said, 'but he's nothing more than a trained New York City crook. My back was against the wall. I'm not proud of it. But it had to be done.'

Apple's income would no longer pass through ABKCO, and until the settlement of the dissolution of The Beatles' partnership could be reached (it would take until 1975), the four ex-members were given a monthly stipend. Lennon, Harrison and Starr accepted large loans from Klein. James Spooner, a partner in a City firm of accountants, was appointed as receiver of The Beatles' business interests pending a further trial.

In what must be the lowest moment of the band's collective relationships, it was reported that John, George and Ringo drove to St. John's Wood, where John threw two bricks through the windows of Paul and Linda's house in Cavendish Avenue. Paul's last public appearance for several months took place the following day when he collected a Grammy award for *Let It Be*.

Badfinger delivered their new album in March 1971. This was, unfortunately, bad timing, coming at the same time as the High Court ruling to appoint a receiver to take charge of Apple's business and the resignation of Jack Oliver. The album was rejected by Apple, who wanted a more polished sound. George Harrison offered to produce further sessions at EMI.

Ringo's first hit single, 'It Don't Come Easy', would enter the top four in both the UK and the US in spring 1971. Versions from February 1970 remain unreleased: the final version has some Beatle-y arpeggios, and terrific slide guitar from George Harrison – an unreleased take with George's guide vocals is equally wonderful. Quite rightly, 'It Don't Come Easy' was a big hit for Ringo, the first of his eight top tenners in the US between 1971 and 1975. The B-side, 'Early 1970', is equally good, as Ringo sings with great affection about Paul ('lives on a farm, got plenty of charm'), John ('with his mama by his side, she's Japanese') and George ('a long-haired, cross-legged guitar picker').

Ronnie Spector's 'Try Some, Buy Some' was recorded for a proposed album in February 1971. Spector, wife of Phil and former lead singer with The Ronettes, had a glorious soulful voice and 'Try Some, Buy Some', when issued in April, deserved to be huge. The song was written by George Harrison, a leftover from *All Things Must Pass*, and lavishly co-produced by George and Phil Spector. The single's B-side was 'Tandoori Chicken', an unconvincing bluesy Harrison/Spector collaboration. Other songs recorded include 'You' and 'When Every Song Is Sung', both written by George, and a cover of Lennon-McCartney's 'Two Of Us'. Ronnie Spector's album was left incomplete, hindered by her spouse's erratic behaviour. According to George in his memoirs, *I, Me, Mine*: 'We only did four or five tracks before Phil fell over...'

May 1971: A Celtic Requiem, Ram, The Radha Krsna Temple

Paul and Linda and their children, along with Ringo and Maureen, attended Mick and Bianca Jagger's wedding on 12 May in St. Tropez, marking the first time that Paul and Ringo had socialised together since The Beatles' split the previous year.

Apple released their second and final recording of John Tavener's music as recorded by the London Sinfonietta on 14 May 1971. *A Celtic Requiem* had premiered in August 1969 and, like *The Whale*, is a religious commentary. In the piece, phrases from the traditional *Requiem Mass* are juxtaposed against Irish children's rhymes and games that deal with death. The instrumentation included bagpipes, electric guitar, soprano voices and a children's choir. John Tavener was delighted that Apple Records was supportive of his early works. 'It was marvellously refreshing because serious music at that time was very humourless and narrow,' he said, 'and if recorded at all, therefore tended to be on very obscure labels. To have Apple take on *The Whale* and *A Celtic Requiem* was wonderful.'

George Harrison fulfilled his promise to produce sessions for Badfinger the same month. The songs 'Name Of The Game' and 'Suitcase' were re-recorded, the newie 'I'd Die Babe' was laid down and George played slide guitar on Pete Ham's 'Day After Day'. Joey Molland remembered: 'Pete and I had done the backing track, and George came in the studio and asked if we'd mind if he played ... It took hours, and hours, and hours, to get those two guitars in sync'. Sessions were paused after these four songs because of George's commitments to organising his charity concert, which took place on 1 August.

Paul and Linda McCartney's *Ram* followed later in May, by which time, *All Things Must Pass* had been available for six months, and *John Lennon/Plastic Ono Band* for five. Fans, especially Paul's more demanding UK followers, could have forgiven the home-made whimsy of *McCartney* and the trite 'Another Day' if *Ram* had been more than half a great album ('Ram On', 'Dear Boy', 'Uncle Albert/Admiral Halsey', 'Monkberry Moon Delight', 'Long Haired Lady' and 'The Back Seat Of My Car' are good songs). *Ram* is well crafted and displays a marvellous balance between gritty fun and expert execution, but has very little in the way of depth. It went all the way to number one in the UK and to number two in the US. Buyers would be less forgiving with Paul's next two albums.

'When we decided to do the new album, we wanted to make it fun,' Paul told *Life* in April 1971, 'because it isn't worth doing anything if you can't have fun doing it. The album will be out early in May, and then I'm thinking about getting a band together – another band – because I don't like to just sit around. I really like to play music.'

'The first time I heard it, I thought it was awful', John Lennon told *Hit Parader* in early 1972. 'And then the second time, ahem, I fixed the record player a bit, and it sounded better. I enjoyed a couple like 'My Dog It's Got Three Legs' or something, and the intro to 'Uncle Albert'. In general, I think the other album he did was better in a way. At least there were some songs on it. I don't like all this dribblin' pop-opera jazz. I like pop records that are pop records.'

'I feel sad with Paul's albums,' Ringo told *Melody Maker* in July 1971, 'because I believe he's a great artist, incredibly creative, incredibly clever, but he disappoints me on his albums. I don't think there's one tune on ... *Ram*. I just feel he's wasted his time.'

The opening 'Too Many People' is a thinly disguised attack on John Lennon – 'That was your first mistake/You took your lucky break and broke it in two/Now what can be done for you?' It's a dynamic pop song with a driving bassline and a pulsing lead vocal. '3 Legs' is a straightforward, shallow blues song which could have fitted onto *The White Album*. Strummed ukulele and electric piano drive 'Ram On', a simple, fresh, atmospheric song, named for Paul's 1960 stage name. 'Dear Boy' is Paul's epistle to himself about Linda. The melody, phrasing and vocal arrangements are terrific, with definite hints of The Beach Boys and Burt Bacharach. The piano triplets betray serious songwriting craft. As a follow-up single to 'Another Day', 'Uncle Albert/Admiral Halsey' was perhaps just too trite and self-indulgent with its many changes and silly vocals to be taken seriously, despite giving Macca his first post-Beatles number one. McCartney's gift for melody means that it's impossible not to sing along in the 'hands across the water' section. 'Smile Away' is a shuffling rocker with a ripping vocal, driving fuzz bass and an important message about personal hygiene, and 'Heart Of The Country' skips along with jazzy overtones. It's pleasant but inessential. 'Monkberry Moon Delight' is another of those songs on *Ram* that work better in isolation, away from the less inspired songs elsewhere on the album. Paul sings at full throttle with uncharacteristic aggression, and Linda's backing vocals are very strong. It's silly, but lots of fun. Paul sings about the virtues of domestic bliss in 'Eat At Home', a Buddy Holly rocker with a twangy riff, tight, muted guitar chords and plenty of echo on the vocals. 'Long Haired Lady' was written for Linda, whose unique, edgy vocals (a compliment) add much to this song and to the album as a whole. This jaunty love song includes some 'Hey Jude' chord changes in the 'love is long' section, along with a fabulous horn arrangement. 'Ram On (Reprise)' is a direct continuation of 'Ram' with a few chords from 'Big Barn Bed' for good measure. The album closes with the multi-sectioned 'The Back Seat Of My Car', a piano ballad with swelling orchestration, upbeat rock sections and a rousing finale. This was released as a single in the UK on 13 August 1971, but only reached number 39.

Radha Krishna Temple (London) followed their two singles with a full album, *The Radha Krsna Temple,* in May 1971. Adding to the singles previously issued, sessions took place at Trident Studios between January and March 1970, again produced by George Harrison. *The Radha Krsna Temple* is an album of Sanskrit hymns to Krishna and to the movement's spiritual masters, some of them nearly nine minutes long. It is very much of its time, but, as with The Modern Jazz Quartet and John Tavener, it's another example of Apple's adventurous approach and willingness to fund music not necessarily associated with Western pop.

Although inactive since August 1969, Apple Electronics finally wound up in May 1971. The company name remained registered at Companies House.

June – July 1971: 'God Save Oz', 'Bangla Desh', 'Wings Take Flight'

Mary Hopkin's sixth single for Apple was an earnest English translation of a song by the French producer-composer Georges Châtelain, 'Quand Je Te Regarde Vivre'. 'Let My Name Be Sorrow' once again attempts to evoke the European feel of 'Those Were They Days' and the French-only single 'Prince En Avignon', but Hopkin never seems to fully engage. It stalled at number 46.

John Lennon would often hang his hat on political and 'underground' causes in the early 1970s, so his support of the magazine *Oz* – a mixture of satire, humour, current affairs and political issues – was hardly a surprise. With issue 28, published in May 1970, *Oz* editors unwisely included an adaptation of a Robert Crumb cartoon to include the Rupert Bear cartoon character in an explicitly sexual situation. This, whilst mild by Crumb's standards, made John's banned lithographs look like The Bash Street Kids. A high-profile obscenity case ran from June 1971 to August 1971. 'Some people from *Oz* rang up,' John told *Sounds* later that year, 'and said, 'Will you make us a record?' and I thought, 'Well, I can't', because I'm all tied up contractually and I didn't know how to do it. So then we got down to, would I write a song for them? I think we wrote it the same night, didn't we?' The song was initially recorded in April at John's home studio, with Klaus and Ringo, then re-recorded midway through sessions for *Imagine,* using the same musicians employed for that album. Lead vocals are by Bill Elliott, who recorded several demos for Apple as part of the band Halfbreed and would later form Splinter, signing to George Harrison's Dark Horse Records. The trial's defendants, editors Richard Neville, Felix Dennis and Jim Anderson, were sentenced to up to 15 months' imprisonment. This was later quashed on appeal by the Lord Chief Justice. Without Lennon's patronage (and record company to release it), 'God Save Oz' would have been forgotten long ago.

George Harrison's 'Bangladesh' would be released at the end of July. It was pop music's first charity single and, despite its genuine intent, is not particularly memorable. It was recorded with Phil Spector in Los Angeles – George's first recording session in the US – and gave George a big hit at the height of his popularity as a solo artist. The B-side, 'Deep Blue', is a hidden gem of an understated and intimate folk-blues song, written by Harrison in honour of his mother Louise, who had died the previous year. The singing and playing are sublime and moving.

During the summer, Billy Preston asked to be released from his Apple contract. This must have been a surprise to his bosses, particularly George Harrison, who had brought Preston into The Beatles' orbit and had supported his career significantly. Preston went on to significant commercial success with A&M Records, including two number-one hits with 'Will It Go Round In Circles' and 'Nothing From Nothing' in 1973-1974.

Paul McCartney formed a band in which he was very much first amongst equals. 'I've always said we could have put some very professional group together and gone and done things very much like The Beatles, and just sort of carried on,' Paul said in 2018, 'but I didn't want to do that. I wanted to try to relearn what it is to be in a band. So, yeah, we just kind of threw it together. And then the decision to have Linda in the band singing was a really tough one because she's never sung professionally. She'd just sung at school in the Glee Club and around the house, sort of thing. But it was: whatever we do, we're not going to do what The Beatles did … Well, we followed what the early Beatles did, which was form a band of people who couldn't play very well, couldn't write very well, and just do it a lot until it gets good!' Paul wanted to recruit the musicians who had played on *Ram*: drummer Denny Seiwell and guitarist Hugh McCracken.

Seiwell: '[Paul] called me three or four months after *Ram* was out and said, 'C'mon over. Let's have a little vacation.' I took my wife and went up to the farm in Scotland. When we got to Scotland, he said, 'Let's put a band together.' I said, 'Yeah. That sounds like a good idea.' So, we went back to New York City and packed everything up and moved to England and formed the band Wings with Paul.' When Hugh McCracken declined to take part, Paul called on an old mate.

'I actually knew Paul before Wings', Denny Laine told CrypticRock.com in 2018. 'We are all pretty good friends of The Beatles in The Moody Blues. We did their second British tour, and we were all friends. I felt like I was working with someone I knew very well, and that made it easier. I think it made it easier for him, too. It was about chasing a musical idea rather than living in the past. Paul wanted to change his whole image in a way from being a Beatle into being a solo artist. He had to do his own music to do that. I admired him for that. For me, it was more of a learning experience. I was able to spend a lot more time in the studio than I ever did. I had a fun time before that. Also, touring, travelling the world, meeting a lot of great people was a big part of it as well.'

In Denny Laine, Paul found a musical partner who was nothing if not versatile – a great rock singer, Laine could also write and play guitar, bass, harmonica and piano. Laine and McCartney's partnership lasted nearly ten years, from July 1971 to April 1981. Thus, Wings are formed.

August 1971: The Concert For Bangladesh, Ravi Shankar, El Topo
George's Concert For Bangladesh took place on 1 August. George and Ringo performed on stage together for the first time since 1966, in a band comprising Harrison, Starr, Billy Preston, Leon Russell, Eric Clapton, Jesse Ed Davis, Jim Horn, Klaus Voormann and all four members of Badfinger. The shows were a pioneering charity event, in aid of the displaced Bengali refugees of the Bangladesh Liberation War, and set the model for future multi-artist rock benefits such as Live Aid (1985) and the Concert for New York City (2001). Bob Dylan played a set, his first major concert appearance in the US in five years, as did Ravi Shankar and Ali Akbar Khan. Notably absent, though: Lennon and McCartney.

> Well, at first I thought, 'Oh, I wish I'd been there', you know, with Dylan and Leon ... they needed a rocker. Everybody was telling me, 'You should have been there, John', but I'm glad I didn't do it in a way because I didn't want to go on as 'The Beatles'. And with George and Ringo there, it would have had that connotation of Beatles – now let's hear Ringo sing 'It Don't Come Easy'. That's why I left it all. I don't want to play 'My Sweet Lord'. I'd as soon go out and do exactly what I want.
> John Lennon interviewed for *Apple To The Core*, September 1971

> You know, I was asked to play George's concert in New York City for Bangladesh, and I didn't. Well, listen. Klein called a press conference and told everyone I had refused to do it – it wasn't so. I said to George that the reason I couldn't do it was because it would mean that all the world's press would scream that The Beatles had got back together again, and I know that would have made Klein very happy. It would have been a historical event, and Klein would have taken the credit. I didn't really fancy playing anyway.
> Paul McCartney interviewed for *Melody Maker*, November 1971

With a live album promised, Harrison was unable to devote further time to Badfinger's album sessions. American studio wunderkind Todd Rundgren was called in, even though the band had never heard of him.

Apple's next release, eight days after the concert, was a three-track EP *Joi Bangla* by Ravi Shankar and Ali Akbar Khan. It had been recorded in mid-July in Los Angeles with George producing. 'Joi Bangla' and 'Oh Bhaugowan' are vocal compositions sung in Bengali. The third selection is a spell-bindingly beautiful sitar/sarod duet by Shankar and Khan.

John and Yoko flew to New York City on 31 August 1971. He would never return to his home country. One Saturday night, Allen Klein's nephew, Michael Kramer, took Lennon to the Elgin Theater on the corner of 19th Street and Eighth Avenue in the Chelsea neighbourhood of Manhattan. Together, they saw the midnight screening of *El Topo*, a controversial underground psychedelic spaghetti Western from South America. Lennon loved the film and raved about it to Allen Klein, who bought the rights and arranged national distribution. At Lennon's request, the soundtrack was re-recorded by John Barham for release on Apple in December 1971.

September – October 1971: Imagine, Fly

John Lennon's *Imagine* album (released in September in the US and October in the UK) has a much warmer, fuller production in comparison to its predecessor. It was mostly recorded at John's Ascot Sound studios at his home in Berkshire. Sessions had lasted around five weeks between May and July. George Harrison added his liquid slide guitar to 'Crippled Inside', 'I Don't Want To Be A Soldier', 'Gimme Some Truth' and 'How Do You Sleep?'. Phil Spector once again co-produced, giving a commercial warmth to the sound but without the grandiloquence of *All Things Must Pass*.

'It's the best thing I've ever done', Lennon told *NME* that autumn. 'This will show them. It's not a personal thing like the last album, but I've learned a lot, and this is better in every way. It's lighter, too. I was feeling very happy. There's a guy called George Harrison on it and he does some mother of solos. George used to be with The Bubbles or somebody. Eighty per cent was recorded in Britain in seven days. I took them, re-mixed them, and took it to America like they used to do in the old days. It took me nine days to make this album, and ten to make the other before ... so I'm getting faster.'

The songs are coloured by the disintegration of Lennon's relationship with Paul McCartney, especially 'How Do You Sleep?', which is brutal in its message and delivery. 'I like his *Imagine* album, but I didn't like the others', Paul told *Melody Maker* in November 1971. '*Imagine* is what John is really like, but there was too much political stuff on the other albums. You know, I only really listen to them to see if there's something I can pinch.'

John's response in a letter to *Melody Maker*, published on 4 December 1971: 'So, you think 'Imagine' ain't political? It's 'Working Class Hero' with sugar on it for conservatives like yourself! You obviously didn't dig the words. Imagine! You took 'How Do You Sleep?' so literally. Your politics are very similar to Mary Whitehouse's – saying nothing is as loud as saying something.'

Much has been written about the song 'Imagine'. It was described in *The Guardian* as 'Britain's favourite lyric' (9 October 1999), 'the lyrical anthem of atheism' (17 November 1999) and 'the greatest number-one single of all time' (7 January 2001). But *The New York City Post* asked, 'Is John Lennon's 'Imagine' the worst song of all time?' (28 October 2016). The truth is somewhere in between. Taken alone, 'Imagine' appears to describe a humanist utopia – imagine no countries, no possessions, all the people, sharing all the world. Some observers have suggested that Lennon is overly sentimental, naïvely patronising and irritatingly earnest – that a millionaire can hardly be truthful about having 'no possessions' while singing from his country estate. This misses the point of the chorus: 'You may say I'm a dreamer/But I'm not the only one/I hope someday you will join us/And the world will live as one'. Through gentle instrumentation with simple piano, a superb vocal and stirring strings, 'Imagine' still manages to convey an important message: that hope is vulnerable and that imagination, in itself, is never enough. The hundreds of cover versions have not diluted that message. 'Imagine' was released as a single in the US on 11 October 1971, reaching number three. It was not released as a British single until October 1975, promoting Lennon's *Shaved Fish* compilation. Yoko Ono was given official co-writing credit in 2017.

'Crippled Inside' is a cheerful song about depression; the double-time rhythm hides the brutal, self-examining lyric: 'You can go to church and sing a hymn/You can judge me by the colour of my skin/You can live a lie until you die/One thing you can't hide is when you're crippled inside'. George Harrison plays a lovely dobro solo in the instrumental break. 'Jealous Guy' dates from 1968 when it was recorded as a demo called 'Child Of Nature'. The 1971 version is rewritten as an honest and open confessional in which Lennon addresses his feelings of inadequacy and his failings as a lover and husband. In contrast to the raw recordings of *John Lennon/Plastic Ono Band*, 'Jealous Guy' has a rich production with layered acoustic guitars, orchestral strings, vibraphone and Nicky Hopkins' fabulous piano part. Then, there's Lennon's voice – one of the great rock voices – singing superbly, with great feeling and regretful asides. The combination of the vocals, lyrics and production gives us a true classic of the genre, the equal of anything written and recorded by this artist. The basic tracks for 'It's Hard' were recorded during the first batch of sessions in February 1971 – it was the first song recorded at John's new home studio at Tittenhurst Park. King Curtis' squalling saxophone colours this straight hard blues. There's also a piano played by John Tout, the keyboard player for the British classically-tinged progressive rock band Renaissance. 'I Don't Want To Be A Soldier, Mama, I Don't Wanna Die' started as a funky blues jam. The churning final version, with wide-open production and minimalist lyrics, harks back to *John Lennon/Plastic Ono Band* in its simplicity. The bitter and cynical 'Gimme Some Truth' was started as early as The Beatles' trip to India in 1968, and rehearsed, or at least tried out, in January 1969. The song expresses Lennon's frustration with politicians' hypocrisy: 'No short-haired, yellow-bellied son of Tricky Dicky's gonna Mother Hubbard soft soap me with just a pocket full of hopes. Money for dope, money for rope'. It's still relevant. John's voice is full tilt angry, and he uses one of his classic home-made words: 'hypocritics'. George Harrison's scintillating slide guitar solo starts at 0:49. The beautiful 'Oh My Love' is in direct contrast to the bitterness of 'Gimme Some Truth'. The shimmering, opening electric guitar is played by Harrison, and once again, Nicky Hopkins plays a lyrical, melodic and quite gorgeous piano accompaniment. The conviction in Lennon's lead vocal speaks volumes.

And then we have 'How Do You Sleep?' ... The fall-out from The Beatles' split was not pleasant, with both McCartney and Lennon goading each other in print and in song. Lennon made defamatory remarks about The Beatles in a December 1970 interview with *Rolling Stone*. McCartney responded by taking full-page advertisements in the music press wearing clown costumes and sitting in a bag, a cheeky poke at Lennon and Yoko Ono. McCartney admitted that the song 'Too Many People' from *Ram* was directed at Lennon. 'How Do You Sleep?' is a nasty, sometimes puerile, song that responds to all of this. George Harrison plays some piercing slide guitar – his presence endorsing the song's sentiments. Lennon commented: 'That's the best he's ever fucking played in his life. He'd go on forever if you'd let him.' 'I think it's silly', Paul told *Melody Maker* in November 1971. Nine years later, speaking to *Playboy*, John said: 'You know, I wasn't really feeling that vicious at the time. But I was using my resentment toward Paul to create a song, let's put it that way. He saw that it pointedly refers to him, and people kept hounding him about it. But, you know, there were a few digs on his album before mine. He's so obscure that other people didn't notice them, but I heard them. I thought, well, I'm not obscure, I just get right down to the nitty-gritty. So, he'd done it his way, and I did it mine.'

A startling contrast to the vitriolic 'How Do You Sleep?', 'How' sits alongside 'Jealous Guy' as a confession of insecurity. The arrangement is sophisticated, with the massed acoustic guitars and strings 'chocolate coating' heard elsewhere on the album, but with a stop-start uncertainty that mirrors the lyrical message. The album closes with 'Oh Yoko!', a jubilant, simple love song based on an old Lonnie Donegan track called 'Long Lost John'. Credit again must go to Nicky Hopkins, whose piano playing is superlative. John plays some bar-room harmonica, and Phil Spector sings harmony vocals, giving an upbeat, positive end to a varied album.

September 1971 saw the release, in the US only, of the soundtrack album to the Saul Swimmer film *Cometogether*, an Italian-American road movie funded by ABKCO.

Also appearing that month would be Yoko Ono's album *Fly*. Yoko's musical talent has confounded listeners for almost 60 years. The first half of this double album rocks hard, with a band comprising, for the most part, John Lennon, Klaus Voormann and Jim Keltner. Where Yoko sings rather than merely gabbles or shrieks, there is much to admire. There's a kind of hypnotic tension to the 17-minute 'Mind Train', which manages to stay on a single chord and evokes the more avant-garde work of the German experimental rock band Can. It's raw and fully committed. John's guitar playing is quite brilliant. A tight 4:45 edit was released as a single in January

1972. 'Mrs Lennon', issued as a single in September 1971, is quite lovely, with its echoing piano and acoustic guitar. The lyrics show deep insight into a fragile marriage, and Yoko's singing is appropriately sombre. Likewise, the shimmering, acoustic blues of 'Mind Holes' is captivating.

Side three of *Fly* comprises three long tracks of Ono performing with automated sound machines created by Fluxus musician Joe Jones. These are bold and experimental, remarkable and fascinating, sounding very modern to these ears – the pounding rock/blues and screaming vocals are replaced with ambient soundscapes and echoing crooning. They're much better than you might expect and, in retrospect, wholly worthwhile.

Side four comprises Yoko's impersonation of a boiling kettle mating with a toad for 15 minutes, followed by seven minutes of bluesy slide acoustic guitar (backwards masked, then detuned) and more random squeaking. It's a challenging listen. The album ends with a phone ringing six times. Yoko answers it and says, 'Hello, this is Yoko'. Different variants are available on the US, UK and Japan versions of *Fly*.

The album also includes the previously released 'Don't Worry Kyoko (Mummy's Only Looking For Her Hand In The Snow)', the B-side of 'Cold Turkey', and a renamed 'Open Your Box' (now called 'Hirake'), the B-side of 'Power To The People'.

One can argue that *Fly* is exactly why Apple Records was founded: to issue music that's a long, long way from a mainstream arguably personified by the work of The Beatles. *Fly* bemuses and thrills in equal measure, and every fan of post-war popular music should give it a listen. At least once, anyway.

Apple Studios in the basement at Savile Row finally opened on 30 September 1971 – the sessions for *Get Back* in January 1969 had used borrowed equipment. George attended an opening event and said, 'It's a bit sad now that Apple is in the position all four of us planned three years ago [to have their own studio]. I just wish Paul would use the studio if he wants to. It's silly not to. I can't see the four of us working together again, but I'd like us to be friends. We all own the business, and it's doing well. I'd like all four of us to enjoy it now.' Promotional brochures, given away at the launch, indicate that the studio is available at £37 per hour for 16-track recording and £31 an hour for 8-track. The studio manager, Geoff Emerick, had moved across from EMI in June 1969. Emerick had worked with The Beatles as early as 1963 and engineered *Revolver*, *Sgt. Pepper's Lonely Hearts Club Band* and *Abbey Road*.

The first artists to record at Apple's new studio, with sessions stretching from September to December, were a new signing, the label's first since the departure of Peter Asher two years before. Lon and Derrek Van Eaton, songwriting brothers from New Jersey, came to George Harrison's attention via a demo tape sent to Apple's New York City office. George called them, met them at the time of the Concert For Bangladesh and offered to produce a single. They travelled to London soon afterwards and recorded 'Sweet Music' at EMI's Abbey Road studio. Musicians included Peter Frampton on guitar and Ringo Starr on drums. 'Sweet Music' sounds like an outtake from *All Things Must Pass*, and is therefore rather good.

These sessions were followed by those for an album, *Brother*, produced by Klaus Voormann at Apple Studios. The engineer, at least at first, was Geoff Emerick, who later wrote about the sessions in his memoirs. 'Lon and Derrek ... were a couple of American blokes, and they were quite pleasant to deal with, but their problem was that they couldn't match the feel of the demonstration tape that had gotten them their record deal in the first place. It's actually a common enough occurrence – in recording studio parlance, it's a phenomenon known as 'chasing the demo'. Artists, especially inexperienced ones, are often much more relaxed when they're making a rough recording at home that they know will never be released. But when they get into a professional studio and the pressure is on, they sometimes freeze up and give a less inspired performance. Harrison started out producing the brothers' album, with me doing the engineering, but then he got fed up and frustrated, so he had his old friend Klaus Voormann take over as producer. He and I just didn't click, though, so I begged off from the project and turned the reins over to another engineer.'

A full album would be recorded at Apple, but when 'Sweet Music' failed to be a hit after its release as a single the following spring, a rethink was needed. The May-June release date would be pushed back by four months to allow the brothers to record more songs in New York City.

The Van Eaton sessions at Apple were followed by American band Fanny, who recorded their third album there between 4 and 18 December 1971. It was released the following year on Reprise. Harry Nilsson, Nicky Hopkins, Wishbone Ash, Viv Stanshall, Stealers Wheel, Lou Reizner, Clodagh Rodgers and Marc Bolan also worked at Apple in the next few years.

October 1971: Earth Song/Ocean Song

Just as commercial interest in Mary Hopkin had begun to wane, she released a wonderful album, *Earth Song/Ocean Song*, and single, 'Water, Paper And Clay'.

By now, Hopkin had tired of the pop stylings of her previous few singles. *Earth Song/Ocean Song* returns Hopkin to her folk roots, with songs by Gallagher and Lyle, Harvey Andrews, Ralph McTell, Tom Paxton, Cat Stevens and others. The musicians include McTell, with Dave Cousins and Dave Lambert of The Strawbs, Pentangle's bassist Danny Thompson and future Sky member Kevin Peek. It's an album of depth, supreme musicianship and some genuinely affecting singing by a confident-sounding Hopkin.

The single 'Water, Paper And Clay' is a lovely folk waltz, with Hopkin's pure voice lifting across a simple backing. 'I was so enchanted by that [song]', Hopkin said in 2010. 'It has the quality of an anthem. I liked the fact that I didn't quite understand the lyrics. I liked the mystery. The recording was fun, too. I played the harmonium. I couldn't play and pump the pedals at the same time, so Danny and Ralph are on their knees, pumping the pedals while I played the keyboard. Then, we all went off to the pub and the guys had a few beers, and then we did the slightly inebriated, very loud and free backing vocals. Dave Lambert from The Strawbs joined us for that, and he was the only one who could hit the high note.'

The album is sparingly and tastefully produced by Tony Visconti. Visconti and Hopkin would marry in November 1971. *Earth Song/Ocean Song* would be Hopkin's last album for 18 years.

November – December 1971: 'Happy Xmas (War Is Over)', Raga, Wild Life, Straight Up, The Concert For Bangladesh

Paul launched Wings on 8 November 1971 at a party in London's Empire Ballroom. He was interviewed by Chris Charlesworth of *Melody Maker* about his previous band a couple of days later. 'I just want the four of us to get together somewhere and sign a piece of paper saying it's all over,' he admitted, 'and we want to divide the money four ways. No-one would be there, not even Linda or Yoko or Allen Klein. We'd just sign the paper and hand it to the business people and let them sort it out. That's all I want now. But John won't do it. Everybody thinks I am the aggressor, but I'm not, you know, I just want out.'

For his part, John recorded a Christmas song, which, as Christmas songs go, is less irritating than most. Lennon 'borrowed' the verse melody note-for-note from the folk song 'Stewball', recorded in 1963 by Peter, Paul And Mary, and added his own lyrics and chorus melody. It was issued on 1 December 1971 in the US, and a year later in the UK.

The 96-minute Apple film *Raga*, a documentary about the life and music of Ravi Shankar, was given a press screening on 22 November. The soundtrack album followed on 7 December 1971 on Apple Records, the same day that Wings released *Wild Life*.

Wild Life had been recorded at EMI in late July and early August. Five of the eight songs were first takes: it sounds like a band of half-decent musicians with a fabulous bass player warming up as the tape rolled. According to *Rolling Stone*, who never forgave Paul for leaving The Beatles, *Wild Life* is 'rather flaccid musically and impotent lyrically, trivial and unaffecting.' The rushed feel resulted in a poor commercial and critical reception – it charted significantly lower than *McCartney*, *All Things Must Pass*, *Ram*, *John Lennon/Plastic Ono Band* and *Imagine* – but gives modern listeners an emotional honesty that's missing in Paul's later albums. 'People like it a lot more now because of its rawness', Denny Laine told the *Tallahassee Democrat* in 2018. 'The point was we were just trying out the band on that album. It was just a case of let's just rehearse a few songs and go into the studio. Let's not get too big time about it. I like that album.'

'Mumbo' is rough and rowdy, but has a full-throated McCartney vocal. The lyrics are nonsense, but the performance is full of life. As a whimsical tribute to Carl Perkins with a touch of 'Back Off Boogaloo', 'Bip Bop' could have been recorded for *McCartney*. 'Love Is Strange', a tossed-off reggae rendition of the 1956 Mickey And Sylvia song, completes the third of three consecutive shallow songs that open *Wild Life*. Denny Laine's slide guitar lifts the track, and Macca eventually lets rip with a strong vocal, but there's not much to get excited about.

And finally, we come to 'Wild Life', one of those lost classics in the solo Beatles catalogue. It's a three-chord riff which builds and builds over six minutes to give a real feeling of tension between the possibly multi-faceted lyrics (ostensibly worrying about the fate of animals – sometimes 'aminals' – in the zoo, but perhaps something deeper) and the powerful emotion of McCartney's singing. This is a raw sound, not so far from *John Lennon/Plastic Ono Band*, and perhaps reflects some of the turmoil that Paul experienced in 1970-1971. "Wild Life' was to do with me having gone on safari and actually seeing that sign that I sing about: 'The animals have the right of way'. Which really impressed me', Paul commented in 2018. 'You just realise the sort of dignity and strength of wild animals because here they've got the right of way. Whereas we're all so full of our own importance. It's kind of nice, you know. You're just a guy in a Land Rover. You don't matter so much! So, that was why I wrote that song. Man, you know, we're the 'top species', and yet we're the ones who eff it up, which is not right.'

The second side of the album opens with 'Some People Never Know', a humble, lightweight acoustic ballad with a typically classic McCartney bridge, lifting to a slide guitar solo and some genuinely beautiful harmonies from Linda. This is followed by 'I Am Your Singer', a Paul and Linda duet, which proves that Linda, cool lady as she was, should have stuck to those harmonies. As proof that Paul McCartney is incapable of making more than half a completely awful record, Paul and bandmates close their debut album with two great songs, 'Tomorrow' and 'Dear Friend', as well as the brief instrumental 'Mumbo Link'. 'Tomorrow' takes arpeggio piano and a leaping lead vocal as a direct counterpoint to 'Yesterday', a way of looking ahead post-breakup. Is Paul, literally, putting the Fabs behind him? Or is he simply revisiting his drive for The Beatles to 'get back' and capture the energy of their pre-fame days? 'Tomorrow' sounds remarkably like Queen. Or David Cassidy, take your pick. Often cited as Paul's response to 'How Do You Sleep?', 'Dear Friend' is a plea for reconciliation, with a touch of vulnerability; the balance between pain and love proves just how good a singer McCartney is with the right material, and just how much he means what he sings.

Paul in 2018: 'With 'Dear Friend', that's sort of me talking to John after we'd had all the sort of disputes about The Beatles break-up. I find it very emotional when I listen to it now. I have to sort of choke it back. But, for me, it is a bit like that. I'm trying to say to John, 'Look, you know, it's all cool. Have a glass of wine. Let's be cool.' And luckily, we did get it back together, which was like a great source of joy because it would have been terrible if he'd been killed as things were at that point, and I'd never got to straighten it out with him. This was me reaching out. So, I think it's very powerful in some very simple way. But it was certainly heartfelt.'

Paul chose not to release a single from the album, nor play any live dates with his new band for the time being.

The triple live album *The Concert For Bangladesh*, credited to George Harrison And Friends, comprises heavily edited highlights from the two benefit shows in New York City on 1 August 1971. George sings seven songs, Ringo forgets the words to 'It Don't Come Easy', there is one song each from Leon Russell and Billy Preston (both of whom threaten to steal the show) and five from Bob Dylan. Ravi Shankar's opening set is marred by the audience applauding his tuning up. Despite its hefty price tag, *The Concert For Bangladesh* would reach number one in the UK (one week in January 1972) and number two in the US. It won the Grammy Award for Album Of The Year in 1973. A film of the shows would follow. *The Concert For Bangladesh*, coupled with the earlier success of *All Things Must Pass*, confirmed George Harrison as the most commercially successful ex-Beatle in 1971-1972.

Bandfinger's *Straight Up* was completed on the third attempt. Most of the sessions with Geoff Emerick from early in the year were scrapped, with several re-recorded throughout the year. The four songs recorded with George Harrison in May-June and two of the initial batch were remixed by Todd Rundgren, who also recorded four new songs with the band: 'Sometimes', 'It's Over', 'Baby Blue' and 'Take It All', which captures Pete Ham's reflections on performing at the Concert For Bangladesh. The album was released in December 1971 in the US, and two months later in the UK. As with *No Dice*, *Straight Up* is full of great songs, despite its chequered path to release. Todd Rundgren's production is bright and commercial.

Pete Ham's moody 'Take It All' starts the album reflectively, leading into his wonderful, soulful, confessional 'Baby Blue', which, in due course, would become one of the band's best-known songs. Ham wrote three other superb songs on *Straight Up*. 'Perfection' marries some smart chord changes with brilliant production, and the gorgeous 'Name Of The Game' should have been a big hit. 'Day After Day' was one, reaching number four on the *Billboard* charts. Guitarist Joey Molland added 'Suitcase', 'Sweet Tuesday Morning' and 'Sometimes', which are loud and edgy power pop.

And, quietly at the end of 1971, one of the original staff who had joined Apple in 1968, promotions manager Tony Bramwell, resigned from Apple to join his former boss Ron Kass at Hillary Music Publishing.

1972

January 1972: 10cc

Early in 1972, Apple received an acetate of a fresh-sounding song by a new Manchester band called 10cc. All four members were veterans of the 1960s music scene. Graham Gouldman had written hits for The Hollies and The Yardbirds. His songwriting partner, Eric Stewart, had played with Wayne Fontana And The Mindbenders. They were joined by Lol Creme and Kevin Godley. The group were overflowing with ideas, but Apple didn't see any commercial merit in 'Waterfall', which was perhaps too close to the sound of The Eagles or Crosby, Stills & Nash. Undeterred, 10cc signed to UK records and, perhaps to make a point, issued 'Waterfall' as the B-side to their first number-one single, the effervescent 'Rubber Bullets'.

Badfinger started recording a new album with Todd Rundgren on 17 January, laying down two tracks, 'The Winner' and 'I Can Love You'. Rundgren left the sessions due to an ongoing row over his lack of production credits on 'Day After Day' from *Straight Up*. The band elected to produce the rest of the album themselves.

Paul was also at work on 17 January, rehearsing at the Scotch of St. James club in London and finalising his preferred live lineup of Wings. He recruited former Grease Band guitarist Henry McCulloch and, across 12 days, they worked up a set for a series of dates in February. 'I was in The Grease Band,' McCulloch told journalist Colin Harper in 1997, 'and we were hanging around London not doing very much. Denny Laine used to come round and hang out with us, and he said to me one day, 'McCartney's looking for a guitar player – he wants to know if you'd come down and have a bit of a play'. And I said, 'Well, Jesus, no bother!' and went down, I think, to The Revolution Club – one of those clubs in London anyway – and played 'Long Tall Sally' and a few things like that. It wasn't really an audition, more a play – but it was an audition really, to make sure I wasn't into hard drugs and stuff like that. Anyway, we played, had a chat, and he said, 'Can you come back tomorrow?' and I said, 'Of course', and came back the following day. By the third day, we were on a stage at the ICA. We went through a lot of stuff over that period, and on the third day, he asked me if I wanted to join – and who wouldn't!'

At the end of the month, Paul and Linda flew to New York City for a few days, where they had dinner with John and Yoko.

February 1972: 'Give Ireland Back To The Irish'

Wings' first single, 'Give Ireland Back To The Irish', would be released on Apple at the end of February 1972. It's a powerful rocker with lots of guitars and a mindlessly trite lyric: a simplistic look at a complex political situation. Banned by the BBC, it's not Paul's finest moment. 'I figure I'm just a fella, livin'', Paul said to *Record Magazine* in 1984. 'I got four kids, I'm a ratepayer. So, that entitles me to an opinion. I'm livin' in the West, so we're allowed to talk over here, right? So, when the English paratroopers, my army who I'm payin' rates for, go into Ireland and shoot down innocent bystanders, for the first time in my life, I go, hey, wait a minute, we're the goodies, aren't we? That wasn't very goody. And I'm moved to make some kind of a protest. So, I did 'Give Ireland Back To The Irish', which was promptly banned in England. But it was number one in Spain, of all places. That was rather odd – Franco was in power.'

The song marks the studio debut of Henry McCullough and went to the top of the charts in Ireland, not surprisingly. This was followed by the band's first appearance on *Top Of The Pops* and an 11-date UK tour. 'We'd just turn up at a university,' McCulloch recalled, 'find the Students' Union, and, of course, the minute he stuck his head out the window … 'Can we play tonight?' 'Yes, of course!' And the word went out, and the place'd be packed. But then, instead of getting hotels, it would be, like, Mrs McGonagle's for B&B, you know! It was unusual, alright, but it was very exciting at the same time, 'cos it was my first trip out with him – and splitting the money up evenly after the gigs meant I made more on that than when I became a fully-fledged member!'

In New York City, Allen Klein told his stockholders that, due to the improved relationship between John and Paul, he expected that Paul would sell his 25% stake in Apple to the other three ex-Beatles. In London, Paul's assistant Shelley Turner said, 'Paul is interested in the proposed offer … but has seen no statement yet.'

Meanwhile, with a cruel irony, Harry Nilsson's cover of Badfinger's 'Without You' would reach the top of the US singles chart on 19 February, where it stayed for four weeks. Nilsson has been sourcing songs for his *Nilsson Schmilsson* album over a drink or two at a friend's house. Here, he heard 'Without You', but the next morning, he could not remember who the song was by. 'After sobering up the next day, I said, 'What was that Lennon tune we were listening to last night?' We went through a bunch of [Beatles] albums and couldn't find it. Finally, I said, 'No! It wasn't The Beatles, it was another group. It was Grapefruit or something.' We finally realised it was Badfinger. I took this to [producer] Richard Perry and said, 'I think this should be a number-one hit.' I wish I had written it.'

At the end of the month, Wings flew to Los Angeles to start work on their second album, *Red Rose Speedway*.

March 1972: 'Baby Blue', 'Back Off Boogaloo'

With Nilsson's version of Badfinger's 'Without You' at number one in the US – and earning a fortune for Apple Publishing – a remix of 'Baby Blue' was lifted as a single from *Straight Up* in the US in March 1972. Bizarrely, Apple chose not to release 'Baby Blue' as the single in the UK, stalling the momentum from 'Day After Day'.

Ringo's next single, 'Back Off Boogaloo', is a piece of enjoyable fluff. Ringo's drumming and George's slide guitar are terrific. Such was the post-break-up goodwill that it went into the top ten in the US and better still in his home country, where it was held off the top spot by (would you believe) 'Amazing Grace' by the Pipes And Drums And The Military Band Of The Royal Scots Dragoon Guard. This had replaced Nilsson's 'Without You' as the UK's best-selling single.

John: 'Imagine there's no heaven. It's easy if you try.'
Paul: 'Maybe I'm amazed at the way you love me all the time.'
George: 'My sweet Lord. I really wanna see you...'
Ringo: 'Wake up, meathead, don't pretend that you are dead.'

April 1972: The Pope Smokes Dope

One assumes that John Lennon had not heard of David Peel until the Englishman moved permanently to New York City in 1971. 'Harold Smith [*Village Voice* journalist and radio personality] was showing me and Yoko around [Greenwich] Village', John said. 'He was an old friend of Yoko's, and I got to know him. And he took us down to Washington Square, and there [Peel] was.'

Peel was a songwriter and street entertainer who led a band called The Lower East Side. 'Peel mixed anti-government, pro-marijuana polemics with wry satires on New York life among 'the cockroaches ... living in a garbage can', writes Philip Norman in his biography of Lennon's life. 'John became a keen follower of the Lower East Side's street-corner happenings, which to him recalled skiffle gigs around Woolton in the late 1950s.' Lennon and Peel became friends. 'He was such a great guy', John declared. 'We loved his music and his spirit and his whole philosophy.'

Peel appeared with John at the John Sinclair Freedom Rally in Ann Arbor, Michigan, on 10 December 1971, and later that month recorded an appearance on the *David Frost Show*. This was broadcast early in 1972: they perform Peel's 'The Pope Smokes Dope' with John on tea-chest bass. Lennon and Ono produced Peel's album, also called *The Pope Smokes Dope*, for release by Apple in April 1972, along with the singles 'F Is Not A Dirty Word' (US) and 'The Hippie From New York City' (UK). 'F Is Not A Dirty Word' was banned just about everywhere (it covers much of the same ground as 'King Of Fuh').

'People say, 'Peel can't sing', or, 'he can't really play'', John said. 'He writes beautiful songs, and even as simple as his basic chord structures are, supposedly, well, Picasso spent 40 years trying to get as simple as that. David Peel is a natural.' Presumably, John was attracted by the simplicity of Peel's anti-establishment stance. The album is very much a snapshot of the early 1970s in Greenwich Village, but it has very little musical merit. Peel recorded more material for Apple in 1973, but the disintegration of the record company precluded any releases.

John's single 'Woman Is The Nigger Of The World' saw US release on 24 April 1972. What was he thinking? Whereas it's impossible to deny Lennon's belief in what he was singing – opposition to misogyny and women's subservience to men in all cultures – the execution leaves much to be desired. The message is unsubtle, heavy-handed and overblown. Releasing this as a single in America was surely short-sighted: the song was banned by many US radio stations and stalled at number 57.

May – July 1972: 'Mary Had A Little Lamb', Some Time In New York City

Wings' version of the traditional nursery rhyme 'Mary Had A Little Lamb' is inoffensive. It peaked at number nine in charts that included Slade, Sweet and, ahem, Gary Glitter. The B-side, 'Little Woman Love', is an infectious piano rocker with a riff that sounds exactly like David Bowie's later 'TVC15'.

Surely the low point of John Lennon's post-Beatles career, *Some Time In New York City* (released on Apple in June in the US, but not until September in the UK) was the crushingly disappointing follow-up to *Imagine*. As Madinger and Easter write '... [a] wretched piece of work … a didactic batch of half-baked songs that sounded as if they had been penned by a high school current events student.'

The genesis of this album can be traced to August 1971, when John and Yoko moved to New York City. He was immediately embroiled in a lengthy battle with the US immigration authorities, who wanted to deny permanent residency. Not wanting to lose his chance of not being allowed back into the US, Lennon's simple solution was simply not to leave. *Some Time In New York City* was recorded between December 1971 and March 1972. Lennon's choice of backing band was a now-forgotten New York City boogie outfit called Elephant's Memory, who would release their own album on Apple as well as record two with Yoko Ono.

Each of the songs on *Sometime In New York City* has an overt political message: women's rights ('Woman Is The Nigger Of The World'), race relations ('Angela'), police brutality ('Attica State'), Britain's role in Northern Ireland ('Sunday Bloody Sunday' and 'The Luck Of The Irish') and Lennon's difficulties in obtaining a green card ('New York City'). The album was released to abysmal reviews, and despite the honesty and conviction in Lennon's performances and a lovely production touch from Phil Spector, it remains a challenging and ultimately unfulfilling listen. American listeners voted with their pocketbooks – number 48 was its highest chart position. A second disc of *Some Time In New York City* comprises an unlistenable live album. Don't remember him this way.

Two of the most obscure Apple releases are a pair of singles by the British singer-songwriter Chris Hodge, who was signed to the record label by Ringo Starr. The uninspiring UFO-themed single, 'We're On Our Way', was released in June 1972, reaching number 44 in the US (and number 26 in the Netherlands). The dreary country-flavoured follow-up, 'Goodbye Sweet Lorraine' (March 1973), was not released in the UK, nor was it a hit in the US.

Badfinger were something of a schizophrenic band in that their live shows were much louder and rowdier than their albums. This is evidenced in two recordings they made for the BBC in June 1972 and August 1973. The band elected not to play (or, at least, the BBC did not broadcast) their best-known songs such as 'No Matter What', 'Day After Day', 'Baby Blue' and 'Without You'. A 15-track live album, released in 1997, illustrates Badfinger's rockier side.

The *Wings Over Europe* tour comprised 25 dates between 9 July and 24 August. It was during these dates that Paul's 1961 Höfner 500/1 bass guitar was stolen and presumed lost until 2024. During this period, Apple office staff were moved to offices at 54 St. James's Street in Picadilly as the Savile Row office was given a major renovation. This reconfigured all of the rooms on the upper floors, thus ending the physical manifestation of Apple since 1968.

September – November 1972: Elephant's Memory, Brother, Those Were The Days

Drummer Mike Gibbins quit Badfinger in September 1972 to be replaced by Robbie Stawinski for a tour and further sessions for *Ass*. Gibbins rejoined the following month, but it would be more than a year before *Ass* would see release. Meanwhile, the band's management had lost patience with Apple. Badfinger would fulfil their Apple contract in due course, but signed a new deal with Warner Bros. Records in October 1972.

Elephant's Memory were the NYC bar band that backed John and Yoko both in the studio and in concert between 1971 and 1973. They played unpretentious rock music. Their album for Apple Records, issued in September (US) and November (UK) and produced by John and Yoko, has the distinction of never being re-released. Ignored at the time, the less frantic elements of music of Elephant's Memory might, ironically, have made a stir a few years later as part of the CBGBs scene in New York City – remove the boogie stylings and it's not so far from a pumped-up Television or a less arty Talking Heads with added saxophones. In the UK, an edit of the song 'Liberation Special' would be the accompanying single. In the US, 'Power Boogie' would have the honours.

Lon and Derrek Van Eaton's album *Brother* would be issued in September 1972 in the US, and in February the following year in the UK. The final track list comprised six songs from the original running order (including the original demo of 'Warm Woman' that opens the album and failed to trouble the UK singles charts in the spring of 1973), plus five newer songs recorded with session musicians in New York City.

As a debut album, *Brother* is certainly impressive. Stephen Holden in *Rolling Stone* wrote, 'This staggeringly impressive first album … displays more energy, good feeling and sheer musical talent than any debut record I've heard this year. Derrek's lead singing is amazing. His style ranges from a weird, tremulous falsetto to the hardest rock holler, and he is capable of shading in the difference as well.'

With minimal promotion from Apple, however, *Brother* was a commercial failure. The album remained out of print until 2012. Lon and Derrek started work on a second album for Apple before the end of the year, including one track with George Harrison on slide guitar, and both musicians played on Ringo's 'Photograph' single, recorded in March 1973. This led them to producer Richard Perry, who would helm their next album after their release from Apple.

Mary Hopkin's contract with Apple expired in March 1972. A compilation album of her singles for Apple, called *Those Were The Days*, followed along with a re-release of her Eurovision single, 'Knock Knock, Who's There?'.

October 1972 saw the US release of 'Saturday Nite Special' by The Sundown Playboys, a Louisiana Cajun band who had already been together almost 30 years by this point (and are active today). A UK release followed in November 1972 and was promoted by a limited edition 78rpm single and a flyer which reads:

> THE SUNDOWN PLAYBOYS
> From the moss-covered Evangeline oaks to the winding, picturesque bayous, the incomparable complacence of CAJUN life paces forward with the traditions and customs of yesteryear.
>
> And perhaps the most distinct characteristic still prevalent today is CAJUN MUSIC. Historically, CAJUN MUSIC was handed down generation to generation and is still very popular today. The 'fais-do-do' (weekly dance where entire family groups would meet at a particular designated place) gave way to the larger nightclubs, and that CAJUN good life is celebrated on weekends, particularly Saturday nights.
>
> THE SUNDOWN PLAYBOYS are six happy CAJUNS who love to play that CAJUN music and are considered tops by CAJUN music fans. They play professionally at night and during the weekends. Lesa and Larry work for an oil refinery in Lake Charles, Darrel is a candyman (vending route), Wallace operates a grocery, Danny is a freshman at McNeese State College and Pat is a senior at St. Louis High School in Lake Charles.
>
> The SATURDAY NIGHT SPECIAL represents the joys and excitement of a CAJUN weekend dance, where you can 'let it all hang out', dance, laugh, sing, drink and forget about life's troubles.
>
> RING 01 247 9856

December 1972: 'Hi, Hi, Hi'

Wings' next single, 'Hi, Hi, Hi', is a terrific Macca rocker which was already the regular set-closer for the band. It's a boogie, most likely celebrating Paul's fondness for the high life, which led the BBC to ban the song for 'lyrical content problems'. The inoffensive reggae-lite flip side, 'C Moon', was given lots of radio play and helped give Paul another top-five hit in the UK.

The classic *Phil Spector's Christmas Album* (originally called *A Christmas Gift For You* and issued in 1963) was re-released by Apple in December 1972. It sold well, reaching number six in the US. In the UK, its high point of number 21 was the highest chart placing for a non-Beatles album for three years.

Earlier that year, a box set of Beatles songs called *Alpha Omega* appeared in the US, released by Audio Tape, Inc. in New Jersey. This 60-song four-LP collection was advertised in print and on TV and radio stations in the Midwest and was sold by mail order for $13.95 (well over $100 in current value). This compilation was sourced from Capitol LPs featuring the edits found exclusively on those albums and was an attempt to exploit the Sound Recording Amendment of 1971, which extended federal copyright protection to sound recordings fixed on or after 15 February 1972. Sound recordings before that date would remain subject to state or common law copyright. State law in New Jersey was lax, and restricting the sale of the set to mail order ensured that Audio Tape could hide behind pirate-friendly laws. A second volume followed. In response to the promotion of *Alpha Omega*, Allen Klein filed a lawsuit on behalf of George Harrison, Capitol Records and Apple Records against Audio Tapes, Inc., as well as the TV network ABC and local affiliates who had aired commercials. This was filed in February 1973 and found in the plaintiffs' favour.

The success of *Alpha Omega* had identified a market demand for a Beatles career retrospective. Within two months of the ruling, Apple/EMI issued the hugely successful *1962-1966* and *1967-1970*. Press ads pointedly noted that these were 'the only authorised collections of the group's music'.

1973

January 1973: Ass Is Rejected

1973 marks the high-water mark of the ex-Beatles' top ten single successes as solo artists. George scored a US number-one with 'Give Me Love (Give Me Peace On Earth)'; Ringo went one better with two – 'Photograph' and 'You're Sixteen', and another top five US hit with 'Oh My My'. Wings' 'Live And Let Die' reached number two in the US, with top-ten placings for 'Helen Wheels' and 'Jet'. Lennon's 'Mind Games' reached number ten. The solo Beatles scored six big hits in the UK, with 'You're Sixteen' achieving the highest placing.

This brought significant income to Apple. But Badfinger continued to struggle. They had completed work on their new album, *Ass*, and this was mixed at Trident and Air during the first two weeks of 1973. The track listing was strong:

Side One:
'Get Away'
'When I Say'
'Apple Of My Eye'
'The Winner'

Side Two:
'Piano Red'
'Cowboy'
'Regular'
'I Can Love You'
'Timeless'

They returned from a US tour in late February to learn that Apple had once again rejected their work. Chris Thomas, then working for Apple as an engineer, was asked to improve the recordings and make new track selections.

February 1973: Approximately Infinite Universe

Approximately Infinite Universe, Yoko Ono's follow-up to *Fly*, sees her moving away from the experiments of her first two solo albums towards a more conventional rock sound with actual singing – all on her own terms, of course. It was recorded at the Record Plant in New York City between mid-October and mid-November 1972, with backing by Elephant's Memory.

Approximately Infinite Universe includes ballads, slow rockers and smooth funk amongst its 22 songs. Her singing ranges from the soft croon of 'Death Of Samantha' to the more strident piano-led 'What A Bastard The World Is'. 'You know half the world is occupied by you pigs', she declares. 'I can always get another pig like you'. 'Winter Song' is stately and proud, and 'I Want My Love To Rest Tonight' has a commercial shine. 'Now Or Never' is a waltz-time acoustic protest song which veers towards preaching.

Are we gonna keep pushing our children to drugs?
Are we gonna keep driving them insane?
Are we gonna keep laying empty words and fists?
Are we gonna be remembered as the century that failed?

Approximately Infinite Universe is beautifully produced, never less than intriguing and very often extremely listenable. The songs, all written by Ono, are really strong but marred by her frequently pitchy singing. For all of her qualities as an artist, Yoko's musicality often sounds forced.

Apple released two singles from *Approximately Infinite Universe*, namely 'Now Or Never' (US only, November 1972) and 'Death Of Samantha' (US: February 1973/UK: May 1973). There was little prospect of these being commercially successful; therefore, their release would have been financially draining for Apple. Likewise, both *Fly* and *Approximately Infinite Universe* were costly productions, recorded at Abbey Road and The Record Plant with top-class session musicians. One suspects that all of this expenditure was merely to keep Ono happy.

March 1973: 'I'm The Greatest', 'My Love'

Ringo continued work on his next solo album. On 13 March, he was reunited with George and John at Sunset Sound Recorders in Los Angeles to record John's 'I'm The Greatest'.

And, at last, another classic from Paul. 'My Love', released on 23 March 1973 (UK) and on 9 April 1973 (US), was the second of seven number-one US singles for Paul and/or Wings between 1971 and 1980. 'My Love' is one of those unforced ballads that McCartney can toss off in his sleep. As love songs go, this one is a cracker, with simple lyrics giving a direct message: 'And when the cupboard's bare/I'll still find something there with my love/ It's understood/It's everywhere with my love'. Linda certainly inspired some of Paul's best work. 'I'm very proud of 'My Love'', he said on paulmccartney.com in 2018. 'This was early days for me and Linda, so it's a love song to her, really. One of the things I was proud of, funnily enough, was that it charted. It did very well.'

The song had been recorded live, with an orchestra, at Abbey Road in March 1972. Paul plays electric piano, Denny covers bass, and, in his finest moment as a member of Wings (only a few weeks after joining), Henry McCulloch performs a quite beautiful guitar solo. As Paul told *Mojo* in 2010: 'I'd sort of written the solo, as I often did write our solos. And he walked up to me right before the take and said, 'Hey, would it be alright if I try something else?' And I said, 'Er ... yeah.' It was like, 'Do I believe in this guy?' And he played the solo on 'My Love', which came right out of the blue. And I just thought, fucking great. And so there were plenty of moments like that where somebody's skill or feeling would overtake my wishes.'

Elephant's Memory recorded a new single, 'Everglade Woman', this month, but as with further sessions by David Peel and Chris Hodge in 1973, the release was cancelled.

April 1973: Red Rose Speedway, In Concert 1972

Allen Klein's management contract with John, George and Ringo was signed in March 1969 and renewed in 1970, 1971 and 1972. But by early 1973, it was clear that it would not be renewed a fourth time. His inability to reach a settlement with Paul McCartney with regard to the dissolution of The Beatles' partnership proved too much for Lennon, Harrison and Starr. The management contract expired on 31 March 1973. John and Yoko employed former ABKCO attorney Harold Seider to manage their affairs. George partnered with Denis O'Brien, whom he would eventually sue for allegedly cheating him out of £16m over a 12-year period. Ringo retained Hilary Gerard as his business manager and has worked with the accountant Bruce Grakel for the last 50 years.

John was interviewed about this on 6 April in Los Angeles for London Weekend Television.

> John Fielding (LWT): 'Can you tell me what happened with Allen Klein? Why did you and the other two finally decide to get rid of him?'
> John: 'There are many reasons why we finally gave him the push, although I don't want to go into the details of it. Let's say possibly Paul's suspicions were right ... and the time was right.'
> Fielding: 'His contract was coming up for renewal anyway ... wasn't it?'
> John: 'The contract expired, I think, in February, and we were extending it at first on a monthly basis and then finally on a two-week basis, and then finally we pushed the boat out.'
> Fielding: 'When did you personally decide that Klein probably wasn't the man you thought he was?'
> John: 'Well, you're concluding that I thought he was something. My position has always been a 'Devil and the deep-blue sea', and at that time, I do whatever I feel is right. Although I haven't been particularly happy personally for quite a long time with the situation, I didn't want to make any quick moves, and I wanted to see if maybe something would work out.'

A month after 'I'm The Greatest' took Ringo back into the studio with John and George, another partial reunion took place at Apple Studios when Ringo and Paul recorded 'Six O'clock' on 16 April. This appears to be the only time that Paul worked at Apple Studios as a solo artist.

In the meantime, Badfinger were working on new tracks and remixes at Olympic Studios in Barnes, with producer/engineer Chris Thomas.

In the UK, *Wild Life* had sold less than even Ringo's *Sentimental Journey*. The follow-up, *Red Rose Speedway*, would hedge its bets, being credited to

Paul McCartney And Wings and including a major hit single. It was the first of five consecutive number-one albums for Wings; 1973 to 1978 remains Paul's most commercially successful period outside The Beatles.

It opens with 'Big Barn Bed', a simple, happy song, with a thumping guitar riff and nonsense lyrics. Paul's ear for melody is in evidence here – it's unerringly catchy despite leaning almost entirely on two chords. 'My Love' is followed by 'Get On The Right Thing' with thrumming pedal-note bass and piano with chord changes above, propelling this simple rocker into classic Wings territory. Recorded during sessions for *Ram*, the wide-open spaces and harmonies in the chorus point towards *Band On The Run*. Paul's lead vocals are simply splendid – he gradually gets more and more unhinged. 'One More Kiss' is a country song with chiming guitars. As Paul said in 2018: 'Mary was three or four around this time, so just a little kid. And you know how fathers often fuss over their kids? So I was fussing over her; she was a really cute baby. And I'm fussing away, going, 'Give me a kiss. Come on, give me a kiss!' And she'd get fed up with me and sort of go: 'Dad. Alright. But only one more kiss.' So, I got one more kiss ... and a song! It suggested a country and western thing. And I was thinking that when we just listened back to it. A country singer should cover it!'

Paul's immediate post-Beatles career was roundly lambasted by the rock critics ('most of the songs are so lightweight, they float away even as Paulie layers them down with caprices. If you're going to be eccentric, for goodness sake, don't be pretentious about it', wrote Robert Christgau on *Ram*). But every now and then, simply great songs were tucked away on albums or B-sides. 'Little Lamb Dragonfly' is one of those songs that proves how much the critics got it wrong about Paul between 1971 and 1973. It floats on a bed of wonderful guitar playing, has a devastatingly strong lead vocal with occasional bursts of angst and an infectious melody that any other songwriter would sell their children to write. 'Single Pigeon' is a melancholy-but-catchy Broadway piano song with an irresistible, closely-mic'd lead vocal. Paul uses his tender voice, as heard on 'Martha My Dear', and there is a brief flourish of horns to conclude. Linda's harmonies – a key element of the Wings sound – are simply lovely. 'When The Night' is a mellow song with Denny and Henry noodling on acoustic guitars and Paul playing his patented 'Penny Lane' piano arpeggios. Wings go prog rock on the remarkable 'Loup'. What sounds like an in-the-studio two-chord jam morphs into a trippy instrumental suite with Pink Floyd organ, sound effects and fat bass. Paul in 2018: 'Because it's an album track, we had a bit more room to manoeuvre. And I think it's the rebellious aspect of *Wild Life* coming back in. So, you've got 'My Love', and that's a proper song. You've got some other proper songs on the album. But then we've got something like 'Loup', where it was sort of a bit of fun for us.' The album ends with 'Medley: Hold Me Tight/Lazy Dynamite/Hands Of Love/Power Cut', where Paul rams together four song fragments, the first borrowing its title from a song by his other band. Although none of the songs are world-beaters – the lyrics have an unfinished feel about them – the craft at work is palpable, especially in the closing few minutes when all four songs are blended together.

Red Rose Speedway finally kick-started Paul's post-Beatles career, hitting number one in the US, Australia and Spain, and number five in the UK.

The double live album *In Concert 1972* by Ravi Shankar and Ali Akbar Khan provides almost two hours of glorious Indian classical music. It was recorded at the Philharmonic Hall, New York City, in October 1972. The album was produced by George Harrison, tabla player Zakir Hussain and former Beatles engineer Phil McDonald. It comprises just three pieces: 'Raga Hem Bihag' and 'Raga Sindhi Bhairavi' bookend the hour-long 'Raga Manj Khamaj'. The music is sublime throughout. *In Concert 1972* was the final release by Ravi Shankar on Apple Records, following the *Joi Bangla* EP, the *Raga* soundtrack and the *Concert For Bangladesh* album.

May – September 1973: Number One Singles For George, Paul And Ringo

Badfinger's album *Ass* was completed in May 1973. Half the songs had been written by Joey Molland, but the guitarist, unlike his bandmates, had never signed a publishing contract with Apple Music, preferring to assign individual copyrights only for his songs that were selected for Badfinger albums. Badfinger's business manager, Stan Polley, learned of this and attempted to use Apple's lack of a publishing agreement with Molland to block the release of the album, presumably in lieu of a better deal. Ultimately, the writing credits for all of the songs on *Ass* were credited to the group as a whole, not to the individual writers. Eventually, Badfinger's management company sued Apple for unpaid publishing royalties. The band themselves saw none of the readies.

The success of Wings' 'My Love' was matched by its follow-up, three months later, 'Live And Let Die', arguably Wings' first truly classic song. Recorded mid-way through sessions for *Red Rose Speedway*, 'Live And Let Die' is the pomp-rock theme song from the *James Bond* film of the same name – Roger Moore's debut as the titular spy, released the same month as Wings' single. Produced by George Martin at his Air Studios in London, the song is arranged with keen dynamics and combines a piano ballad with a powerful up-tempo middle section, bolstered by a full-on orchestra and a reggae interlude. 'I read the *Live And Let Die* book in one day,' Paul commented as the film was being shot, 'started writing that evening and … finished it by the next evening. I sat down at the piano, worked something out and then got in touch with George Martin, who produced it with us. Linda wrote the middle reggae bit of the song. We rehearsed it as a band, recorded it and then left it up to him. I'm good at writing to order with things like that.' 'Live And Let Die' – the most commercially successful Bond theme to date at that time – was nominated for the Academy Award for Best Original Song in 1974 but lost out to the eponymous theme song from *The Way We Were*.

We should also mention here the TV special *James Paul McCartney*, recorded in February-March 1973 and broadcast in April (US) and May (UK). Along with 'Hi, Hi, Hi' (December 1972) and 'My Love' (March 1973) and the soon-to-be-released 'Live And Let Die' (June 1973), this was another important component of Paul's commercial strategy after an underwhelming 1972. Unfortunately, *James Paul McCartney* was panned by the critics. *The New York Times*: 'a series of disconnected routines strung together with commercials for Chevrolet.' *The Washington Post*: 'Mrs. McCartney's previous careers … do not qualify her to perform in public.' *Melody Maker*: 'overblown and silly.' A highly stylised dance number, 'Gotta Sing, Gotta Dance', saw McCartney wearing a pink tuxedo and a fake moustache, accompanied by dancers wearing a half male tuxedo and half a glittery gown. Paul's fans really wanted him to just play the music – as he does on *James Paul McCartney* in an all-too-short full-throttle sequence of 'The Mess', 'Maybe I'm Amazed' and 'Long Tall Sally' (and 'Hi, Hi, Hi' for the British broadcast). At this time, Wings were midway through an eight-week British tour, Paul's first, officially, since 1965.

By mid-1973, it had been almost three years since George's grand opus, *All Things Must Pass*. Its follow-up, *Living In The Material World*, is an album of new songs of spiritual devotion combined with a sense of confusion at his newfound solo fame and reflection on his disintegrating marriage. It was recorded between October 1972 and March 1973 with a tight core band of Gary Wright, Klaus Voormann, Jim Keltner and Nicky Hopkins. The album was keenly anticipated and preceded by his second US number-one single, 'Give Me Love (Give Me Peace On Earth)'. *Living In The Material World* contains some of Harrison's best guitar playing and singing as a solo artist.

> The material world is like the physical world, as opposed to the spiritual. For me, living in the material world just meant being in this physical body with all the things that go along with it.
> George Harrison, *Crawdaddy*, 1977

'Give Me Love (Give Me Peace On Earth)' is an honest and pure song, soothing and beautifully produced, with lots of George's gorgeous and intricate slide guitar playing. The lyrics have a simple, universal message wrapped in Harrison's spirituality. As George wrote in his autobiography, 'Sometimes you open your mouth, and you don't know what you are going to say, and whatever comes out is the starting point. If that happens and you are lucky, it can usually be turned into a song. This song is a prayer and personal statement between me, the Lord, and whoever likes it.' When released as a single in the US on 7 May 1973, 'Give Me Love (Give Me Peace On Earth)' knocked 'My Love' off the US top spot, which must have peeved McCartney no end. It reached number eight in the UK. 'Sue Me, Sue You Blues' is an 'up yours' in song, originally given to American guitarist Jesse Ed Davis, who had performed at the Concert For Bangladesh. The song reflects on The Beatles' court case in February-March 1971: 'Hold the block on money flow/Move it into joint escrow/Court receiver, laughs, and thrills/But in the end we just pay those lawyers their bills'. 'The Light That Has Lighted The World' is an appeal for release from public attention, originally written for Cilla Black, but George wisely kept it for himself. The scheduled second single from *Living In The Material World*, 'Don't Let Me Wait Too Long' echoes 'My Sweet Lord' in structure and sound. An upbeat pop-soul secular love song with a repetitive and attractive melody, it has a strong production employing the Spector Wall Of Sound and would have been a certain hit. Quite why this wasn't released as a single remains unexplained.

'Who Can See It' is a very earnest and dramatic ballad in shifting time signatures, with Beatles-era, Leslied electric guitar and one of George's most expressive vocal performances, surely influenced by Roy Orbison. John Barham's orchestrations colour the arrangement rather than overwhelming it. It's a long, long way from 'Don't Bother Me' ten years before, even if the underlying lyrical message is similar: 'I only ask, that what I feel/Should not be denied me now/As it's been earned, and I have seen my life belongs to me'.

The album's title track deploys two of George's songwriting tropes: developing a bluesy shuffling tension between minor and major keys and melding Western and Eastern music. The loud, shuffling 'Get Back' style verses and choruses (Ringo and Jim Keltner on a double drums barrage) include a sublime slide guitar solo, George swapping bars with Jim Horn's expressive saxophone. Meditative Indian interludes feature tabla, flute and sitar. This duality is reflected in the lyrics as George struggles to reconcile his commitment to a spiritual path with the wider world of simply material concerns. 'We are not these bodies,' George wrote in his autobiography, 'we are in these material bodies in the physical world.' He takes the opportunity to name-check his erstwhile band mates with a wry pun on rich/Richie: 'Met them all here in the material world/John and Paul here in the material world/Though we started out quite poor/We got Richie on a tour'. The line is followed by a classic Starr drum fill.

Once again, George pushes his moralising spiritual message on the very live-sounding, gospel-flavoured funk/blues of 'The Lord Loves The One (That Loves The Lord)'. George sticks to acoustic guitar and some electric slide interjections. The horns revisit 'Savoy Truffle'. The marvellous 'Be Here Now' comes off as a meditation prayer set to music. It's quiet, fragile, hypnotic and reflective, with a lethargic, dreamlike arrangement and thoughtful lyrics ('A mind, that wants to wander 'round a corner/Is an un-wise mind'). It's very much an offspring of an illicit union between 'Long, Long, Long' and 'Blue Jay Way'. The previously unheard take 10, released in 2024, is one of the most beautiful pieces of music that George ever recorded. 1971 is revisited in 'Try Some, Buy Some', recorded for Ronnie Spector's abandoned solo album. Here, George took the backing track – recorded at Abbey Road with Leon Russell, Gary Wright, Pete Ham, Klaus Voormann and Jim Gordon – remixed it and added his own new lead vocal. The key is slightly too high for George, giving his singing a keening quality as he struggles to hit the top notes.

'The Day The World Gets 'Round' is a song about hope, written immediately after the Bangladesh concert and with lyrics still as relevant today as in 1973: 'The day the world gets 'round to understanding where it's gone/Losing so much ground/killing each other, hand in hand/Such foolishness in man/I want no part of their plan'. The song radiates optimism, bolstered by John Barham's gorgeous orchestral arrangement. George's singing is magnificent. The uplifting conclusion to a fabulous album, 'That Is All', is a slow, romantic ballad with a rising chord sequence, lovely orchestral backing, a devotional lead vocal and a short, melodic guitar solo. The listener cannot be certain whether George is singing to Patti or to God, but as George himself said to *Rolling Stone* in 1976, 'I think all love is part of a universal love. When you love a woman, it's the God in her that you see.'

Thus ends George's second solo album and second masterpiece. *Living In The Material World,* however, seems to have been forgotten about. George's singing, playing and songwriting on this album are every inch as good as any of his other solo albums.

Despite these huge worldwide hit albums and singles, the Apple offices in New York City closed in July.

October – November 1973: Mind Games, Feeling The Space, Ringo, Ass

Paul McCartney And Wings' next single was the rocking 'Helen Wheels', a hard-edged, fast-moving, one-note boogie-rocker, named after Paul and Linda's Land Rover. The song describes a journey from Glasgow to London, taking in Kendal, Liverpool and Birmingham against loud guitars, bass and drums. It reached number 12 in the UK and number ten in the US.

John's *Mind Games* would see release in November 1973, with the title track as the lead single. It's Lennon's first true solo album since *Imagine*, a solid but uninspiring collection of introspective songs with very little of the drive of his earlier work. It was recorded at the beginning of his 'Lost Weekend' – 18 months of separation from Yoko Ono – a full 15 months after the poorly-received *Some Time In New York City.* Other than The Beatlesy title track, and three songs of regret at losing Ono – 'Out The Blue', 'Aisumasen (I'm Sorry)' and 'I Know (I Know)' – there's not much to shout about. It seems much of the grit in Lennon's songs has been ironed out by the New York City session players (and Jim Keltner) employed to record the album. The original mix was muddy, but *Mind Games* was remixed and re-released in 2002 and again in 2024. These are huge improvements, clearer and more defined.

The title track and single 'Mind Games' is an assured and upbeat pop song which had been in Lennon's head for nearly five years – an early version was performed in January 1969 during the *Get Back* sessions. At that time, it was called 'Make Love Not War'. The 'love is the answer' section comes from another song called 'I Promise', one of many examples of John piecing different half-written songs together to make a new one. The song was a minor hit single in America (number 18) and also in the UK (number 26). Had it been released as the follow-up to 'Imagine', then it would surely have been huge. 'Tight A$' is forgettable rockabilly, but 'Aisumasen (I'm Sorry)' delivers a sombre 6/8 blues, with a great guitar solo which rips through the melancholy with clarity and precision – it was performed by David Spinozza, a New York City session player who had also contributed to *Ram*. Lennon's self-doubt is expressed in falsetto in 'One Day (At A Time)'. The song has a strong melody as it moves through gospel, country and choral. The production and arrangement for 'Bring On The Lucie (Freda Peeple)' sound eerily like Phil Spector's work on *All Things Must Pass,* complete with George-style slide guitar. 'Intuition' is an optimistic, cheerful pop song in which John confirms to himself that he has the wherewithal to survive on his own terms. 'Well, my instincts are fine/I had to learn to use them in order to survive/And time after time confirmed an old suspicion/It's good to be alive/ And when I'm deep down and out/And lose communication/With nothing left to say/It's then I realise it's only a condition/Of seeing things that way'. This is in direct contrast to songs like 'Isolation', 'Gimme Some Truth' and the preaching politics of *Some Time In New York City* from the previous few years. Our ears prick up with 'Out The Blue', which is a gorgeous minor-key love song to Yoko, with hints of 'Sexy Sadie' in its chord changes, a folky acoustic introduction, a choral finale and a full-band backing that harks back to the White/Voormann/Hopkins sound of *Imagine*. Lennon's lead vocal starts restrained but gains assurance. 'Only People' sounds a lot like Wings, and 'I Know (I Know)' is something of a throwaway, borrowing the opening riff from 'I've Got A Feeling'. The chorus vocal is full of typical Lennon commitment. 'You Are Here' provides a gentle pedal steel guitar, rich electric piano and massed backing vocals. It's a slow, Latin-tinged version of 'Oh! Yoko' – earnest, elegiac and poetic. The title is reused from John and Yoko's 1968 art exhibition; therefore, Lennon is clearly reaching out to his estranged wife. The final song, 'Meat City', is dissonant and confusing – just like the city it celebrates: New York City. It contains one of Lennon's favourite curses played backwards and sped up.

Mind Games was released in tandem with Yoko's *Feeling The Space*. It's her most conventional album yet, performed by expensive New York City session musicians. The lyrics focus on the issues of being a woman in the 1970s, but the album's production (by Ono herself) is generic and unsurprising, with little of the unpredictability, noise or grit of her earlier works. *Feeling The Space* was accompanied by the singles 'Woman Power' (US) and 'Run, Run, Run' (UK).

To reach a settlement of their accounts, John, George, Ringo and Apple Corps issued a writ against Allen Klein and ABKCO on 2 November 1973. Klein counter-sued. This did not close until 1977.

If Ringo Starr's success is measured by the choice of his collaborators, then his first serious solo album, *Ringo*, is right up there with his greatest achievements. In pure chart terms, three hit singles and an album placing at number two (US) and number seven (UK) is enough to impress anyone who thought that Ringo would be out of work after The Beatles ended.

> Everything just sort of came together like the country album, like an accident, in a way. I [had] worked with Harry Nilsson in London on his album [*Son Of Schmilsson*] with producer Richard Perry. So, Harry and I were invited to do the Grammy Awards, and Richard was saying, 'Remember you were talking to me in the club one night, you know ... you'd like to do something? After the Grammys, why don't you come down to LA for a week?' And we went in. It worked so well; in ten days, we had eight tracks, you see. Once we started, we couldn't stop. And then I got John to write me something, and I got Paul and I got George. You know ... dragged in all me friends, 'cuz I'm lucky. I got a lot of people who'll work for me. I'll work for them, but I always feel very lucky that people will come out for me.
> **Ringo Starr, *Innerview*, August 1977**

> I think it's great. [Richard] Perry's great, Ringo's great, I think the combination was great and look how well they did together. There are no complaints if you're number one.
> John Lennon, *Rolling Stone*, April 1975

Lennon is correct. *Ringo* is a very good album indeed. It kicks off with 'I'm The Greatest'. The recording of this song is the only time that three out of four ex-Beatles performed together in the studio after 1970 in John Lennon's lifetime. With trusty side-men Voormann and Preston (overdubbed later) making up a formidable fivesome, 'I'm The Greatest' ranks as a highlight of any of the solo Beatles' collective discographies. It originates from November 1970 – Lennon recorded it at home that month – but was adapted for *Ringo* two and a half years later. The writing is affectionate, George's arpeggios invoke 1969, and as soon as Lennon joins on harmony vocals, the alchemical magic is right there. It sounds like them and is surely Ringo's signature song. Ringo concludes by declaring himself to be 'the greatest – in this world, in the next world, and in any world!'. On this song, who are we to disagree? 'Have You Seen My Baby' is a catchy song, written by Randy Newman, at that time still better known as a songwriter than a singer/songwriter. It's powered by James Booker's rollicking piano – check out the details of Booker's remarkable life as a musician – and Marc Bolan's boogie guitar. And then we have 'Photograph', written by George and Ringo on a sailing holiday in 1971. This vies with 'It Don't Come Easy' and 'I'm The Greatest' as Ringo's best solo number and shoulder to shoulder with any other post-Beatles song. 'Photograph' was first recorded during sessions for *Living In The Material*

World in late 1972, then re-recorded in Los Angeles, in the spring of 1973 for *Ringo*. Richard Perry gives the song a lavish Phil Spector production, with acoustic guitars, saxophone solo, strings and choir. When released as a single in the US on 24 September 1973, it was a deserved number one. George also donated the next song, 'Sunshine Life For Me (Sail Away Raymond)'. This is a cute, light-hearted country song recorded with members of The Band and harks back to their own 'Rag Mama Rag'. George's harmony vocals ring true as the musicians work up a lovely rock/hootenanny hybrid. 'You're Sixteen' was another big hit for Ringo: his second and final US number-one single. It was also a big hit in the UK, going as high as number four, hitting the top ten at the same time as 'Jet' by Paul McCartney And Wings. 'Oh My My' is the first fruit of the Starkey/Poncia songwriting partnership. It was another big American hit single. 'Step Lightly' has a swampy sound characterised by Tom Scott's winding horns and a spoons solo. Paul, with Linda, gets songwriting credit on 'Six O'Clock'. It was the first time Paul had worked with Ringo since January 1970. 'Six O'Clock' is a charming pop ballad, written directly for Ringo, at his request. It was recorded at Apple on 16 April 1973 with flutes and strings added at Abbey Road soon afterwards. Paul and Linda's familiar harmonies stand out in the choruses – and we hear the occasional trademark 'doooo!' from Paul. Ringo's and Jim Keltner's rock-steady drumming, with a solo, and piping horns characterise 'Devil Woman', one of the weaker tracks on *Ringo*, but George's 'You And Me (Babe)' maintains the high quality of 'Photograph' and 'Sunshine Life For Me (Sail Away Raymond)'. George's guitar solos are subtle, melodic and truly wondrous. The song ends with a roll call of the musicians and technicians involved in the album's making.

The contributions from George, John and Paul on *Ringo* resulted in inevitable rumours of a potential Beatles reunion. Paul was quick to quash these. 'The others did some tracks for it in Los Angeles, and then the material was brought over here for me. I worked on a track called 'Six O'Clock' ... so in a way, there's been some collaboration already, and I think that kind of thing might happen more often. I'm happy to play with the other three, and I'm sure they are, too, if it is physically possible, but more important for me is the new thing [Wings] because I really get turned on by new ideas.'

Badfinger's *Ass* finally saw release (in the US) in November. It had taken so long to get to market that Badfinger had already recorded their self-titled album, the first for Warner Brothers, again with Chris Thomas at the helm. They finally seem to have shaken off the overriding influence of The Beatles on *Ass*, which is full of vibrant songs, mostly written by Joey Molland, who sings well on 'Icicles' and 'I Can Love You'. 'Constitution' is a hard rocker which sounds nothing like the band's previous songs. Pete Ham shines with some thrilling lead guitar. Ham himself provides only two songs: the reflective, dynamic eight-minute 'Timeless', which might lay claim to be the band's best song of all, and the affectionate, melodic 'Apple Of My Eye'.

Ass would prove to be the last original Apple album not made by an ex-Beatle. The US release of *Badfinger* would take place just three months later. In the UK, *Ass* would be delayed until March 1974, by which time their first album for Warners was already in the shops.

December 1973: Band On The Run

If *Red Rose Speedway*, 'My Love' and 'Live And Let Die' helped to bury the spectre of *Wild Life*, then *Band On The Run* was a dramatic return to form that can sit alongside any of Paul's work from the 1960s. The album had a difficult birth. Paul wanted to record outside the UK. Wings had so far only recorded their songs in London, mostly at Abbey Road and Olympic Studios. Paul, perhaps naïvely, selected Lagos, Nigeria, as a suitable venue for an important album. Both guitarist Henry McCulloch and drummer Denny Seiwell were having none of it and quit Wings on the eve of the sessions.

'We were still on this retainer, and we'd been told that as things progressed, we could contribute material, become part of a 'band' as such, but it never ever came to that', McCulloch told Colin Harper in 1997. 'We'd rehearsed *Band On The Run* and were due to go to Lagos [to record it], and I can remember it well – we had a row one afternoon. I wanted to contribute, you know, 'Give me a chance – if it doesn't work out, we'll do it your way'. I felt it was time he allowed the musicians to have some of their own ideas used as part of this 'group' vibe. But all that was slowly being lost – the idea from the university tour, the van, the craic and all that started to go out the window. It wasn't a fierce row, just 'Oh stuff it, I'm away home' sort of thing. There was nothing said. There were a lot of things said in the press, like there was a terrible rumour I'd pulled a gun on him, that I'd hit him over the head with a bottle – really! But I think we both knew in our hearts it was time for me to go, and he left it to me to choose the time of leaving.'

'Henry (McCullough) had just left', Denny Seiwell told Gary James in 2014. 'Here we were getting ready to go to Lagos and cut *Band On The Run*, and we still had no agreement in writing. We had a verbal agreement that didn't hold any water. I'd already made *Wild Life* and *Red Rose Speedway* with that agreement in mind, but I never received a dime from that. It became a financial matter at that point. I said, 'You know what? This is not good. My interests are not being looked after here.' I should have sat him down and talked to him and said, 'Look, I won't do this anymore!' But instead, I was infuriated by a couple of things that happened, and I just called him up and said, 'I'm leaving. I'm done here."

So, it was just the McCartneys and faithful Denny Laine who flew to Nigeria in August 1973 with engineer Geoff Emerick, who had recently quit as head of Apple Studios. EMI's studio in Lagos was outdated and underequipped – and Paul and Linda were robbed at knifepoint during their stay. 'Paul had his cassette of the rehearsals stolen, so we had to start from scratch', says Denny Laine. 'It was a very badly equipped studio.' Paul also suffered from health problems during the sessions. But basic tracks for most of the album were completed by the third week in September. One song was recorded at ex-Cream drummer Ginger Baker's home studio. Work continued at George Martin's AIR studios in London in October, including overdubs of pounding horns, glorious, luscious orchestral arrangements by Tony Visconti and the recording of a new song, 'Jet'. 'We came back to London and finished [the album] off', notes Denny Laine. 'It was just me and Paul, really, in the studio. We just wanted to ... get the feeling right. It was what worked.'

The album is self-confident, effortlessly melodic, dynamic and commercial. The songs have an ebb and flow which harks back, in structure, zip and zing, to *Abbey Road*. *Band On The Run* became the top-selling studio album of 1974 in the United Kingdom, Canada and Australia. *Rolling Stone* reviewer Jon Landau gushed, 'The finest record yet released by any of the four musicians who were once called The Beatles.'

'*Band On The Run* is a great album', John Lennon told *Rolling Stone* in 1975. 'Wings is almost as conceptual a group as Plastic Ono Band. Plastic Ono was a conceptual group, meaning whoever was playing was the band. And Wings keeps changing all the time. It's conceptual. I mean, they're backup men for Paul. It doesn't matter who's playing. You can call them Wings, but it's Paul McCartney's music. And it's good stuff. It's good Paul music.'

American pop fans in 1974 must have become weary of awful number-one hit singles such as Grand Funk's 'The Loco-Motion' (number one for two weeks in May 1974) and Ray Stevens' 'The Streak' (number one for three weeks in May-June 1974). These two songs were superseded at the top of the charts, for a single week, by one of the very best songs of Paul McCartney's career. 'Band On The Run' proves that McCartney would not temper his artistic ambitions to fit the studio mandates of simple pop songs like 'My Love': it is constructed from three distinct parts and hangs together perfectly. It starts with a slow, doe-eyed bluesy ballad, possibly reflecting on the band's tenure in Lagos – 'stuck inside these four walls'. The tempo increases for an agitated 'if we ever get out here' with a funky backbeat underpinned by electric piano – this is not Linda's style, even though she is the only keyboard player credited. After two minutes, a terrific horns and strings blast starts a sun-shiny country-rock section. Laine's 12-string acoustic and sharply defined slide guitar trills may be his best contribution to a Wings' song. This last section was recorded in London some weeks after the rest of the song: the clean, crisp drum sound betrays the use of a technically superior studio – on much of the Lagos material, it sounds as though Paul was playing on wet cardboard. The song's theme is one of freedom and escape. Not coincidentally, its writing and recording coincided with Harrison, Lennon and Starr's acrimonious parting with manager Allen Klein in March 1973, leading to improved relations between McCartney and his fellow ex-Beatles. 'Band On The Run' displays more grit than Lennon, more melody than Harrison and more invention than Starr.

The opening double-whammy concludes with 'Jet', released as a single three months ahead of *Band On The Run*. Lyrically, it is another tribute to a McCartney pet dog – Martha in 1968, Jet in 1974. As with many of the other songs on the album, the lyrics are utter nonsense. The performance, though, is exuberant, driven by Macca's powerful drumming, palm-muted guitars, sparkling harmonies, strings and propellant horns. 'Jet' was recorded entirely at AIR after the band had returned from Nigeria. 'Bluebird' is a gentle acoustic song, with a hint of calypso betraying its origins on a Jamaican holiday. Wings' classic cascading harmonies colour the chorus, and there is a wonderfully warm saxophone solo by Howie Casey, one of Paul's friends from the Merseybeat scene of the early 1960s. The wonderful 'Mrs. Vanderbilt' evokes the central section of 'You Never Give Me Your Money' as Paul employs very similar vocals, rhythm and melody – even the lyrics rhyme: 'out of college, money spent' to 'down in the jungle, living in a tent' – adding powerfully melodic bass playing and a dumb 'ho, hey ho!' chorus. The resolution to the chorus of 'leave me alone, Mrs. Vanderbilt' is pure McCartney, and again we hear some delightful saxophone by Howie Casey. This classic album track is followed by another, 'Let Me Roll It'. This is a slow rocker, allowing Paul to use his full chest voice against squalling guitars and a grinding riff. The production, riff and echoed vocals recall the solo work of John Lennon, although Paul claims that this was not intentional. It seems that Paul enjoys writing songs on holiday – the breezy 'Mamunia' was written in Marrakesh (it means 'safe haven' in Arabic). In sound and structure, it's a cross between 'Mother Nature's Son' and 'Every Night'. It's lightweight, but effortlessly melodic, bolstered by a terrific production, including harmonies and a Moog synthesiser solo that the sleeve notes claim to be performed by Linda, and perhaps it was. 'No Words' is a beautiful love song with outstanding McCartney/McCartney/Laine vocal harmonies, driving guitars and a heart-pulling string quartet arrangement. It's mostly Denny's writing, his first for Wings, starting as two separate songs and linked together at Paul's suggestion with a final verse from Paul himself: 'You wanna turn your head away/And someone's thinking of you/I wish you'd see, it's only me/I love you'. Denny plays a fantastic solo at the end; there's also a definite feel of George Harrison throughout.

Another song written in Jamaica, 'Picasso's Last Words (Drink To Me)' has an intriguing back story. 'A few months before the album, I'd been on holiday,' Paul said as part of a 1993 audio documentary, 'and I'd met Dustin Hoffman, who was filming *Papillon* with Steve McQueen. We went out to dinner together and got to know each other a bit. He asked me 'How do you write songs?' And I was saying, 'You just sort of do it. You pick 'em out of the air and there they are.' He said, 'Could you write one just now? I saw something great today.' He went and got a copy of *Time* magazine.'

Hoffman takes up the story: 'Somehow, we had gotten into a conversation about Picasso because Picasso had just died [8 April 1973]. Paul asked me why I admired Picasso so much, and I talked about Picasso's last days and how the night before [he died], he had said a rather prophetic thing – he raised his glass and said, 'drink to me, drink to my health, you know I can't drink any more.' I was so struck by that sentence. So, I was saying all this to Paul, and he just started strumming [his guitar]. He began singing this song of the story that I had just told him about Picasso. It just came out of him. It's right under childbirth in terms of great events of my life.'

The album ends with 'Nineteen Hundred And Eighty–Five', a smart, up-tempo pop song fashioned from a simple, descending keyboard motif. It has a lively, live-sounding lead vocal and a magnificent orchestral accompaniment to the fade before cascading into a quick reprise of the title track to take the album to an upbeat conclusion.

The aptly named 'Apple Of My Eye' by Badfinger was the last non-Beatles release on Apple Records. It came out in the US on 10 December 1973 and in the UK on 8 March 1974. Despite all of their problems with cancelled singles and rejigged albums, Pete Ham still held affection for his time with Apple Records, and this beautiful song pays a fond farewell.

> Oh, I'm sorry, but it's time to make a stand
> Though we never meant to bite the lovin' hand
> And now, the time has come to walk alone
> We were the children, now we're overgrown

The Apple ideal of supporting diverse artists had lasted six years. Apple Records was now solely a vanity label for the ex-members of The Beatles.

1974-1976

With Allen Klein gone, Neil Aspinall was officially appointed as head of Apple Records on 1 April 1974. That Neil had survived Klein's stewardship of Apple says much about his pragmatic character. As the story goes, Neil was invited to John's home in New York City, where, on behalf of John, George and Ringo, he was asked to take over Apple and promptly threw up. According to Lennon's biographer, Philip Norman, John's pithy response was, 'If I'd been asked to run Apple, I'd have thrown up as well.'

With Paul's approval, a dependable Beatles insider was looking after their Apple-related business affairs. All four of the ex-Beatles trusted him explicitly, and Neil's loyalty stretched back to 1961. George, for his part, formed his own record label, Dark Horse, in May 1974, signing a handful of acts and, eventually, himself. Meanwhile, Yoko Ono recorded her fifth album for Apple, *A Story*, in the middle part of the year. Once again, she hired the Record Plant and employed expensive session musicians, including David Spinozza (who co-produced), Hugh McCracken, Kenneth Ascher, Michael Brecker, Alan Rubin, Randy Brecker and Rick Marotta. The album remained unreleased until the 1992 box set *Onobox*.

There were no new releases on Apple until the autumn, but *Band On The Run* spent 103 consecutive weeks on the UK album charts, peaking at number one for seven weeks between July and September 1974. It topped the Billboard chart on three separate occasions, won a Grammy and went on to sell more than 7 million copies.

John's single 'Whatever Gets You Thru The Night' promoted his album *Walls And Bridges*, released in the UK on 4 October 1974 and in the US on 26 November 1974. *Walls And Bridges* was the fourth and last album of original material by Lennon under his own name in his lifetime, recorded just five years after splitting with his Beatles bandmates.

> I enjoyed doing *Walls And Bridges,* and it wasn't hard when I had the whole thing to go into the studio and do it. I'm surprised it wasn't just all bluuuuggggghhhh. (pause) I had the most peculiar year. And ... I'm just glad that something came out. It's describing the year, in a way, but it's not as sort of schizophrenic as the year really was. I think I got such a shock during that year that the impact hasn't come through. It isn't all on *Walls And Bridges,* though. There's a hint of it there. It has to do with age and God knows what else. But only the surface has been touched on *Walls And Bridges*, you know?
> John Lennon, *Rolling Stone*, April 1975

Mind Games has its moments, but *Walls And Bridges* is very good indeed. And yet it seems to have dropped through the cracks to become John Lennon's forgotten album. It opens with the soulful 'Going Down On Love', full of silky horns and Marvin Gaye percussion. Elton John's involvement in 'Whatever Gets You Thru The Night' was something of a coup for John Lennon. In 1974, Elton John was probably the biggest pop star in the world, with four US number-one albums between 1972 and 1974, with two more to follow in 1975. John and Elton sing in tight harmony on a very funky, very fun tune.

> Elton sort of popped in on the session for *Walls And Bridges* and sort of zapped in and played the piano and ended up singing 'Whatever Gets You Thru The Night' with me. Which was a great shot in the arm. I'd done three-quarters of it, 'Now what do we do?' Should we put a camel on it or a xylophone? That sort of thing. And he came in and said, 'Hey, ah'll play some piano!'
>
> John Lennon, *Rolling Stone*, April 1975

'Whatever Gets You Thru The Night' was John's only US number-one single during his lifetime.

With its jangling piano (Nicky Hopkins again) and strings, 'Old Dirt Road' could be an outtake from *Imagine*. 'What You Got' is a powerfully furious funk/rocker with the riff from 'Back Off Boogaloo', and in the gentle, soulful 'Bless You', John's feelings are explicit, and the power and emotion in this song are plain to hear. 'Scared' has a dynamic, pulsating arrangement with bluesy guitar and parping horns. It sounds like nothing else by Lennon, or any of the other ex-Beatles. The hit single '#9 Dream' is based on John's string arrangement on Harry Nilsson's 'Many Rivers To Cross', which itself may have been inspired by George Harrison's 'Try Some, Buy Some'. The end result takes us into another dimension entirely, with truly warm and gorgeous verses, reflective, dream-like vocals and a nonsense-lyric chorus. It's anyone's guess what 'Ah! böwakawa poussé, poussé' means, though. ''Surprise, Surprise (Sweet Bird Of Paradox)' is a song for May Pang, John's partner during the 'Lost Weekend'. It's one of the lesser songs on *Walls And Bridges*, but it's still sexy and sassy. With its riffs reminiscent of 'Working Class Hero' (verses) and 'How Do You Sleep' (chorus), 'Steel And Glass' is a dark, bitter, emotional song which has been interpreted as an attack on Allen Klein. 'There you stand with your LA tan/And your New York City walk and your New York City talk/Well your teeth are clean but your mind is capped/You leave your smell like an alley cat'.

'It isn't about one person in particular,' John once said, 'but it has been about a few people and, like a novel writer, if I'm writing about something other than myself, I use other people I know or have known as examples. If I want to write a 'down' song, I would have to remember being down, and when I wrote 'Steel And Glass', I used various people and objects. If I had listed who they were, it would be a few people, and you would be surprised. But it really isn't about anybody. I'm loath to tell you this because it spoils the fun. I would sooner have everybody think, 'Who's it about?' and try to piece it together. For sure, it isn't about Paul. It has a few licks like the saxes are playing the guitar licks from 'How Do You Sleep?' I like to compute variations of my own music in the music I do. I steal from myself.'

'Beef Jerky' is a Bowie-esque instrumental with more than a hint of the riff from McCartney's 'Let Me Roll It'. 'Nobody Loves You (When You're Down And Out)' is a lethargic, melancholy, raw ballad with bleary-eyed, cynical lyrics ('Ev'rybody's hustlin' for a buck and a dime/I'll scratch your back and you knife mine'). The album closes with a minute of 'Ya Ya'. Lennon's son, Julian (aged 11), plays drums, and John provides piano and hoarse vocals.

Wings' last single on Apple, 'Junior's Farm', was another big hit – number three in the US. It's a thumping, flat-out rocker that was recorded in Nashville. It's a fun, bouncy bit of musical fluff. New lead guitarist Jimmy McCulloch – only 21 when this song was recorded and whose harder rocking sound would help propel Wings into massive stadia in 1975-1976 – plays a quite superb guitar solo. The B-side, 'Sally G', is a clever and charming country song with Wings supported by Nashville session fiddlers Vassar Clements and Johnny Gimble, and steel guitarist Lloyd Green.

Goodnight Vienna (November 1974), the follow-up to *Ringo*, is once again stuffed with famous friends, hand-picked songs and hit singles. The title track is another great song donated by John Lennon, who also plays piano here. As with the other songs John wrote for Ringo, '(It's All Down To) Goodnight Vienna' suits his voice and character perfectly. In a unique mix, it was Ringo's seventh hit single in the US, although this was the first to miss the top ten. The cover of Allen Toussaint's 'Occapella' has a bright horn line and a funky backbeat. 'Oo–Wee' is one of the best Starkey/Poncia songs, with a strong horn arrangement, gospel backing vocals and a classic Dr John piano solo. 'Husbands And Wives' is a sweet, sad country waltz, sung with much sincerity. Elton John appears on his second solo Beatles album, writing and playing on 'Snookeroo'. Elton plays effervescent piano (and counts the song in), and the Band's Robbie Robertson plays a thrilling guitar solo. A serviceable Starkey/Poncia original, 'All By Myself', has New Orleans horns and Dr John's tinkling piano. Ringo revisits 'Don't Pass Me By' in the simple, three-chord 'Call Me'. Without Ringo's inherent charm, this would be very limp – but the arrangement shines. 'No No Song' was a number-three US hit in February 1975, Ringo's last top-ten single. It's a wry anti-drugs song, as our Ritchie avoids the temptations of drugs and booze. The second verse starts 'A woman that I know came from Majorca, Spain/she smiled because I did not understand. Then she held out a ten-pound bag of cocaine…' Ah, the nineteen-seventies! Originally recorded by The Platters in 1955, 'Only You (And You Alone)' was released as a single ahead of the album, reaching number six in the US. The backing track, recorded at the same session as the album's title track, is played by the crack band of Starr, Lennon, Klaus Voormann, Jim Keltner, Billy Preston, Jesse Ed Davis and Steve Cropper. It sounds effortless. Ringo's voice is exposed in 'Easy For Me', a piano/

orchestra ballad, written by Harry Nilsson. Again, one cannot doubt Ringo's sincerity – any technical limitations are overcome by the earnest and genuine performance. The album closes with a reprise of 'Goodnight Vienna', with John demanding, 'Okay, with gusto, boys, with gusto!'

Although John and Ringo were working together once again, the likelihood of a Beatles reunion remained distant.

> It's all fantasy, the idea of putting The Beatles together again. If we ever do that, I'll tell you, the reason will be that everybody's broke. And even then, to play with The Beatles, I'd rather have Willy Weeks on bass than Paul McCartney. That's the truth, with all respect to Paul. Since I made *All Things Must Pass*, it was so nice for me to be able to play with other musicians. I don't think The Beatles are that good. I mean, they're fine. Ringo's got the best backbeat I've ever heard, and he'll play a great backbeat 24 hours a day. Paul is a fine bass player, a little overpowering at times, and John has gone through his scene, but it feels to me like he's come around. I mean, to tell you the truth, I'd join a band with John Lennon any day, but I couldn't join a band with Paul McCartney. But that's nothing personal. It's just from a musical point of view.
> George Harrison, press conference, Los Angeles, October 1974

At this time, George was about to set off on a challenging 45-date US tour, which launched his record label and new album, both called *Dark Horse*. The tour was critically savaged, and recordings confirm that George pushed his voice too far, committing himself to so many concerts in seven weeks. *Dark Horse*, released towards the end of the tour, was tarred with the same brush. The songs on *Dark Horse* reflect a difficult period in Harrison's life, as he separated from his wife, Patti, tackled tricky business issues and resorted to drugs and drink to push on through. The album missed the UK charts completely – in contrast to Ringo's *Goodnight Vienna*, released three weeks before and a top ten hit in the UK.

The opening tune is 'Hari's On Tour (Express)', a smooth, jazzy slide guitar and saxophone instrumental, written for George's live tour dates. George's band here are The LA Express, an American jazz fusion ensemble who had formed the previous year and played on a number of Joni Mitchell's albums in 1973-1976. 'Hari's On Tour (Express)' was recorded at George's home studio the day after George saw Mitchell in London and invited the band to record with him. The L.A. Express give a clean, professional, polished sound. 'Simply Shady' was recorded towards the end of the sessions for the album. It's a bluesy country rocker, and George's voice is clearly starting to suffer from the laryngitis that marred his live concert dates. 'So Sad' is a bleak song about the end of a marriage: George and Patti's. The arrangement is sympathetic, shimmering 12-string and beautiful trademark slide guitar with some rich Nicky Hopkins' piano stylings. There is a wry quote from 'Here Comes The

Sun' in the closing moments – a song from a happier time in George and Patti's relationship. 'Bye Bye, Love' follows 'So Sad'. George plays and sings everything here, working up a new melody line and a new verse (with a pointed dig at Eric Clapton). Billy Preston's rich electric piano, full of Ray Charles fills and trills, gives 'Māya Love' a smoky, funky sound. There is also a healthy dose of George's sweet slide guitar. The lyrics are a philosophical reflection on George's failed marriage. 'Ding Dong, Ding Dong' is a very simple 'welcome to the New Year' song with a Phil Spector 'wall of sound' production, a trite, repetitive lyric and a dull, forgettable musical backing. It was released as a single in the UK on 6 December 1974 (B-side 'I Don't Care Any More') and reached number 38; it went two places higher in the US, released on 23 December 1974. The very silly contemporary promotional film shows George in his 1963 and 1967 Beatles suits, amongst other costumes from years past. 'Dark Horse' was also released as a single and would have the unfortunate accolade of being the first Beatles solo single not to make the charts in the UK. Under George's hoarse vocals, it's an urgent, acoustic-driven jazz/funk song, especially the bouncy chorus. Recorded with George's live band, Billy Preston once again cooks up a storm on electric piano. 'Far East Man' is George Harrison's only writing collaboration with Ronnie Wood, who was still with The Faces in 1974. It's George's first real exercise in soul music and reflects the troubled private lives of the co-composers, each of whom, it seems, had affairs with the other's wife in 1973-1974. Wood recorded the song himself on his album *I've Got My Own Album To Do*, released ten weeks before *Dark Horse*. Finally, 'He' (Jai Sri Krishna)', the only spiritual song on *Dark Horse*, is an unusual mix of gospel keyboards, folky acoustic guitar, Indian percussion instruments and Moog synthesiser, wobble board and a gububbi, an Indian percussion string instrument – George can be heard playing this under the choruses. His singing is clear and far from the hoarser sound elsewhere on the album.

After years of red tape, the official papers for the dissolution of the Beatles & Company partnership were due to be signed at the Plaza Hotel in New York City at midnight on 19 December 1974. Paul and Linda, who attended George's solo concert earlier that evening, had arranged to fly in and be present, while Ringo had signed the documents earlier in London, not wanting to travel to New York City and risk being served with court papers by Allen Klein. John, however, did not turn up. It was another nine days before he agreed to sign after some changes were made to the agreement. In a twist that's still impossible to believe, Lennon signed the paperwork at Disney World, where he was staying with his son at the Polynesian Village Hotel. The Beatles officially ended in Disney World, Florida, on 27 December 1974. Beatles & Company was formally brought to London's High Court on 9 January 1975 with a view to dissolution.

Now officially and legally no longer tied to each other, Lennon, Starr and Harrison's commerciality began to falter. *Rock 'N' Roll*, Lennon's last album for five years, sees an artist with nothing new to say. The genesis of *Rock 'N' Roll* was The Beatles' song 'Come Together', which used a line from an old Chuck Berry song – 'Here come old flat top' are the opening words of 'You Can't Catch Me'. Berry's publisher, Morris Levy, decided to sue for copyright infringement, based on those five words. As part of the settlement, Lennon agreed to record three Levy-owned songs – this idea became a full album. Recording commenced in October 1973 with the working title *Back To Mono*, later *Oldies But Moldies*. Lennon called in Phil Spector, but initial sessions in Los Angeles fell into disarray, and the unreliable Spector made off with the master tapes.

'It started in '73 with Phil and fell apart', John told *Rolling Stone* in 1975. 'I ended up as part of mad, drunk scenes in Los Angeles, and I finally finished it off on me own. And there were still problems with it up to the minute it came out. I can't begin to say, it's just barmy, there's a jinx on that album. I don't like to tell tales out of school, y'know. But I do know there was an awful loud noise in the toilet of the Record Plant West.'

Finally, over five productive days in October 1974, Lennon completed the album in New York City. Wanting to assure Levy that progress was being made, Lennon gave him a rough mix of 15 songs. Levy promptly released an album on his own record label called *Roots: John Lennon Sings The Great Rock & Roll Hits*. *Rock 'N' Roll* was released in February 1975, and Levy's album was withdrawn from sale, ensuring that original copies of *Roots* are sought-after collectors' items.

As an album, it's as well-crafted as you would expect from one of rock's great voices with the best session players money can buy. John gives spirited attempts at songs from Little Richard, Chuck Berry, Fats Domino, Buddy Holly and others. 'Stand By Me' is very fine indeed, with a wide-open production and a full-throated Lennon lead vocal, as is a slower and funkier arrangement of 'Do You Wanna Dance?' and a scintillating Sam Cooke medley. But one feels that John's heart isn't really in it, and even the most ardent Beatles fanatics have probably only played it a handful of times.

Rock 'N' Roll was released in mid-February, with the single 'Stand By Me' following in March (US) and April (UK). By now, Yoko was pregnant, and John stepped back from his career for the next five years.

In the meantime, Paul and George were seen socialising together for the first time in almost five years on 24 March at a party in Long Beach to celebrate the end of recording sessions for Wings' *Venus And Mars*. Two weeks later, on 9 April 1975, the lawsuit was settled, and The Beatles' formal business partnership was finally dissolved. 'It's '75 now, isn't it?' John Lennon asked *Rolling Stone*. 'Well, I've just settled The Beatles settlement. It must've happened in the last month. Took three years. (pause) And on this day that you've come here, I seem to have moved back in here [to New York City]. In the last three days. By the time this goes out, I don't know ... That's a big change. Maybe that's why I'm sleeping funny. As a friend says, I went out for coffee and some papers, and I didn't come back. (chuckles) Or vice versa. It's always written that way, y'know.'

More change was coming. Paul had delivered the requisite number of albums for Apple under the original Apple/EMI deal and was free to sign with Capitol for his next album with Wings. Both *Venus And Mars* and 'Listen To What The Man Said' were US number ones.

An announcement on 6 May 1975 confirmed that Apple Records would cease operations early in 1976 when The Beatles' nine-year contract with EMI was due to expire. Neil Aspinall would continue to head up Apple Corps, with a handful of employees, to gather royalties and fight lawsuits. Apple Studios ceased operations on 16 May when Apple Corps sold its freehold interest in 3 Savile Row.

The last album of original material on Apple Records was George's *Extra Texture (Read All About It),* released on 22 September in the US and three weeks later in the UK. It kicks off with the wailing saxophone of 'You', the lead-off single. 'You' is an energetic, radio-friendly, upbeat soul/R&B song owing a definite debt to 'What Is Life?', and was recorded in February 1971 as part of Ronnie Spector's unfinished album. The end result is joyous, and it was a minor hit in the US and the UK. A request for tolerance and a reflection on the nature of relationships, 'The Answer's At The End' initiated with an inscription at George's Friar Park home: 'Scan not a friend with a microscopic glass. You know his faults, now let his foibles pass'. The arrangement again takes much from contemporary soul music, especially the jazzy piano and the swelling strings – George also quotes himself singing 'Isn't it a pity' in the final moments. 'This Guitar (Can't Keep from Crying)' is a sequel, of sorts, to 'While My Guitar Gently Weeps'. It is inevitably compared to George's Beatles classic, but stands as an excellent song in its own right, yearning and expressive. George fights back against what he felt was undue criticism, calling out *Rolling Stone* in particular: 'While you attack, create offence/I'll put it down to your ignorance'. When released as the final single on Apple, until 1994, 'This Guitar (Can't Keep From Crying)' was the first solo Beatles single not to register on either the US or UK charts. 'Ooh Baby (You Know That I Love You)' is a soul ballad in the style of Smokey Robinson, whereas 'World Of Stone' is a delicate ballad which morphs into a shuffling rocker. The pop-gospel-soul 'Philly Sound' ballad 'Can't Stop Thinking About You' has lush strings and rich backing vocals, and 'Tired Of Midnight Blue' is a sideways love song to Olivia as George laments the shallow lifestyle of the LA scene: 'I don't know where I had been/But I know what I had seen/ Made me chill right to the bone/Made me wish that I'd stayed home'. With upfront jangly piano and lots of slide guitar, it's a highlight of *Extra Texture*. 'Grey Cloudy Lies' is a dour song. Listen to George's voice break on 'Now I only want to live/With no teardrops in my eyes/But at times it feels like no chance/No clear blue skies'. As George himself described it when talking to Paul Gambaccini, 'one of those depressing, 4 o'clock in the morning sort of songs' (Radio 1 interview, 1975). It's not an uplifting listen. 'His Name Is Legs (Ladies And Gentlemen)' is a light-hearted finish to a downbeat album.

Extra Texture (Read All About It) could only reach number 16 in the UK but was still a marked improvement on *Dark Horse*.

With Apple winding down, two compilations sought to claim some final pennies. John's *Shaved Fish* gathered ten of the singles that he had issued as a solo artist. It was the only compilation of Lennon's non-Beatles recordings released during his lifetime and peaked at number eight in the UK and number 12 in the US. In parallel, 'Imagine' would finally be released as a single in the UK on the same day, 24 October 1975. It reached number six. Ringo's *Blast From Your Past* collects ten songs from his solo career. Seven of these were top-ten hits in the US, and two of them were number ones, 'Photograph' and 'You're Sixteen'. Despite being full of great songs, *Blast From Your Past* failed to chart in the UK and peaked at number 30 in the US.

1976 started with the sad news of the death of Mal Evans. Evans, who adored The Beatles, was killed by the Los Angeles Police Department when he reportedly threatened them with an air rifle while in a drunken rage. Mal was cremated, and his ashes were sent back to his family in the UK. In a twist which is almost too sad to report, Mal's remains were lost by the airline repatriating the urn. They were later found in the lost luggage office of an airport. They were recovered and given to his family, who spread them at South West Middlesex Crematorium.

The ex-Beatles' nine-year contract with EMI expired on 26 January. The final singles on the Apple label would be by Ringo and George. The belated UK release of Ringo's 'Oh My My' happened almost two years after it had been a top-five hit in the US. Released to promote *Blast From Your Past*, it predictably failed to chart. George's single 'This Guitar (Can't Keep From Crying)', 6 February 1976, marked the end of Apple Records. EMI in the UK re-released all 22 singles by The Beatles on 5 March, along with a new pairing of 'Yesterday'/'I Should Have Known Better'. 'Yesterday' rose to number eight, and five others entered the top 40.

With John on sabbatical and without a record deal, George signed himself to his own Dark Horse Records. Ringo went to Polydor (UK) and Atlantic (US), but only one of his future albums would crack the top 30 in either of these major markets.

Also in 1975, John Lennon applied for the green card that would allow him permanent residence in the US. Once granted, John held up the precious paper to the press cameras. 'It's been a long and slow road,' he said, 'but I am not bitter. Now I'm going home to crack open a tea-bag and start looking at some travel catalogues.'

Apple Records Since 1976

For the next 30 years, Apple would be managed by The Beatles' old friend Neil Aspinall. Lawsuits continued to take up much of his time. The tangled legal dispute between the former Beatles and Allen Klein was finally settled in 1977. Klein was to relinquish all managerial rights for a one-time payment of just over $5 million, plus undisputed retention of all previous commissions and expenses. Klein was subsequently charged with three felony counts of income tax evasion. The court case ended in a mistrial because of a deadlocked jury, but at a second trial in 1979, he was found guilty of a misdemeanour charge for false accounting. He was fined $5,000 and sentenced to two months in jail. Klein was later appointed Phil Spector's business manager, a development which deserves a book of its own. He died in 2004. Both Yoko Ono and Sean Lennon attended his funeral.

In 1978, Neil Aspinall instigated the first of three lawsuits against the newly formed Apple Computer Inc. Aspinall had kept Apple Electronics as a registered company and sued for trademark infringement. The case was settled in 1981, with an estimated £41,000 ($80,000) paid to Apple Corps by Apple Computer Inc., and an agreement that Apple Computer could use their name and logo as long as they did not enter the music business. Eight years later, a second suit was settled after Apple Computer Inc. included a 32-channel synthesiser chip in their Apple IIGS desktop model. This time, the payout was a rather higher £13.5 million. Apple Computer Inc. was sued for the third time in 2003 following the introduction of the iTunes Music Store and the iPod music player. The eight-week trial in 2006 ended in a victory for Apple Computer Inc. when the judge ruled the company's iTunes Music Store did not infringe on the trademark of Apple Corps.

'With great respect to the trial judge,' Neil Aspinall noted in a subsequent press release, 'we consider he has reached the wrong conclusion. We felt that during the course of the trial, we clearly demonstrated just how extensively Apple Computer had broken the agreement. We will accordingly be filing an appeal and putting the case again before the Court of Appeal. We have been advised by our legal team, including two eminent specialist QCs and our solicitors, Eversheds, that we have every prospect of reversing this decision on appeal.' No appeal was filed. Within months, Apple Inc. (owner of Apple Computers) paid Apple Corps the astounding sum of $500 million to assume global ownership of the Apple trademarks. The Granny Smith logo would then be licensed back to Apple Corps.

By now, iTunes was a major distributor of digital music. And yet, The Beatles' songs were not available on the streaming platform because Apple and EMI had yet to decide how to handle the digital music rights. 'The Beatles all want to be on iTunes,' Steve Jobs later recalled, 'but they and EMI are like an old married couple. They hate each other but can't get divorced. The fact that my favourite band was the last holdout from iTunes was something I very much hoped I would live to resolve.'

It would take until the summer of 2010 for the resolution. In a press statement, Paul McCartney said, 'We're really excited to bring The Beatles' music to iTunes. It's fantastic to see the songs we originally released on vinyl receive as much love in the digital world as they did the first time around.' Steve Jobs died of cancer in October 2011 and therefore lived to see The Beatles' music on iTunes. Neil Aspinall, sadly, did not. Neil remained with Apple until 2007 and died the following spring. By then, The Beatles' business dealings were all but resolved. The green Apple logo has been seen on all new Beatles albums released since 1994, including *Live At The BBC* (1994), *Anthology 1* (1995), *Anthology 2* and *Anthology 3* (both 1996), *Yellow Submarine Songtrack* (1999), *1* (2000), *Let It Be... Naked* (2003), *Love* (2006) and *On Air: Live At The BBC Vol. 2* (2013) and *Anthology 4* (2025).

2021 saw a new box set called *Good As Gold (Artefacts Of The Apple Era 1967-1975),* which includes previously unheard (or very rare) Apple recordings and demos by Grapefruit, Timon, Contact, Drew And Dy, Focal Point, Gallagher And Lyle and Jackie Lomax.

It seems appropriate that The Beatles' final single, 'Now And Then', was an Apple release in 2023.

Postscript

Badfinger signed to Warner Bros. in late 1973. Their advance, $2 million, sounded good, but it was for six albums in just three years. Once the advance had been split six ways – managers Bill Collins and Stan Polley took their share, too – and the cost of the albums they had to pay for themselves was deducted, then the deal didn't look quite so sweet. Badfinger's self-titled sixth album, again recorded with Chris Thomas, was released in February 1974 to mixed reviews. Neither single from the album was a hit, and the best song, Pete Ham's wistful 'Lonely For You', was overlooked.

As usual, bad luck followed Badfinger. Stan Polley's financial machinations resulted in a lawsuit by their record company over £250,000 of missing money that was supposed to reside in an escrow account. Warners withdrew from the marketing of the magnificent album *Wish You Were Here,* and this cut off the band's income. The songs 'Just A Chance', 'Know One Knows' and 'Dennis' are outstanding but remained barely known until the album's 2020 release.

The lawsuit against Badfinger Enterprises resulted in Stan Polley being accused of mishandling the band's affairs. It would drag on through the courts for years, tying up millions of dollars. Pete Ham left the band and was replaced by guitarist/keyboardist Bob Jackson, but was persuaded to return. The five-piece Badfinger went into Apple Studios to record their third album under their Warners contract with Kiss producers Kenny Kerner and Richie Wise. The album, to be called *Head First*, was recorded in 11 days in December 1974. Warners, however, were unable to accept *Head First* because of the ongoing legal case. The album was shelved.

Stan Polley was finally ditched by Badfinger, but the band were unable to book live concerts due to restrictive contracts and impending legal actions. Pete Ham had recently bought a house in Surrey, and his girlfriend was expecting a child. Ham reportedly tried to contact Polley during the early months of 1975, but was not able to reach him. On the night of 23 April 1975, Pete Ham received a phone call telling him that Polley and the band's money had disappeared. Later that night, he met Tom Evans and, after a long session in the pub where he drank ten whiskies, Pete hanged himself in his garage studio. His suicide note read: 'I will not be allowed to love and trust everybody. This is better. P.S. Stan Polley is a soulless bastard. I will take him with me.' A month after that, Warner Bros. terminated their contract with Badfinger, and the band officially broke up. Two years later, Molland and Evans reformed Badfinger and released two albums before splitting once more. Stan Polley was finally forced to pay an undisclosed amount of money to Warner Bros. in 1978.

By the early 1980s, both Molland and Evans were leading two separate bands, both named Badfinger. They had a heated argument on the evening of 18 November 1983 and, ground down, Evans hanged himself in his garden.

Head First was finally released in 2000 using a rough mix that had been prepared at the end of the recording sessions in December 1974. This was the last Badfinger studio album to include Pete Ham and Mike Gibbins, and the only one to feature Bob Jackson as a group member.

Mike Gibbins passed away in his sleep on 4 October 2005 at the age of 56 due to a brain aneurysm. Stan Polley lived a long life, dying aged 87 in 2009.

All of Badfinger's albums for Apple were released in 2010 with many bonus tracks. An exhaustive 17-CD box set called *Fresh From Apple Records* includes these albums, along with *Post Card*, *Earth Song/Ocean Song*, *Is This What You Want?*, *Under The Jasmin Tree*, *Space*, *That's The Way God Planned It*, *Encouraging Words*, *The Radha Kṛṣṇa Temple*, *The Whale*, *A Celtic Requiem*, *James Taylor* and *Doris Troy*. This also included a disc of 20 rare or unreleased tracks by Badfinger.

In 2013, the song 'Baby Blue' from *Straight Up* was prominently featured in the closing moments of the final episode of *Breaking Bad*. It charted in the UK for the first time at number 73. *Badfinger* and *Wish You Were Here* saw a re-release in 2020. In 2024, the original multi-track masters of *Head First* were found, and Bob Jackson (the sole surviving member of this lineup) remixed the entire album for release in December 2024, 50 years after they were recorded.

Joey Molland died from complications of diabetes at a hospital in St. Louis Park, Minnesota, on 1 March 2025. He was 77. Bob Jackson continues to tour under the Badfinger name.

Guess I got what I deserved
Kept you waiting there too long, my love
All that time, without a word
Did you really think that I'd forget
Or I'd regret
The special love I have for you
My baby blue

Apple Records UK And US Discographies

Singles And EPs

The Beatles, 'Hey Jude'/'Revolution' (UK: 30 August 1968, US: 26 August 1968)

Mary Hopkin, 'Those Were The Days'/'Turn! Turn! Turn!' (UK: 30 August 1968, US: 26 August 1968)

Jackie Lomax, 'Sour Milk Sea'/'The Eagle Laughs At You' (UK: 6 September 1968, US: 26 August 1968)

John Foster & Sons Ltd. Black Dyke Mills Band, 'Thingumybob'/'Yellow Submarine' (UK: 6 September 1968, US: 26 August 1968)

The Iveys, 'Maybe Tomorrow'/'And Her Daddy's A Millionaire' (UK: 15 November 1968)

White Trash, 'Road To Nowhere'/'Illusions' (UK: 24 January 1969, US: 3 March 1969)

The Iveys, 'Maybe Tomorrow'/'And Her Daddy's A Millionaire' (US: 27 January 1969)

James Taylor, 'Carolina In My Mind'/'Taking It In' (UK: 17 February 1969, US: 17 March 1969). Re-released in November 1970 with 'Something's Wrong' as the B-side.

Mary Hopkin, 'Goodbye'/'Sparrow' (UK: 28 March 1969, US: 7 April 1969)

The Beatles With Billy Preston, 'Get Back'/'Don't Let Me Down' (UK: 11 April 1969, US: 5 May 1969)

Jackie Lomax, 'New Day'/'Fall Inside Your Eyes' (UK), 'Thumbin' A Ride' (US) (UK: 9 May 1969, US: 2 June 1969)

Brute Force, 'King Of Fuh'/'Nobody Knows' (UK: 16 May 1969)

The Beatles, 'The Ballad Of John And Yoko'/'Old Brown Shoe' (UK: 30 May 1969, US: 4 June 1969)

Billy Preston, 'That's The Way God Planned It'/'What About You' (UK: 27 June 1969, US: 14 July 1969)

Plastic Ono Band, 'Give Peace A Chance'/'Remember Love' (UK: 4 July 1969, US: 7 July 1969)

Various Artists, 'Wall's Ice Cream EP' (UK: 18 July 1969)

Radha Krishna Temple (London), 'Hare Krishna Mantra'/'Prayer To The Spiritual Masters' (UK: 29 August 1969, US: 21 August 1969)

Trash, 'Golden Slumbers-Carry That Weight'/'Trash Can' (UK: 26 September 1969, UK: 15 October 1969)

The Beatles, 'Something'/'Come Together' (UK: 31 October 1969, US: 6 October 1969)

Hot Chocolate Band, 'Give Peace A Chance'/'Living Without Tomorrow' (UK: 10 October 1969, US: 27 October 1969)

Billy Preston, 'Everything's Alright'/'I Want To Thank You' (UK: 17 October 1969, US: 10 November 1969)

Plastic Ono Band, 'Cold Turkey'/'Don't Worry Kyoko' (UK: 24 October 1969, US: 20 October 1969)

Badfinger, 'Come And Get It'/'Rock Of All Ages' (UK: 5 December 1969, US: 2 February 1970)
Mary Hopkin, 'Temma Harbour'/'Lontano Dagli Occhi' (UK: 16 January 1970, US: 9 February 1970)
Billy Preston, 'All That I've Got'/'As I Get Older' (UK: 30 January 1970, US: 16 February 1970)
Jackie Lomax, 'How The Web Was Woven'/'Thumbin' A Ride' (UK), '(I) Fall Inside Your Eyes' (UK: 6 February 1970, US: 23 March 1970)
Lennon/Ono/Plastic Ono Band, 'Instant Karma!'/'Who Has Seen The Wind?' (UK: 6 February 1970, US: 20 February 1970)
Doris Troy, 'Ain't That Cute'/'Vaya Con Dios' (UK: 13 February 1970, US: 16 March 1970)
The Beatles, 'Let It Be'/'You Know My Name (Look Up The Number)' (UK: 6 March 1970, US: 11 March 1970)
Radha Krishna Temple (London), 'Govinda'/'Govinda Jai Jai' (UK: 6 March 1970, UK: 24 March 1970)
Mary Hopkin, 'Knock, Knock Who's There?'/'I'm Going To Fall In Love Again' (UK: 23 March 1970)
The Beatles, 'The Long And Winding Road'/'For You Blue' (US: 11 May 1970)
Mary Hopkin, 'Que Sera, Sera'/'Fields Of St. Etienne' (US: 15 June 1970)
Doris Troy, 'Jacob's Ladder'/'Get Back' (UK: 28 August 1970, US: 21 September 1970)
Ringo Starr, 'Beaucoups Of Blues'/'Coochy-Coochy' (US: 5 October 1970)
Mary Hopkin, 'Think About Your Children'/'Heritage' (UK: 16 October 1970, US: 2 November 1970)
Badfinger, 'No Matter What'/'Carry On Till Tomorrow' (US), 'Better Days' (UK) (US: 19 October 1970, UK: 6 November 1970)
George Harrison, 'My Sweet Lord'/'Isn't It A Pity' (US: 23 November 1970)
Billy Preston, 'My Sweet Lord'/'Little Girl' (US: 14 December 1970)
John Lennon/Plastic Ono Band, 'Mother'/'Why' (US: 28 December 1970)
George Harrison, 'My Sweet Lord'/'What Is Life' (UK: 15 January 1971)
George Harrison, 'What Is Life'/'Apple Scruffs' (US: 15 February 1971)
Paul McCartney, 'Another Day'/'Oh Woman, Oh Why' (UK: 19 February 1971, US: 22 February 1971)
John Lennon/Plastic Ono Band, 'Power To The People'/'Open Your Box' (UK), 'Touch Me' (US) (UK: 12 March 1971, US: 22 March 1971)
Ringo Starr, 'It Don't Come Easy'/'Early 1970' (UK: 9 April 1971, US: 16 April 1971)
Ronnie Spector, 'Try Some, Buy Some'/'Tandoori Chicken' (UK: 16 April 1971, US: 19 April 1971)
Mary Hopkin, 'Let My Name Be Sorrow'/'Kew Gardens' (UK: 18 June 1971)
Jackie Lomax, 'Sour Milk Sea'/'I Fall Inside Your Eyes' (US: 21 June 1971)
Bill Elliot And The Elastic Oz Band, 'God Save Us'/'Do The Oz' (UK: 16 July 1971, US: 7 July 1971)

George Harrison, 'Bangladesh'/'Deep Blue' (UK: 30 July 1971, US: 28 July 1971)
Paul & Linda McCartney, 'Uncle Albert/Admiral Halsey'/'Too Many People' (US: 2 August 1971)
Paul & Linda McCartney, 'The Back Seat Of My Car'/'Heart Of The Country' (UK: 13 August 1971)
Ravi Shankar, 'Joi Bangla'/'Oh Bhaugowan'/'Raga Mishri' (UK: 27 August 1971, US: 31 August 1971)
Yoko Ono, 'Mrs. Lennon'/'Midsummer New York City' (UK/US: 29 September 1971)
John Lennon, 'Imagine'/'It's So Hard' (US: 11 October 1971)
Badfinger, 'Day After Day'/'Money' (US: 15 November 1971)
Mary Hopkin, 'Water, Paper And Clay'/'Jefferson' (UK), 'Streets Of London' (US) (UK/US: 26 November 1971)
John & Yoko/Plastic Ono Band, 'Happy Xmas (War Is Over)'/'Listen, The Snow Is Falling' (US: 1 December 1971)
Badfinger, 'Day After Day'/'Sweet Tuesday Morning' (UK: 14 January 1972)
Yoko Ono, 'Mind Train'/'Listen, The Snow Is Falling' (UK: 21 January 1972)
Wings, 'Give Ireland Back To The Irish'/'Give Ireland Back To The Irish (Version)' (UK: 25 February 1972, US: 28 February 1972)
Ringo Starr, 'Back Off Boogaloo'/'Blindman' (UK: 18 March 1972, US: 20 March 1972)
Badfinger, 'Baby Blue'/'Flying' (UK: 20 March 1972)
Lon & Derrek Van Eaton, 'Sweet Music'/'Song Of Songs' (US: 20 March 1972)
David Peel & The Lower East Side, 'F Is Not A Dirty Word'/'The Ballad Of New York City/John Lennon-Yoko Ono' (US: 20 April 1972)
John Lennon/Plastic Ono Band, 'Woman Is The Nigger Of The World'/'Sisters, O Sisters' (UK: 24 April 1972)
Wings, 'Mary Had A Little Lamb'/'Little Woman Love' (UK: 12 May 1972, US: 29 May 1972)
Chris Hodge, 'We're On Our Way'/'Supersoul' (UK: 9 June 1972, US: 29 May 1972)
David Peel And The Lower East Side, 'The Hippie From New York City'/'The Ballad Of New York City/John Lennon-Yoko Ono' (UK: 16 June 1972)
The Sundown Playboys, 'Saturday Nite Special'/'Valse De Soleil Coucher' (UK: 17 November 1972, US: 31 October 1972)
Yoko Ono, 'Now Or Never'/'Move On Fast' (UK: 13 November 1972)
Mary Hopkin, 'Knock Knock, Who's There?'/'International' (UK: 13 November 1972)
John & Yoko/Plastic Ono Band, 'Happy Xmas (War Is Over)'/'Listen, The Snow Is Falling' (UK: 24 November 1972)
Elephant's Memory, 'Liberation Special'/'Madness' (UK: 30 November 1972)
Elephant's Memory, 'Power Boogie'/'Liberation Special' (US: 1 December 1972)

Wings, 'Hi, Hi, Hi'/'C Moon' (UK: 1 December 1972, US: 4 December 1972)
Yoko Ono, 'Death Of Samantha'/'Yang Yang' (UK: 4 May 1973, US: 26 February 1973)
Lon & Derrek Van Eaton, 'Warm Woman'/'More Than Words' (UK: 9 March 1973)
Chris Hodge, 'Goodbye, Sweet Lorraine'/'Contact Love' (US: 31 March 1973)
Paul McCartney & Wings, 'My Love'/'The Mess' (UK: 23 March 1973, US: 9 April 1973)
George Harrison, 'Give Me Love (Give Me Peace On Earth)'/'Miss O'Dell' (UK: 25 May 1973, US: 7 May 1973)
Wings, 'Live And Let Die'/'I Lie Around' (UK: 1 June 1973, US: 18 June 1973)
Ringo Starr, 'Photograph'/'Down And Out' (UK: 19 October 1973, US: 24 September 1973)
Yoko Ono, 'Woman Power'/'Men Men Men' (US: 24 September 1973)
Paul McCartney & Wings, 'Helen Wheels'/'Country Dreamer'. (UK: 26 October 1973, US: 12 November 1973)
John Lennon, 'Mind Games'/'Meat City' (UK: 16 November 1973, US: 29 October 1973)
Yoko Ono, 'Run, Run, Run'/'Men Men Men' (UK: 9 November 1973)
Ringo Starr, 'You're Sixteen'/'Devil Woman' (US: 3 December 1973)
Badfinger, 'Apple Of My Eye'/'Blind Owl' (US: 10 December 1973, UK: 8 March 1974)
Paul McCartney & Wings, 'Jet'/'Mamunia' (US: 28 January 1974)
Ringo Starr, 'You're Sixteen'/'Devil Woman' (UK: 8 February 1974)
Paul McCartney & Wings, 'Jet'/'Let Me Roll It' (UK: 15 February 1974, US: 18 February 1974)
Ringo Starr, 'Oh My My'/'Step Lightly' (UK: 18 February 1974)
Paul McCartney & Wings, 'Band On The Run'/'Zoo Gang' (UK), 'Nineteen Hundred And Eighty-Five' (US) (UK: 28 June 1974, US: 8 April 1974)
John Lennon, 'Whatever Gets You Thru The Night'/'Beef Jerky' (UK: 4 October 1974, US: 23 September 1974)
Paul McCartney & Wings, 'Junior's Farm'/'Sally G' (UK: 25 October 1974, US: 4 November 1974)
Ringo Starr, 'Only You (And You Alone)'/'Call Me' (UK: 15 November 1974, US: 11 November 1974)
George Harrison, 'Ding Dong, Ding Dong'/'I Don't Care Anymore' (UK), 'Hari's On Tour (Express)' (UK: 6 December 1974, US: 23 December 1974)
John Lennon, '#9 Dream'/'What You Got' (US: 16 December 1974)
Ringo Starr, 'No No Song'/'Snookeroo' (US: 27 January 1975)
John Lennon, '#9 Dream'/'What You Got' (UK: 31 January 1975)
Ringo Starr, 'Snookeroo'/'Oo-Wee' (UK: 21 February 1975)
George Harrison, 'Dark Horse'/'Hari's On Tour (Express)' (UK: 28 February 1975)
John Lennon, 'Stand By Me'/'Move Over Ms. L' (UK: 18 April 1975, US: 10 March 1975)

Ringo Starr, '(It's All Down To) Goodnight Vienna'/'Oo-Wee' (US: 2 June 1975)
George Harrison, 'You'/'World Of Stone' (UK: 12 September 1975, US: 15 September 1975)
John Lennon, 'Imagine'/'Working Class Hero' (UK: 24 October 1975)
George Harrison, 'This Guitar (Can't Keep From Crying)'/'Māya Love' (US: 8 December 1975)
Ringo Starr, 'Oh My My'/'No No Song' (UK: 9 January 1976)
George Harrison, 'This Guitar (Can't Keep From Crying)'/'Māya Love' (UK: 6 February 1976)

Albums

George Harrison, *Wonderwall Music*. (UK: 1 November 1968, US: 2 December 1968)
The Beatles, *The Beatles* (UK: 22 November 1968, US: 25 November 1968)
John Lennon & Yoko Ono, *Unfinished Music No.1: Two Virgins* (UK: 29 November 1968, US: 17 January 1969)
James Taylor, *James Taylor* (UK: 6 December 1968, US: 17 February 1969)
Modern Jazz Quartet, *Under The Jasmin Tree* (UK: 6 December 1968, US: 17 February 1969)
The Beatles, *Yellow Submarine* (UK: 17 January 1969, US: 13 January 1969)
Mary Hopkin, *Post Card* (UK: 21 February 1969, US: 3 March 1969)
Jackie Lomax, *Is This What You Want?* (UK: 14 March 1969, US: 17 May 1969)
John Lennon & Yoko Ono, *Unfinished Music No. 2: Life With The Lions* (UK: 9 May 1969, US: 26 May 1969)
George Harrison, *Electronic Sound* (UK: 9 May 1969, US: 26 May 1969)
The Iveys, *Maybe Tomorrow* (Released In July 1969 In Japan, West Germany And Italy)
Billy Preston, *That's The Way God Planned It* (UK: 22 August 1969, US: 10 September 1969)
The Beatles, *Abbey Road* (UK: 26 September 1969, US: 1 October 1969)
John Lennon & Yoko Ono, *Wedding Album* (UK: 7 November 1969, US: 20 October 1969)
Modern Jazz Quartet, *Space* (UK: 24 October 1969, US: 10 November 1969)
Plastic Ono Band, *Live Peace In Toronto 1969* (UK/US: 12 December 1969)
Badfinger, *Magic Christian Music* (UK: 9 January 1970, US: 16 February 1970)
The Beatles, *Hey Jude* (US: 26 February 1970)
Ringo Starr, *Sentimental Journey* (UK: 27 March 1970, US: 24 April 1970)
Paul McCartney, *McCartney* (UK: 17 April 1970, US: 20 April 1970)
The Beatles, *Let It Be* (UK: 8 May 1970, US: 18 May 1970)
Doris Troy, *Doris Troy* (UK/US: 11 September 1970)
Billy Preston, *Encouraging Words* (UK/US: 11 September 1970)
London Sinfonietta / John Tavener, *The Whale* (UK: 25 September 1970, US: 15 October 1970)

Ringo Starr, *Beaucoups Of Blues* (UK: 25 September 1970, US: 28 September 1970)
Badfinger, *No Dice* (UK: 9 November 1970, US: 27 November 1970)
George Harrison, *All Things Must Pass* (UK: 30 November 1970, US: 27 November 1970)
Yoko Ono/Plastic Ono Band, *Yoko Ono/Plastic Ono Band* (UK/US: 11 December 1970)
John Lennon/Plastic Ono Band, *John Lennon/Plastic Ono Band* (UK/US: 11 December 1970)
The Beatles, *From Then To You* (UK: 18 December 1970)
London Sinfonietta/John Tavener, *A Celtic Requiem* (UK: 14 May 1971)
Paul & Linda McCartney, *Ram* (UK: 28 May 1971, US: 17 May 1971)
Radha Krishna Temple (London), *The Radha Krsna Temple* (UK: 28 May 1971, US: 21 May 1971)
John Lennon, *Imagine* (UK: 8 October 1971, US: 9 September 1971)
Stelvio Cipriani, *Cometogether* (US: 20 September 1971)
Yoko Ono, *Fly* (UK: 3 December 1971, US: 20 September 1971)
Mary Hopkin, *Earth Song/Ocean Song* (UK: 1 October 1971, US: 3 November 1971)
Original Soundtrack Recording, *Raga* (US: 7 December 1971)
Wings *Wild Life* (UK/US: 7 December 1971)
Badfinger. *Straight Up* (US: 13 December 1971, UK: 4 February 1972)
George Harrison And Friends, *The Concert For Bangladesh* (US: 20 December 1971, UK: 10 January 1972)
Original Soundtrack Recording, *El Topo* (US: 27 December 1971)
David Peel & The Lower East Side, *The Pope Smokes Dope* (US: 17 April 1972)
John & Yoko/Plastic Ono Band, *Some Time In New York City* (UK: 15 September 1972, US: 16 June 1972)
Elephant's Memory, *Elephant's Memory* (UK: 10 November 1972, US: 18 September 1972)
Lon & Derrek Van Eaton, *Brother* (UK: 9 February 1973, US: 22 September 1972)
Mary Hopkin, *Those Were The Days* (UK: 24 November 1972, US: 25 September 1972)
Various Artists, *Phil Spector's Christmas Album* (UK: 8 December 1972, US: 1 December 1972)
Yoko Ono, *Approximately Infinite Universe* (UK: 16 February 1973, US: 8 January 1973)
The Beatles, *1962–1966* (UK: 19 April 1973, US: 2 April 1973)
The Beatles, *1967–1970* (UK: 19 April 1973, US: 2 April 1973)
Paul McCartney & Wings, *Red Rose Speedway* (UK: 4 May 1973, US: 3 April 1973)
Ravi Shankar & Ali Akbar Khan, *In Concert 1972* (UK/US: 13 April 1973)
George Harrison, *Living In The Material World* (UK: 22 June 1973, US: 30 May 1973)

John Lennon, *Mind Games* (UK: 16 November 1973, US: 2 November 1973)
Yoko Ono, *Feeling The Space* (UK: 23 November 1973, US: 2 November 1973)
Ringo Starr, *Ringo* (UK: 23 November 1973, US: 2 November 1973)
Badfinger, *Ass* (US: 26 November 1973, UK: 8 March 1974)
Paul McCartney & Wings, *Band On The Run* (UK: 7 December 1973, US: 5 December 1973)
John Lennon, *Walls And Bridges* (UK: 4 October 1974, US: 26 November 1974)
Ringo Starr, *Goodnight Vienna* (UK: 15 November 1974, US: 18 November 1974)
George Harrison, *Dark Horse* (UK: 20 December 1974, US: 9 December 1974)
John Lennon, *Rock 'N' Roll* (UK: 21 February 1975, US: 17 February 1975.
George Harrison, *Extra Texture (Read All About It)* (UK 3 October 1975, US: 22 September 1975)
John Lennon, *Shaved Fish* (UK/US: 24 October 1975)
Ringo Starr, *Blast From Your Past* (UK: 12 December 1975, US: 20 November 1975)

Bibliography

Badman, K., *The Beatles After the Break-up 1970-2000* (Omnibus Press, London, 1993)
Beatles, The, *The Beatles Anthology* (Cassell & Co, London, 2000)
Blake, M., *Pretend You're In A War: The Who And The Sixties* (Aurum, London, 2015)
Bramwell, T. & Kingsland, R., *Magical Mystery Tours* (St. Martin's Press, New York City, 2005)
Brown, P. and Gaines. S., *The Love You Make: An Insider's Story Of The Beatles* (Penguin, London, 2002)
Brown, P. and Gaines. S., *All You Need Is Love* (St. Martin's Press, New York City, 2024)
Doggett, P., *You Never Give Me Your Money* (The Bodley Head, London, 2009)
Day-Webb, R., *Badfinger On Track* (Sonicbond, Tewkesbury, 2022)
Egan, S. [ed], *The Mammoth Book Of The Beatles* (Constable & Robinson, London, 2009)
Goldman, A., *The Lives Of John Lennon* (Bantam, London, 1988)
Goodman, F., *Allen Klein: The Man Who Bailed Out The Beatles* (Haughton Mifflin Harcourt, Boston, 2015)
Granados, S., *Those Were The Days: The Beatles And Apple* (Cherry Red Books, London, 2021)
Hammack, J., *The Beatles Recording Reference Manual: Volume 4: The Beatles Through*
Yellow Submarine (Late 1966-1967) (CreateSpace, 2019)
Hammack, J., *The Beatles Recording Reference Manual: Volume 5: Let It Be Through Abbey*
Road (1969-1970) (CreateSpace, 2020)
Harrison, G., *I Me Mine* (Weidenfeld & Nicholson, London, 2002)
Harry, B., *The Encyclopaedia Of Beatles People* (Blandford, London, 1997)
Isaacson, W., *Steve Jobs: The Exclusive Biography* (Simon & Schuster, New York City, 2011)
Leslie, I., *John and Paul, A Love Story In Songs* (Faber & Faber, London, 2025)
Lewisohn, M., *The Beatles Recording Sessions* (Hamlyn, London, 1988)
Lewisohn, M., *The Complete Beatles Chronicle* (Pyramid Books, London, 1992)
McCabe, P. and Schonfeld, R.D., *Apple To The Core: The Unmaking Of The Beatles* (Martin Brian & O'Keefe, London, 1972)
Miles, B., *Many Years From Now* (Secker & Warburg, London, 1997)
Miles, B., *The Beatles: A Diary* (Omnibus Press, London, 1998)
Miles, B., *The Zapple Diaries* (Peter Owen Publishers, London, 2015)
Norman, P., *Shout!* (Corgi, London, 1981)
Norman, P., *John Lennon: The Life* (Harper, 2009)
O'Dell, C., and Ketcham, K., *Miss O'Dell: My Life With The Beatles, The Stones, Bob Dylan And The Women Who Loved Them* (Touchstone, London, 2009)

Rice, T., *Oh, What A Circus* (Coronet Books, London, 1999)
Taylor, D., *As Time Goes By* (Davis-Poynter, London, 1973)
Wenner, J., *Lennon Remembers* (Penguin, Harmondsworth, 1973)
White, T., *James Taylor: Long Ago And Far Away* (Omnibus Press, London, 2011)
Zimmer, D., *Crosby, Stills & Nash: The Biography* (Da Capo, Boston, 2000)

Also available from Sonicbond

On Track series

AC/DC – Chris Sutton 978-1-78952-307-2
Allman Brothers Band – Andrew Wild 978-1-78952-252-5
Tori Amos – Lisa Torem 978-1-78952-142-9
Aphex Twin – Beau Waddell 978-1-78952-267-9
Asia – Peter Braidis 978-1-78952-099-6
Badfinger – Robert Day-Webb 978-1-878952-176-4
Barclay James Harvest – Keith and Monica Domone 978-1-78952-067-5
Beck – Arthur Lizie 978-1-78952-258-7
The Beat, General Public, Fine Young Cannibals – Steve Parry 978-1-78952-274-7
The Beatles 1962-1996 – Alberto Bravin and Andrew Wild 978-1-78952-355-3
The Beatles Solo 1969-1980 – Andrew Wild 978-1-78952-030-9
Blue Oyster Cult – Jacob Holm-Lupo 978-1-78952-007-1
Blur – Matt Bishop 978-178952-164-1
Marc Bolan and T.Rex – Peter Gallagher 978-1-78952-124-5
David Bowie 1964 to 1982 – Carl Ewens 978-1-78952-324-9
David Bowie 1963 to 2016 – Don Klees 978-1-78952-351-5
Kate Bush – Bill Thomas 978-1-78952-097-2
The Byrds – Andy McArthur 978-1-78952-280-8
Camel – Hamish Kuzminski 978-1-78952-040-8
Captain Beefheart – Opher Goodwin 978-1-78952-235-8
Caravan – Andy Boot 978-1-78952-127-6
Cardiacs – Eric Benac 978-1-78952-131-3
Wendy Carlos – Mark Marrington 978-1-78952-331-7
The Carpenters – Paul Tornbohm 978-1-78952-301-0
Nick Cave and The Bad Seeds – Dominic Sanderson 978-1-78952-240-2
Eric Clapton Solo – Andrew Wild 978-1-78952-141-2
The Clash (revised edition) – Nick Assirati 978-1-78952-325-6
Elvis Costello and The Attractions – Georg Purvis 978-1-78952-129-0
Crosby, Stills and Nash – Andrew Wild 978-1-78952-039-2
Creedence Clearwater Revival – Tony Thompson 978-1-78952-237-2
Crowded House – Jon Magidsohn 978-1-78952-292-1
The Damned – Morgan Brown 978-1-78952-136-8
David Bowie 1964 to 1982 – Carl Ewens 978-1-78952-324-9
David Bowie 1964 to 1982 – Carl Ewens 978-1-78952-324-9
Deep Purple and Rainbow 1968-79 – Steve Pilkington 978-1-78952-002-6
Deep Purple from 1984 – Phil Kafcaloudes 978-1-78952-354-6
Depeche Mode – Brian J. Robb 978-1-78952-277-8
Dire Straits – Andrew Wild 978-1-78952-044-6
The Divine Comedy – Alan Draper 978-1-78952-308-9
The Doors – Tony Thompson 978-1-78952-137-5
Dream Theater – Jordan Blum 978-1-78952-050-7
Bob Dylan 1962-1970 – Opher Goodwin 978-1-78952-275-2
Eagles – John Van der Kiste 978-1-78952-260-0
Earth, Wind and Fire – Bud Wilkins 978-1-78952-272-3
Electric Light Orchestra – Barry Delve 978-1-78952-152-8
Emerson Lake and Palmer – Mike Goode 978-1-78952-000-2
Fairport Convention – Kevan Furbank 978-1-78952-051-4
Peter Gabriel – Graeme Scarfe 978-1-78952-138-2
Genesis – Stuart MacFarlane 978-1-78952-005-7
Gentle Giant – Gary Steel 978-1-78952-058-3
Gong – Kevan Furbank 978-1-78952-082-8
Green Day – William E. Spevack 978-1-78952-261-7
Steve Hackett – Geoffrey Feakes 978-1-78952-098-9
Hall and Oates – Ian Abrahams 978-1-78952-167-2
Peter Hammill – Richard Rees Jones 978-1-78952-163-4
Roy Harper – Opher Goodwin 978-1-78952-130-6
Hawkwind (new edition) – Duncan Harris 978-1-78952-290-7
Jimi Hendrix – Emma Stott 978-1-78952-175-7

The Hollies – Andrew Darlington 978-1-78952-159-7
Horslips – Richard James 978-1-78952-263-1
The Human League and The Sheffield Scene – Andrew Darlington 978-1-78952-186-3
Humble Pie –Robert Day-Webb 978-1-78952-2761
Ian Hunter – G. Mick Smith 978-1-78952-304-1
The Incredible String Band – Tim Moon 978-1-78952-107-8
INXS – Manny Grillo 978-1-78952-302-7
Iron Maiden – Steve Pilkington 978-1-78952-061-3
Joe Jackson – Richard James 978-1-78952-189-4
The Jam – Stan Jeffries 978-1-78952-299-0
Jefferson Airplane – Richard Butterworth 978-1-78952-143-6
Jethro Tull – Jordan Blum 978-1-78952-016-3
J. Geils Band – James Romag 978-1-78952-332-4
Elton John in the 1970s – Peter Kearns 978-1-78952-034-7
Billy Joel – Lisa Torem 978-1-78952-183-2
Journey – Doug Thornton 978-1-78952-337-9
Judas Priest – John Tucker 978-1-78952-018-7
Kansas – Kevin Cummings 978-1-78952-057-6
Killing Joke – Nic Ransome 978-1-78952-273-0
The Kinks – Martin Hutchinson 978-1-78952-172-6
Korn – Matt Karpe 978-1-78952-153-5
Led Zeppelin – Steve Pilkington 978-1-78952-151-1
Level 42 – Matt Philips 978-1-78952-102-3
Little Feat – Georg Purvis – 978-1-78952-168-9
Magnum – Matthew Taylor – 978-1-78952-286-0
Aimee Mann – Jez Rowden 978-1-78952-036-1
Ralph McTell – Paul O. Jenkins 978-1-78952-294-5
Metallica – Barry Wood 978-1-78952-269-3
Joni Mitchell – Peter Kearns 978-1-78952-081-1
The Moody Blues – Geoffrey Feakes 978-1-78952-042-2
Motorhead – Duncan Harris 978-1-78952-173-3
Nektar – Scott Meze – 978-1-78952-257-0
New Order – Dennis Remmer – 978-1-78952-249-5
Nightwish – Simon McMurdo – 978-1-78952-270-9
Nirvana – William E. Spevack 978-1-78952-318-8
Laura Nyro – Philip Ward 978-1-78952-182-5
Oasis – Andrew Rooney 978-1-78952-300-3
Phil Ochs – Opher Goodwin 978-1-78952-326-3
Mike Oldfield – Ryan Yard 978-1-78952-060-6
Opeth – Jordan Blum 978-1-78-952-166-5
Pearl Jam – Ben L. Connor 978-1-78952-188-7
Tom Petty – Richard James 978-1-78952-128-3
Pink Floyd – Richard Butterworth 978-1-78952-242-6
The Police – Pete Braidis 978-1-78952-158-0
Porcupine Tree (Revised Edition) – Nick Holmes 978-1-78952-346-1
Procol Harum – Scott Meze 978-1-78952-315-7
Queen – Andrew Wild 978-1-78952-003-3
Radiohead – William Allen 978-1-78952-149-8
Gerry Rafferty – John Van der Kiste 978-1-78952-349-2
Rancid – Paul Matts 978-1-78952-187-0
Lou Reed 1972-1986 – Ethan Roy 978-1-78952-283-9
Renaissance – David Detmer 978-1-78952-062-0
REO Speedwagon – Jim Romag 978-1-78952-262-4
The Rolling Stones 1963-80 – Steve Pilkington 978-1-78952-017-0
Linda Ronstadt 1969-1989 – Daryl O. Lawrence 987-1-78952-293-8
Roxy Music – Michael Kulikowski 978-1-78952-335-5
Rush 1973 to 1982 – Richard James 978-1-78952-338-6
Sensational Alex Harvey Band – Peter Gallagher 978-1-7952-289-1
The Small Faces and The Faces – Andrew Darlington 978-1-78952-316-4

The Smashing Pumpkins – Matt Karpe 978-1-7952-291-4
The Smiths and Morrissey – Tommy Gunnarsson 978-1-78952-140-5
Soft Machine – Scott Meze 978-1078952-271-6
Sparks 1969-1979 – Chris Sutton 978-1-78952-279-2
Spirit – Rev. Keith A. Gordon – 978-1-78952- 248-8
Stackridge – Alan Draper 978-1-78952-232-7
Status Quo the Frantic Four Years – Richard James 978-1-78952-160-3
Steely Dan – Jez Rowden 978-1-78952-043-9
The Stranglers – Martin Hutchinson 978-1-78952-323-2
Talk Talk – Gary Steel 978-1-78952-284-6
Talking Heads – David Starkey 978-178952-353-9
Tears For Fears – Paul Clark – 978-178952-238-9
Thin Lizzy – Graeme Stroud 978-1-78952-064-4
Tool – Matt Karpe 978-1-78952-234-1
Toto – Jacob Holm-Lupo 978-1-78952-019-4
U2 – Eoghan Lyng 978-1-78952-078-1
UFO – Richard James 978-1-78952-073-6
Ultravox – Brian J. Robb 978-1-78952-330-0
Van Der Graaf Generator – Dan Coffey 978-1-78952-031-6
Van Halen – Morgan Brown – 9781-78952-256-3
Suzanne Vega – Lisa Torem 978-1-78952-281-5
Jack White And The White Stripes – Ben L. Connor 978-1-78952-303-4
The Who – Geoffrey Feakes 978-1-78952-076-7
Roy Wood and the Move – James R Turner 978-1-78952-008-8
Yes (new edition) – Stephen Lambe 978-1-78952-282-2
Neil Young 1963 to 1970 – Oper Goodwin 978-1-78952-298-3
Frank Zappa 1966 to 1979 – Eric Benac 978-1-78952-033-0
Warren Zevon – Peter Gallagher 978-1-78952-170-2
The Zombies – Emma Stott 978-1-78952-297-6
10CC – Peter Kearns 978-1-78952-054-5

Decades Series
The Bee Gees in the 1960s – Andrew Mon Hughes et al 978-1-78952-148-1
The Bee Gees in the 1970s – Andrew Mon Hughes et al 978-1-78952-179-5
Black Sabbath in the 1970s – Chris Sutton 978-1-78952-171-9
Britpop – Peter Richard Adams and Matt Pooler 978-1-78952-169-6
Phil Collins in the 1980s – Andrew Wild 978-1-78952-185-6
Alice Cooper in the 1970s – Chris Sutton 978-1-78952-104-7
Alice Cooper in the 1980s – Chris Sutton 978-1-78952-259-4
Curved Air in the 1970s – Laura Shenton 978-1-78952-069-9
Donovan in the 1960s – Jeff Fitzgerald 978-1-78952-233-4
Bob Dylan in the 1980s – Don Klees 978-1-78952-157-3
Brian Eno in the 1970s – Gary Parsons 978-1-78952-239-6
Faith No More in the 1990s – Matt Karpe 978-1-78952-250-1
Fleetwood Mac in the 1970s – Andrew Wild 978-1-78952-105-4
Fleetwood Mac in the 1980s – Don Klees 978-178952-254-9
Focus in the 1970s – Stephen Lambe 978-1-78952-079-8
Free and Bad Company in the 1970s – John Van der Kiste 978-1-78952-178-8
Genesis in the 1970s – Bill Thomas 978178952-146-7
George Harrison in the 1970s – Eoghan Lyng 978-1-78952-174-0
Kiss in the 1970s – Peter Gallagher 978-1-78952-246-4
Manfred Mann's Earth Band in the 1970s – John Van der Kiste 978178952-243-3
Marillion in the 1980s – Nathaniel Webb 978-1-78952-065-1
Van Morrison in the 1970s – Peter Childs – 978-1-78952-241-9
Mott the Hoople & Ian Hunter in the 1970s – John Van der Kiste 978-1-78-952-162-7
Pink Floyd In The 1970s – Georg Purvis 978-1-78952-072-9
Suzi Quatro in the 1970s – Darren Johnson 978-1-78952-236-5
Queen in the 1970s – James Griffiths 978-1-78952-265-5
Roxy Music in the 1970s – Dave Thompson 978-1-78952-180-1
Slade in the 1970s – Darren Johnson 978-1-78952-268-6

Status Quo in the 1980s – Greg Harper 978-1-78952-244-0
Tangerine Dream in the 1970s – Stephen Palmer 978-1-78952-161-0
The Sweet in the 1970s – Darren Johnson 978-1-78952-139-9
Uriah Heep in the 1970s – Steve Pilkington 978-1-78952-103-0
Van der Graaf Generator in the 1970s – Steve Pilkington 978-1-78952-245-7
Rick Wakeman in the 1970s – Geoffrey Feakes 978-1-78952-264-8
Yes in the 1980s – Stephen Lambe with David Watkinson 978-1-78952-125-2

Rock Classics Series

90125 by Yes – Stephen Lambe 978-1-78952-329-4
Bat Out Of Hell by Meatloaf – Geoffrey Feakes 978-1-78952-320-1
Bringing It All Back Home by Bob Dylan – Opher Goodwin 978-1-78952-314-0
Californication by Red Hot Chili Peppers - Matt Karpe 978-1-78952-348-5
Crime Of The Century by Supertramp – Steve Pilkington 978-1-78952-327-0
The Dreaming by Kate Bush – Peter Kearns 978-1-78952-341-6
Let It Bleed by The Rolling Stones – John Van der Kiste 978-1-78952-309-6
Pawn Hearts by Van Der Graaf Generator – Paolo Carnelli 978-1-78952-357-7
Purple Rain by Prince – Matt Karpe 978-1-78952-322-5
The White Album by The Beatles – Opher Goodwin 978-1-78952-333-1

On Screen Series

Carry On… – Stephen Lambe 978-1-78952-004-0
David Cronenberg – Patrick Chapman 978-1-78952-071-2
Doctor Who: The David Tennant Years – Jamie Hailstone 978-1-78952-066-8
James Bond – Andrew Wild 978-1-78952-010-1
Monty Python – Steve Pilkington 978-1-78952-047-7
Seinfeld Seasons 1 to 5 – Stephen Lambe 978-1-78952-012-5

Other Books

1967: A Year In Psychedelic Rock 978-1-78952-155-9
1970: A Year In Rock – John Van der Kiste 978-1-78952-147-4
1972: The Year Progressive Rock Ruled The World – Kevan Furbank 978-1-78952-288-4
1973: The Golden Year of Progressive Rock 978-1-78952-165-8
Dark Horse Records – Aaron Badgley 978-1-78952-287-7
Derek Taylor: For Your Radioactive Children – Andrew Darlington 978-1-78952-038-5
Eric Clapton Sessions – Andrew Wild 978-1-78952-177-1
Ghosts – Journeys To Post-Pop – Matthew Restall 978-1-78952-334-8
The Golden Age of Easy Listening – Derek Taylor 978-1-78952-285-3
The Golden Road: The Recording History of The Grateful Dead – John Kilbride 978-1-78952-156-6
Hoggin' The Page – Groudhogs The Classic Years – Martyn Hanson 978-1-78952-343-0
Iggy and The Stooges On Stage 1967-1974 – Per Nilsen 978-1-78952-101-6
Jon Anderson and the Warriors – the Road to Yes – David Watkinson 978-1-78952-059-0
Magic: The David Paton Story – David Paton 978-1-78952-266-2
Misty: The Music of Johnny Mathis – Jakob Baekgaard 978-1-78952-247-1
Musical Guide To Red By King Crimson – Andrew Keeling 978-1-78952-321-8
Nu Metal: A Definitive Guide – Matt Karpe 978-1-78952-063-7
Philip Lynott – Renegade – Alan Byrne 978-1-78952-339-3
Remembering Live Aid – Andrew Wild 978-1-78952-328-7
Thank You For The Days - Fans Of The Kinks Share 60 Years of Stories – Ed. Chris Kocher 978-1-78952-342-3
The Sonicbond On Track Sampler – 978-1-78952-190-0
The Sonicbond Progressive Rock Sampler (Ebook only) – 978-1-78952-056-9
Tommy Bolin: In and Out of Deep Purple – Laura Shenton 978-1-78952-070-5
Maximum Darkness – Deke Leonard 978-1-78952-048-4
The Twang Dynasty – Deke Leonard 978-1-78952-049-1

... and many more to come!

Would you like to write for Sonicbond Publishing?

We are mainly a music publisher, but we also occasionally publish in other genres including film and television. At Sonicbond Publishing we are always on the look-out for authors, particularly for our two main series, On Track and Decades.

Mixing fact with in depth analysis, the On Track series examines the entire recorded work of a particular musical artist or group. All genres are considered from easy listening and jazz to 60s soul to 90s pop, via rock and metal.

The Decades series singles out a particular decade in an artist or group's history and focuses on that decade in more detail than may be allowed in the On Track series.

While professional writing experience would, of course, be an advantage, the most important qualification is to have real enthusiasm and knowledge of your subject. First-time authors are welcomed, but the ability to write well in English is essential.

Sonicbond Publishing has distribution throughout Europe and North America, and all our books are also published in E-book form. Authors will be paid a royalty based on sales of their book. Further details about our books are available from www.sonicbondpublishing.com. To contact us, complete the contact form there or email info@sonicbondpublishing.co.uk